Praise for *Free Birds Revolution*

"With *Free Birds Revolution*, Miles Everson has crafted a smart and useful guide to the independent workforce revolution. His blend of data-driven analysis and practical wisdom offers invaluable insights for those seeking to spread their wings in a perilous but promising new economy."

—Daniel H. Pink, #1 *New York Times* Bestselling Author,
The Power of Regret, Drive, and *To Sell Is Human*

"Miles has identified a lost civilization of Americans living among us: 72 million free agents ready to work but on their terms. They are born with an insatiable need for freedom in both work and life. Miles offers a solution where these free spirits can soar to freedom and financial heights with no limits, using their unique talents in their own way and on their own terms—doing it Frank Sinatra's 'My Way.'"

—Jim Clifton, Chairman, Gallup

"*Free Birds Revolution* is an essential first stop for anyone venturing into the world of independent work or looking to go deeper—and Miles Everson is the ultimate independent-thinking guide, offering a unique perspective from his unique vantage point on the front lines."

—Elaine Pofeldt, Independent Journalist and Author, *The Million-Dollar, One-Person Business* and *Tiny Business, Big Money*

"*Free Birds Revolution* explores the entrepreneurial spirit that resonates deeply with my own journey in business, nonprofit, and public service. As Governor of Arkansas, I prioritized creating a fertile ground for small businesses to flourish, understanding that entrepreneurship is the lifeblood of our free market economy. This book encapsulates the essence of breaking free from conventional constraints to forge one's path to success. It is a must-read for anyone inspired to take control of their destiny, much like the independent ventures I have championed throughout my career. Plus, it's full of stories from rock-and-roll legends—so, it's entertaining too."

—Mike Huckabee, 44th Governor of Arkansas, former Republican presidential candidate, Host of TBN's *Huckabee*, bestselling author, and grandfather of 7

"*Free Birds Revolution* is a powerful manifesto for those ready to redefine their work lives with authenticity and intentionality. Miles Everson's insights align beautifully with the IEP Method®—a framework I champion for cultivating energy, presence, and impact. This book invites readers to embrace independence and craft a career that resonates with their true selves. It's an essential read for anyone committed to showing up fully and leading their own revolution in the evolving world of work."

—Anese Cavanaugh, CEO, Active Choices, Inc.; Creator, IEP Method®; Founder, Positive Energy Workplace Initiative®; and Author, *Contagious Culture and Contagious You*

FREE
BIRDS
REVOLUTION

FREE BIRDS
REVOLUTION

THE FUTURE OF WORK
& THE INDEPENDENT MIND

MILES EVERSON

WITH WALTER SCOTT LAMB

Matt Holt Books
An Imprint of BenBella Books, Inc.
Dallas, TX

Matt Holt is an imprint of BenBella Books, Inc.
8080 N. Central Expressway
Suite 1700
Dallas, TX 75206
benbellabooks.com
Send feedback to feedback@benbellabooks.com

BenBella and *Matt Holt* are federally registered trademarks.

Printed in the United States of America
10 9 8 7 6 5 4 3 2 1

Library of Congress Control Number: 2024033586
ISBN 9781637745755 (hardcover)
ISBN 9781637745762 (electronic)

Editing by Katie Dickman
Copyediting by Scott Calamar
Proofreading by Denise Pangia and Cape Cod Compositors, Inc.
Text design and composition by Jordan Koluch
Cover design by Joseph Hearne
Cover image © Shutterstock / NadzeyaShanchuk
Printed by Lake Book Manufacturing

Special discounts for bulk sales are available.
Please contact bulkorders@benbellabooks.com.

From Miles Everson:

This one's for the man who told me, "Define yourself. Never give up your authenticity by letting others define you. There's power in your independence." Thanks Dad.

From Walter Scott Lamb:

To my Dad, the first entrepreneur I ever knew, who died as this project began. Though I know you're with Jesus and I'll see you again, I miss you every day.

Contents

Part 2 THE INDEPENDENT MIND OF A FREE BIRD

IT'S TIME FOR FREE BIRDS TO FLY

Get active in your own rescue.

—Marcus Aurelius

Kevin Cronin, a newly minted high school graduate from the suburbs of Chicago, loved his girlfriend and his guitar—a real six string. To paraphrase Canadian rocker Bryan Adams, Cronin and some guys from school had a band, and they tried real hard. It was the summer of '69 and they were the best days of his life.

But the relationship with the girl fizzled out, as did Cronin's desire to spend four more years in a college classroom. So he hopped in his car and headed west.

"A buddy of mine and I just packed up and went to Colorado in my freshman year at college—my first road trip," Cronin said. "Another guy who'd been at high school with us lived out in Boulder. One morning, we said, 'Let's just go to Boulder. Let's go. We're off!'"[1]

Inspired by the freedom of travel and the beauty of the Rocky Mountains, Cronin strummed a guitar and birthed lyrics about his recently ended relationship.

You said we'd work it out
You said that ya had no doubt
That deep down we were really in love

Oh, but I'm tired of holdin' on
To a feelin' I know is gone
I do believe that I've had enough

As Cronin crooned, the verses took shape.

I've had enough of the falseness
Of a worn-out relation
Enough of the jealousy
And the intoleration
Oh, I make you laugh
And you make me cry

"But I only wrote the verses. I didn't have a chorus for it," Cronin said. "It got as far as 'I make you laugh, you make me cry'—it just didn't quite pay off."[2]

And so, the song remained unfinished.

Two years later, Cronin became the lead singer for a regional band named REO Speedwagon, joining them in an endless string of gigs at bars and clubs in college towns throughout the Midwest. He helped create REO's second album, then left the group in 1974 before rejoining them the next year—this time for good. As one journalist wrote: "When he discovered that he didn't want a solo singing career and neither did the public, he returned in 1975."[3]

This reminds me that when we dissect "the independent mind" in part 2 of this book, we'll see that a career path is rarely a straight line—especially for an entrepreneur. The marketplace often determines just how squiggly *your* line will be—to use a term from the title of Helen Tupper's excellent book, *The Squiggly Career*.[4] If you're still early in your career, I recommend you embrace the mindset that you're going to change jobs, roles, and locations often—because you will, statistically speaking. More on that later.

As REO Speedwagon returned to the recording studio, Cronin brought out his lyrical leftovers, including the breakup ballad from six years earlier. "I always had those verses kinda in the back of my head," he said.[5] But

Cronin got no support for the song. "One of our producers turned that down for our 1976 *R.E.O.* album. He told me it was a crummy song; it only had three chords; it was too slow. It wasn't a REO Speedwagon song."[6]

The producer had a point: REO fans knew them for hard rock, not melodic rock. Cronin persisted. "I started thinking, 'I like this song. If somebody writes it who is in REO Speedwagon, how can it not be an REO Speedwagon song?'"[7] He argued for the creative license to move beyond the portfolio of previous work. No worn-out relations or intolerations, right? But the producer won the debate for that album and shelved the song.

Cronin wasn't pleased. "The sound of a band has to come from the band itself. That's when we decided to fire our producer," Cronin explained. "There's a million ways you can play any song. One way seems to us the way the song wants to be."[8]

Another year passed and REO began working on their next album. Cronin once again dusted off the road-trip lyrics, except that by now, he had the chorus figured out:

Oh, I make you laugh
And you make me cry
I believe it's time for me to fly
Time for me to fly
Oh, I've got to set myself free
Time for me to fly
And that's just how it's got to be
I know it hurts to say goodbye
But it's time for me to fly

Recorded in October 1977 and released in July 1978—nine years after Cronin first worked on the song!—"Time for Me to Fly" became one of REO's top five greatest hits of all time. Cronin called it "the fulcrum of our live set" and says it still gives him chills when he plays it for fans.[9] The song hit the charts again thirty years later in 2020 after the band sang it in a cameo appearance in the Netflix drama *Ozark*.[10] And in 2021, the tourism department of his home state of Illinois used the song in their "Time for Me to Drive" campaign—bringing things full circle with Cronin's 1969 teenage road trip that inspired the song. That's longevity. How many of the creative seeds we plant today will continue to bear fruit fifty years from now?

"You know, our audiences are interesting," Cronin said in 1985. "They're a partying kind of rock 'n' roll audience. But they get as crazy over the slow, romantic ballads as they do over the rock 'n' roll songs. I used to think we had to play fast, loud, and hard all the time."[11]

If you're a millennial or Gen Zer who knows a few REO Speedwagon songs, chances are that none of them are the "fast, loud, and hard" songs. The band remained true to themselves (which, as we will see in part 2, is a core characteristic of the independent mind), and they worked within their skill set. But they also listened to the audience's desire—the market-place. This illustrates what Reid Hoffman, cofounder of PayPal, calls the "three puzzle pieces that shape your career path": your assets (hard and soft), your aspirations/values, and the market realities.[12] REO built success cross-generationally because when it was time for them to adapt to the mar-ketplace, they weren't afraid to fly.

◆ ◆ ◆

It was the summer of '69—yes, again. But this time with a pack of high school musicians in Jacksonville, Florida, who played gigs and practiced relentlessly. They even looked like rock stars, with long hair that got them in trouble with their PE coach, a flat-topped disciplinarian named Leonard Skinner. Having cycled through several names for their band, their founder, Ronnie Van Zant, decided on the name that stuck: Lynyrd Skynyrd.

Allen Collins, Skynyrd's extremely talented seventeen-year-old guitar-ist, had a love affair with music—a fact that his girlfriend, Kathy Johns, took note of as she watched him practice in his mother's living room. Was there room in his life for her too? "If I leave here tomorrow," Kathy asked, "would you still remember me?" Allen heard song lyrics in those words and began immediately setting them to music—a somewhat ironic reaction, given his girlfriend's question and concern. With additional lyrics by Van

Zant, a piano intro, and a lengthy, frenetic guitar solo finale, Lynyrd Skynyrd gave birth to their signature song: "Free Bird."

Allen married Kathy the following year, and Skynyrd played the song at the wedding reception. After all, the song's lyrics meant more than a guy not wanting to settle down with his girl. Van Zant said the lyrics were "about what it means to be free, in that a bird can fly wherever he wants to go. Everyone wants to be free. That's what this country is all about."[13]

Skynyrd would play an extended version of "Free Bird" lasting twelve or more minutes to close out their concerts, with the guitar solo wailing away for over half that time. Music industry executives demanded a short version for radio play, so the band recorded five-minute and nine-minute versions—neither of which exactly qualifies as short. But fans loved the song, sending it into the Top 40 charts. And *Guitar World* ranks the ending as the world's eighth-best guitar solo in rock history. Those free birds you could not change.

UNBUNDLED MELODY

If right this minute, you desired to listen to "Free Bird" or "It's Time for Me to Fly," how would you do it? You know the answer because it's second nature by now. You'd reach for your device of choice (phone, tablet, computer) and open an app or website: YouTube, Apple Music, iTunes, Amazon Music, Spotify—to name just a few.

But would you drive to your local mall to purchase a physical music product (LPs, cassettes, CDs) from a store like Camelot Music or Tower Records? Of course not.

Even if your favorite is the late, great Prince, you're not "going to party like it's 1999"—the year when CDs still dominated sales (and the year when 19-year-old Sean Parker began the music file-sharing application Napster). In the mid-1990s, malls could support multiple music stores. Now, malls themselves are mostly on life support, and finding a brick-and-mortar music store is like spotting a bald eagle in the wild or Taylor Swift on public transit. It's not impossible, but if it happened you'd stop and stare.[14]

Instead, you'd watch the song's video for free on YouTube. Or you'd subscribe to one or more streaming services for about $12/month—giving you unlimited music for less than the price of one CD. You might even *purchase* the digital songs and albums off iTunes or Amazon—though even as I write this sentence, I'm asking myself: "Do people still do this?" If so, why?

But for sure, what you *wouldn't* do is purchase *seven* or more other songs on something called an "album" (digital or physical) to get to that *one* song you've heard of—the *one* you like. You only want "It's Time for Me to Fly."[15] Even when given the option of streaming unlimited songs at no extra cost, most people skip those other songs too.

To paraphrase *The Godfather*: "Leave the album. Take the melody."

That's unbundling and—believe it or not—unbundling is why there's an independent workforce. Not the unbundling of music, but the unbundling of work from something individual people ("songs") do as full-time employees of one company ("album").

One outcome of unbundled work is the growth in size and influence of the independent workforce, and that's what this book is all about. So, in a real sense, unbundled work is what gets me up in the morning, and it's the reason MBO Partners (the company I lead as CEO) exists: to make it easy for enterprises to access people who are choosing to be independent professionals. And it's smart for enterprises to do so because independents make up an increasingly large portion of the US and global workforce. We help people find a way (the independent way) to do what they really love to do when they're working and help enterprises to access this growing segment of the workforce. Unbundled work benefits both sides—the professional as well as the enterprise.

How did unbundling happen? Nicholas Negroponte, a pioneer of the Information Age and the first investor in *Wired* magazine, wrote an international bestselling book in 1993 called *Being Digital*, with a simple predictive exhortation: "Move bits, not atoms."[16] Meaning, the world has gone digital (bits), and your business model should reflect that instead of being tied to the physicality of products and bricks and mortar (atoms).

Negroponte's prophecy was accurate, and he updated it two decades later in 2015: "Anything that can be bits will be. Any process that can be disintermediated will be. *That is old news.* What is new about vaporization is its unexpected consequences that reach far beyond media. Who would have imagined that taxis might be vaporized?"[17]

The idea of everything "being digital" went from a bold prediction to "old news" in only two decades. That's because the rate of change is accelerating (see chapter 1). So I break no new ground here when I describe the digital revolution and its impact on analog media (music, movies, news, print publishing). Because the point *isn't* media. The point is the *information revolution*, and how it is changing *everything* that's analog—or at least, everything that *can* be digitized.[18] And that includes work.

In part 1 we will look at six forces shaping the future of work, so I don't want to oversimplify here in the early pages with an overemphasis on one factor. That said, when I tell you "the future of work *is* independent," that statement *does* rest on the foundation of the digital revolution. But on a more existential level, the future of work is independent because of people's innate desire for a more fulfilling and rewarding vocational life—the kind of work life that can be had when they unbundle themselves from working as an employee of just one organization or enterprise, or when they side-hustle to scratch their entrepreneurial itch.

The traditionally analog world of work has been and is being revolutionized by the digital explosion of the fourth Industrial Revolution. The changes will transform all aspects of work: labor, employment, HR, compensation, benefits, career path planning, training, credentialing, retirement, commercial real estate, office politics, cubicles, and more. Every kind of worker will need to adjust, even workers who opt to remain full-time employees of a single company for long durations.

To future-proof their organizations, employers must first open their eyes to see the totality of their workforce. They must even change how they define the term *workforce* because it no longer includes only captive full-time employees but also their contingent labor sources. The successful employers of tomorrow will leverage this strategic workforce to keep up with deep pools and labor benches of in-demand skills. Savvy employers will strategically recognize and acknowledge this population of skilled independent labor as a significant portion of their workforce.

Top performers no longer wish to be traditional, long-term employees, and acknowledging this truth should drive a shift in HR thinking and strategic planning. The Bureau of Labor Statistics has shown that today's average employee tenure is just 4.1 years, down to the lowest level since 1980.[19] For employees under the age of 35, the average tenure is now down to 2.8 years.[20] Bankrate's 2023 job seeker survey reported that 56% of American workers will look for a new job within the year.[21] The technology sector gets hit the hardest, with a 13% annual turnover rate, and some of the largest tech companies report average employee tenure rates of only one to two years.[22]

That's why I say that the future of work is independent. More workers than ever are opting out of traditional jobs to go independent or are doing independent work in addition to their work as employees. How many? There are now 72 million independent workers in the United States—working either occasionally, part time, or full time. Independents work, but they've unbundled "work" from "full-time employment."

That data comes from original research commissioned by MBO Partners, where we are building the future of work via a deep job platform that connects top independent professionals and enterprises worldwide. Every year we commission a study and release a report full of deep understanding of the "The State of Independence"—it's the longest running study of its kind (more on that in chapter 7).

One thing is for sure: Unbundling work also increases a company's agility and innovation. It enables more specific skills for a specific outcome, rather than assigning an outcome to a predefined role within a company. Unbundling personalizes the work to each person rather than groups of people or functions. And the fractional workforce can significantly impact return on assets, helping the business succeed as it navigates uncertain waters—like times of recession. Further, studies on cost savings have shown a 15–35% reduction in employment expenses when businesses leverage the external workforce. In sum, independent work benefits everyone:

- For the company: Unbundling work enhances agility and innovation, and it benefits the bottom line.

- For the individual: Unbundling work expands freedom of choice, increases satisfaction, and produces higher income levels.

OL' MAN RIVER

The invention of the tiny transistor in 1947 launched the Information Age, but its impact on the economy wasn't felt overnight or even much during the next decade. We're now almost eight decades downstream from that first transistor, so it's safe to say the digital revolution and its economy are not fads. Likewise, in another five years, nobody will be arguing that "remote work" and the independent workforce were transient features of the early twenty-first-century economy.

While the COVID-19 shutdowns accelerated the pace of change, the roots of our great work unbundling go back forty years. The independent workforce isn't a short-term anomaly produced by the pandemic. It's a long-term socioeconomic trend established by irreversible, worldwide advances created by the Information Age technologies. The Mississippi River may not seem formidable in Minnesota (I could jog across its bridge in a minute as a college student at St. Cloud University), but stand along its banks in New Orleans and you'll understand its unstoppable power.

Here's how the stream of change became an independent workforce river. First, as I will explain later in the "Interlude," the social contract that dominated the American workforce for half a century was grounded in one big thing: workers promised loyalty to a business in return for a guaranteed pension for life when they retired. But the pensions and the mutual loyalty are mostly gone now.

Second, the internet and all the technology of the digital revolution flattened information and made the cost of starting up a business negligible. The only capital investment many workers need today is a laptop and a cell phone. From online education to online networks, most workers can get the necessary skills and build friendships and business contacts without leaving their homes. Many of these relationships are as strong or stronger than those forged in a traditional workplace.

And then came the pandemic, accelerating the universal social acceptance of remote work. For the first time, many companies and institutions were forced to adapt to a workforce that was entirely remote. Millions of employees suddenly had a new, albeit strained, form of work-life balance. They got their first taste of what it could be like to work from home. Recruiting went virtual.

Then the "great resignation" followed as people realized they were tired of employers telling them what to do and when. I wrote several articles calling this mass awakening "the great realization" because the workforce began to understand—to realize—that their labor and career *can* be different. Not only can they work from home, but they can also get hired in Boise to work for a company in Boston. And that's when it hit them: They don't have to be full-time employees anymore. They realized they can do it all as independent contractors. And that's when they became "Free Birds."

THE CRITICS

I won't pretend there aren't any critics of independent work. It's not hard to find bleak headlines about the "gig economy" (the most used phrase when talking about the independent workforce):

- "The Gig Economy Is Coming for Your Job"[23]
- "The Gig Economy Celebrates Working Yourself to Death"[24]
- "The Gig Economy: Lower Wages, More Injuries, Horrible Benefits—It's Worse Than You Think"[25]
- "False Freedom: Sharing the Scraps from the Perilous Gig Economy"[26]
- "The Gig Economy: Opportunity or Exploitation?"[27]
- "Yes, the Gig Economy Sucks; No, It's Not Fulfilling Its Promise of Freedom"[28]

Injuries, broken promises, peril, exploitation, and death? Wow. What's up with all that? This view sees independents as huddled masses yearning to breathe free—but who have become slaves of Amazon and its "Mechanical Turk" work. So, is the external workforce trading away their vocational life for dollars on the hour? Did they jump into the freelance economy with aspirations of upward mobility, only to find themselves stuck behind the wheel of their Ubermobile?

Also among the critics are the minimizers, those who describe independents as a lucky elite, a tiny percentage of the overall workforce. They imagine independents as wealthy, white-collar hipsters sitting on a beach or in a coffee shop while posting influencer videos on YouTube, creating graphic designs, or performing IT. This criticism comes with its own tagline: "If only everyone could be so lucky."

And don't forget the passive-aggressive criticism posed as a question: "So, you're in between jobs?" The assumption is that independents wouldn't be doing this kind of work if they had a choice. If they could just land a job, then they'd cycle back out of independent work. That's the argument.

Some critics even hit below the belt, questioning the work ethic of independents—especially that of younger-generation freelancers. These pontificators say things like, "Young people these days are lazy and don't know how to work." In the minds of these critics, work only counts if you're a full-time employee for one employer because that's the only way the critics know work to be done. And how else would you get health insurance or matching contributions to a retirement account? So, only unambitious people would deny themselves such perks by remaining "unemployed," right? Wrong.

Finally, there's the Malcolm Gladwell critic—literally, Malcolm Gladwell, the journalist and bestselling book author. When Gladwell interviewed with Steven Bartlett for Bartlett's *The Diary of a CEO* podcast in late 2022, they discussed how the American workforce seemed unwilling to lose the work flexibility that had come upon them suddenly and unexpectedly by COVID-19. Gladwell, who wrote a half dozen books over the past decade while sitting in coffee shops around the globe, said this: "It's not in your best interest to work at home. I know it's a hassle to come into the office, but if you're just sitting in your pajamas in your bedroom, is that the work-life you want to live?"[29] Although Gladwell's shaming took aim at work-from-home *employees* and not the external workforce in particular, the critique equally hits independents.

Gladwell continued: "As we face the battle that all organizations are facing now in getting people back into the office, it's really hard to explain this core psychological truth, which is we want you to have a feeling of belonging and to feel necessary. And we want you to join our team. And if you're not here it's really hard to do that."

Look, as much as I read and recommend Gladwell's books with their rich insight and page-turning storytelling, all that "pajamas in your bedroom" condescension showed how much he missed the point. Gladwellians want "to get people back into the office"—and they want workers to be happy about that. But as Emily Dickinson wrote and Selena Gomez sang: "The heart wants what it wants." So some workers embraced the RTO (return to office) with joy because that's how they prefer to work. Others, however, checked out because of the mandates.

Admittedly, Gladwell's focus wasn't on the independent workforce per se. But when you aim your argument's gun at employees who prize remote work, your bullets will also be hitting independents. And as we will see later, employees gaining the freedom to work remotely serves as an entry drug to the independent mind.

It's not rocket science and it's not about pajamas: People want *freedom*.

THE PINK CADILLAC OF FREE BIRD PROPHETS

Twenty-plus years ago, in 2001, Daniel Pink wrote a remarkably prescient book titled *Free Agent Nation: How America's New Independent Workers Are Transforming the Way We Live*. Pink, now a veteran bestselling author of many books, had only recently launched his career as a freelance writer, leaving behind a full-time job in the White House as the chief speechwriter for Vice President Al Gore.

As Pink became a "free agent," he looked around the coffee shops and Kinko's he frequented and saw a surging wave of fellow independent workers. He did the journalist's hard work of research and reported on what he saw. In December 1997, *Fast Company* magazine—then just two years old—published his article, and it went viral by the mostly analog standards of the day. Pink developed his book from that article, putting in an additional year of research and interviewing independents.

Keep this in mind: Whatever Pink's prophetic eyes saw about the future of work being independent, he made these observations an entire decade before Steve Jobs introduced the first iPhone, a breakthrough with an impact nobody saw coming—not in 1997. That year, most people used a pager, bulky cell phones were *merely* phones (app-less and Apple-less), fewer than 30% of Americans had access to high-speed internet, and fax machines hit their peak for purchases in the United States (3.9 million).[30] So when Jobs launched the iPhone in 2007, the best even he could do was to analogize the product as "An iPod, a phone, and internet communicator."[31] In 1997, there was no Napster (1999), iPod (2001), iPhone (2007), Myspace (2003), Facebook (2004), Twitter (2006), Uber (2010), or DoorDash (2013).

When Pink wrote his book, Mark Zuckerberg was only in junior high. And yet, there was Pink with these solopreneur stories and a prediction about how the future of work would be a lot more like *them* and a lot less like *The Organization Man* of William Whyte's famous bestselling 1956 book.[32] Pink nailed it.

As often happens to prophets, Pink's article had critics—though their criticisms didn't age well. One writer argued that "free agents" would discover painfully and soon enough just how tough it was to color outside the lines of regular full-time employment. How could they keep current clients happy while also doing their own taxes, HR, marketing, and all a corporation's "back office" functions? He argued that employers benefited most from the rise of the free agent nation because they "get to hire independent contractors without the burden of shelling out for health benefits or sick leaves or pensions."[33]

Throughout this book, I will answer these types of criticisms—they haven't changed much over years. And I will show that employers *do* benefit significantly from the rise of the independent workforce—but not for reasons of exploitation.

Did you know that Tom Cruise has three front teeth? Google it. He chipped a tooth as a teen and got a cap. Okay, so Cruise doesn't *literally* have three front teeth—he just *looks* like he does. His smile has helped him earn a fortune in Hollywood for four decades—even with its lack of symmetry. But here's the thing. You may have never noticed the appearance of his third middle tooth before, but now that I've told you about it and once you see it—you'll never be able to unsee it. Unseeing it is mission impossible.

Likewise, you're not going to be able to unsee independents after reading this book. What I know comes from real-world experience, not theories. You'll read of original data gleaned from independents who report being happier, wealthier, and more financially secure than they ever were as full-time employees of one company. I'm in the trenches every day with business leaders and independents alike—and I want to open your eyes to the "Free Birds Revolution" taking place all around you. Whether you're an independent already, hope to become one, or are a business leader, by reading this book you are going to start seeing independents all over the place.

* * *

I've structured this book in two parts. I think both sections are important for all readers to digest—independents and business leaders alike. That said, if you're a newbie independent or hoping to become one, you may want to go directly to part 2: "The Independent Mind of a Free Bird."

First, I know how important it is for small businesses and executives to keep aware of macro trends—changes that impact their business and the bottom line. These trendlines are the acorn that grew into the oak tree of the independent workforce. So I'll explain these trends in the remainder of part 1, "The Times They Are A-Changin': Six Forces Shaping the Future of Work."

And, not to steal my own thunder here, but no single trend will impact business as much as the labor market. I continually hear an urgent question from executives and business owners: "How do I find, recruit, and retain top talent?" I follow up their question by asking them about their utilization of independents. Every CEO will say that people—their employees—are their most important assets. But it's time they expand the definition of "people" to include external workers because many of the most talented professionals in the workforce choose to be independent.

If less than 20% of an enterprise's workforce are independents, then that's the immediate starting point for improvement. The business models that survive and thrive will be built on a modern understanding of the workforce. Enterprises that view their workforce mostly in terms of having full-time, captive employees will be disrupted. Therefore, I give them a target: 30% of their labor spend should be for independent workers. If this sounds crazy, stick with me because I think you'll feel differently by the end of part 1.

Second, if business leaders are to create the corporate culture, policies, and structures that independents find attractive, then they must first understand what it is that motivates the external workforce. Therefore, in part 2, I'll explain "The Independent Mind of a Free Bird." Practically speaking, an alternative title for this section could be: "Leading Your Business to Become the Client of Choice for the Independent Workforce." If you're a small business owner or a corporate leader (I've been doing both for over thirty years), then you know it's past time to think clearly about the future of work and the proverbial war for talent. Even if you despise war metaphors in business, you know the truth of the analogy. Part 2 can help you design strategies for attracting to your business the talent you need.

And if you are reading this book as an independent—or someone who hopes to become one soon—then this book is about your freedom. You've got to believe that you have the freedom to cultivate and use *your* independent mind to renegotiate *your* relationship with *your* work. After all, the hours you invest vocationally represent one-third of your life—roughly 90,000 hours of your time on this planet.[34] Does your current job or career path make that "one-third" feel like a cage? A prison sentence? Then consider this book a first step in following the counsel of the Roman emperor and Stoic philosopher Marcus Aurelius: "Get active in your own rescue."

* * *

In August 1977, REO Speedwagon opened for Lynyrd Skynyrd to sold-out crowds in Fresno, California, and at Anaheim Stadium. REO played their new song, "It's Time for Me to Fly"—a song so new that they hadn't even recorded it at the time. They put the song on their next album, pulled in countless new fans, and earned their first Top 40 album. REO was ascending.

Lynyrd Skynyrd had been touring coast-to-coast and internationally throughout 1977, playing in a dozen cities each month alongside the best rock bands of the day. But just as everything had come together for Skynyrd, a plane crash in October killed six, including guitarist Steve Gaines, his singer-sister Cassie Gaines, and the leader of the band, Ronnie Van Zant. The surviving band members regrouped years later, but it would never be the same.

Google "Free Bird" and you'll find a live concert video of Lynyrd Skynyrd's July 2, 1977, performance at Oakland Coliseum. With over 70 million views, it's the second most watched video on their YouTube channel. That Oakland concert, part of the famous "Day on the Green" music festivals produced by the legendary Bill Graham, was the seventh to the last time the original band performed together.

Watch them on stage that day, totally rocking and having the best time of their lives in front of tens of thousands of fans who were having an equally fun time. It's a reminder to us all that even without tragic plane crashes, life goes by so quickly, and nothing stays the same for long.

Free Birds, it's time for you to fly.

PART 1

THE TIMES THEY ARE A-CHANGIN'

Six Forces Shaping the Future of Work

1

LIFE IN THE FAST LANE

Force #1: The Rate of Change Is Accelerating

> History and societies do not crawl. They make jumps.
> —Nassim Nicholas Taleb, *The Black Swan*[1]

On that second day of July 1977, when Skynyrd played in Oakland, two music-loving guys in their 20s (both named Steve) were 45 minutes away down in Cupertino, California. Across America, millions of people stood in long lines to see the newly released *Star Wars*—a revolution in moviemaking.

I was thirteen that summer and remember being captivated by George Lucas's amazing blockbuster. Meanwhile, Steve Jobs (22) and Steve Wozniak (27) were leading their one-year-old startup's dozen or so employees in an assembly-line production of a revolution of their own making: the Apple II.

They had no time for distractions but couldn't be happier than being dialed into their passion. One year earlier, as Wozniak was assembling fewer than 200 units of the Apple I, he said, "It's hard not to live, eat, and sleep computer when you're involved with such a responsive new market. But when you're growing as fast as we are, you just don't have time for anything else."[2] By contrast, the Apple II sold triple that amount in the second half of 1977. The company's profits escalated, and the company's products catalyzed the digital revolution.

* * *

The rate of change is accelerating. That's the theme of this chapter and it's the first of the "Six Forces Shaping the Future of Work" that form part 1 of this book. I've talked about these forces in writing and in dialogue with business leaders so often that, for shorthand, I sometimes refer to them as the "Everson's Evolutions." Not that I invented the concepts, of course, but I just think that, when combined, they're core to understanding the future of work. These trends are shaping the future of employers' relationships with their workers and the entire business model of our nation's economy.

Heraclitus, the ancient Greek philosopher, wrote, "Change is the only constant in life." I agree with that quote and use it frequently when I give talks on business and the future. But in today's world we can see that change is not simply constant and continual. Rather, the rate of change has been accelerating throughout most of the second half of the twentieth century and continues to accelerate because of technological advances and the *convergences* of those advances.

Convergences push the rapid pace of innovation. While many focus on a single invention and latch onto that as a panacea, when multiple innovations, or new ideas and capabilities that have not previously existed, converge, we get demonstrable societal change. And don't miss this: Innovations most often spring from independent-minded people who have strong convictions about doing things differently and better than before. This is the "independent mind" at work.

To put some flesh and bones on the "rate of change is accelerating" theme, let's focus in on a single innovation (personal computing) and the independent minds of this particular group of innovators (Jobs, Wozniak, and Gates, in particular). Within the Apple and Microsoft stories, we get not only a simple illustration of rapid change (the growth of the companies themselves) but also the story of how their products became an agent of rapid global change outside of their own industry. These innovators and their innovations became "flywheels"—to use the metaphor made famous by Jim Collins to describe how continuous effort and incremental improvements compound over time. What looks like a sudden big breakthrough was actually built through a series of small, consistent actions. Apple and Microsoft were both flywheels and catalysts for other flywheels outside the industry.[3]

And to think, a humble magazine article sparked the inspiration for these flywheels.

ONE MAGAZINE TO SCHOOL THEM ALL

When the editors of *Popular Electronics* magazine published the January 1975 edition and sent it to their nearly half-million subscribers, the editors could not have predicted that this single issue would be directly responsible for the birth of two companies—Apple and Microsoft—which would revolutionize the world and combine for a market cap of $6 trillion.[4]

The cover showed a picture of what we would describe as some sort of electrical control box with buttons, lights, and knobs. The article's title stated the promise: "World's First Minicomputer Kit to Rival Commercial Models." What you see on the cover, of course, is not what anyone today thinks of when they think of a "minicomputer." Nevertheless, the editors beamed with pride: "For many years, we've been reading and hearing about how computers will one day be a household item . . . the home computer age is here, finally."

Well, it's true that the home computer age had arrived—*if* you knew how to assemble and solder together a box of wires, resistors, and chips. And also program. And also read output displays that consisted of blinking lights. Though this "kit" truly was a game changer, it wasn't designed for the everyman. "You are a weird-type person," the magazine wrote, describing their own readers, "because only weird-type people sit in kitchens and basements and places all hours of the night, soldering things to boards to make machines go flickety-flock."[5] Nevertheless, hundreds of orders poured into Altair, the assembler of the kit, from independent-minded people who wanted to create tech that could disrupt the status quo. These microcomputer enthusiasts believed that computing power belonged to everyone, not just big business and governments who could afford million-dollar equipment.

One such geek was William "Bill" Gates, a sophomore at Harvard, who read the issue of *Popular Electronics* with his friend Paul Allen, and panicked. Here's why: If the home computer revolution had arrived—and that's exactly what they understood the Altair 8800 to represent—then there would be a need for software. Gates knew that hardware doesn't "flickety-flock" without programs. Someone would need to kick-start a personal computer software industry, and Gates wanted to be the early nerd who got the worm of wealth and achievement in this new field. They would have to act quickly because the pace of change was accelerating.

The boys called the company responsible for the Altair and pitched the idea. The man on the phone explained they would buy an operating system "from the first guy who shows up with one."[6] Skipping out on classes and working around the clock, Gates and Allen took BASIC and adapted it to the Altair. They saved the program on paper tape and flew to Albuquerque. But would it work?

Yes, it *did* work! So the Altair's maker bought the software, Gates dropped out of Harvard to found Microsoft in April 1975, and the rest is history.

Meanwhile, up in Menlo Park, California, a group of electronic enthusiasts decided to launch a club where like-minded hobbyists could meet to share ideas and parts. On March 5, 1975, the Homebrew Computer Club held its first meeting, when Steve Wozniak and thirty "enthusiastic people" showed up at the garage of the guy who started the group.[7] It was there that Wozniak saw the *Popular Electronics* issue from January and shared in the group's excitement about the Altair.[8]

Wozniak took home some technical specification sheets about the microprocessor in the Altair, and that's when things began to click for the brilliant young engineer. He realized that this Altair and the microprocessor powering it followed the same basic plan he had designed, on paper, five years earlier. I say "on paper" because Wozniak didn't have the money back then for those expensive parts. But prices had been dropping yearly (we will look at "Moore's law" in chapter 2). Wozniak's epiphany that night was that he could build a computer himself without even ordering the Altair everyone was so excited about. And as he pondered it more throughout the night, he knew his computer would be much better than the Altair.

"It was as if my whole life had been leading up to this point," Wozniak wrote in his autobiography. "I could build my own computer, a computer I could own and design to do any neat things I wanted to do with it for the rest of my life . . . And it was that very night that I started to sketch out on paper what would later come to be known as the Apple I."[9]

Wozniak intended to write up the schematics and "give it away for free to other people" as a way of "socializing and getting recognized."[10] But by the fall of 1975, Jobs had convinced Wozniak that even though die-hard hobbyists might have the time and stamina to solder together a bunch of components and wires, the less-intense hobbyist would probably pay extra to have a pre-assembled computer—just like most people purchase bicycles already assembled. Jobs convinced Woz that the two of them could earn money by constructing Wozniak's computer plan and selling it.

And that's when things began to accelerate.

In April 1976, they decided on "Apple" as the company's name and signed a partnership agreement. They demonstrated the "computer" (i.e., the circuit board with chips) to the Homebrew Club and met the owner of Byte, a pioneering retail computer hobbyist store that opened the previous year. He agreed to purchase fifty units at $500 per unit for this "Apple I" machine.

They flew to Atlantic City for an electronics trade show over Labor Day. They made no sales, but Jobs walked the floor and gathered intel. He realized that their future could be paved with gold, but only if they could produce a completed consumer product—a finished computer in a case, not just a motherboard of chips, wires, and assembly instructions. To do that would require an infusion of capital.

In the fall of 1976, venture capitalist Mike Markkula showed up to the garage, talked with the Steves, and looked at the working models. Markkula was only in his thirties but had retired young after earning a fortune with Gordon Moore's Intel just down the road. He liked what he saw and agreed to invest $250,000, predicting Apple would be a Fortune 500 company in five years. On January 3, 1977, they dissolved the earlier partnership and formed Apple, Inc., with a valuation of $5,309.[11]

In mid-April of 1977, the first West Coast Computer Faire opened in San Francisco, a pioneering two-day event that became the world's most significant computer trade show. Jobs had come up with a beautiful foam molded plastic shell that gave a sleek, finished appearance to complement the engineering wizardry of Wozniak. Jobs hustled and pitched and closed on sales, resulting in three hundred orders at the fair.

Media buzz accelerated. In May, Wozniak published a detailed description of Apple II's engineering in *Byte* magazine, explaining why the vision: "To me, a personal computer should be small, reliable, convenient to use, and inexpensive."[12] Up to that point, the word *computer* had not been linked to *any* of those other words. Hence, the revolution.

Compare Woz's words with a statement published by the Ford Motor Company to describe its founder's vision for the company's pioneering product, the 1908 Model T: "Henry Ford wanted the Model T to be affordable, simple to operate, and durable."[13] Though separated by seventy years and a world of technological advances, these pioneering, independent minds shared the same vision. And though these founders have reaped unprecedented financial windfalls from their labor and ingenuity, they didn't start with *only* the idea of amassing wealth for its own sake. Their products could help improve people's lives—that's the vision.

Most entrepreneurs I know are like this too. It's easy for us to chase our dreams of becoming wealthy someday. However, if we're not careful with how we approach each day and live our lives, we could get stuck, confused, dissatisfied, and unhappy. We could end up missing the real point of why we're working hard and doing our best to earn money! That's why it's important to refrain from thinking about getting wealthy as your end point in living a happy and meaningful life. Money can buy you life satisfaction, but it can't buy you lasting happiness and fulfillment.[14]

Woz and Jobs began shipping the Apple II on June 10, 1977, with high schoolers and other locals quickly hired to assemble, solder, program, and package up the computers.

In July 1977, Apple's advertisement in a national magazine was published in *Byte*, showing a man at a kitchen table using the Apple II to analyze stock market data while his wife stood nearby at the kitchen counter. The point: computers belong in the home.[15]

Elvis died the next month—a fact that has no bearing on our story except to get a sense of proportion for how much time has, and has not, passed since that day. (That said, both Presley and Jobs received the Presidential Medal of Freedom posthumously. Presley by President Trump in 2018 and Jobs by President Biden in 2022.) The following month, Apple closed the books on their fiscal year, showing revenue of $774,000 from 570 units shipped in four months. They went on to sell 7,600 units in 1978 ($7.8M revenue), 35,100 units in 1979 ($47M revenue), and 78,100 units in 1980 ($117M revenue).[16] The Apple II remained in production until 1993 and sold almost six million units. By contrast, it's unlikely that six million people in 1976 had ever even been in a room with a computer. The times they were a-changin'.

The two Steves began Apple in a garage with essentially just this one product, the Apple II. Capitalizing on such rapid success, they took the company public in December 1980 with a market cap of around $1.79 billion—an immense increase from the original $5,309 valuation from four years earlier.

But even more fascinating than the chronicle of Apple's corporate fortune is the story of how this product and company catalyzed the personal computer revolution itself—and how we all do work. With the Apple II leading the way, personal computers ushered in the nascent digital economy as we now know it.

The rate of change in the speed, power, and price of computers accelerated even as rapid advances were being made in software, satellites, silicon, cell phones, and the sharing of information over what came to be known as the internet. That is, not only was the rate of change accelerating in several areas of tech innovations, but there was also a convergence of innovations. The innovations *weren't* siloed. The rapid changes in one area opened or expanded revolutionary changes in adjacent areas. And then, finally, those convergences impacted aspects of society previously untouched by the impact of computers.

CELL PHONES, THE INTERNET, AND INDEPENDENTS

It's incredible how many technological "firsts" happened during those early to mid years of the 1970s. While much focus went to Watergate, Vietnam, and bell-bottoms, the techno foundation of the entire digital revolution was being laid. What a run! And we don't even have time to talk about the accelerated satellite technology of the early 1970s (the first commercial communications satellite went up in 1974).

But I'd be amiss if I didn't mention the date of the world's first mobile phone call: April 3, 1973. Right there in the early 1970s, Martin Cooper, a senior engineer at Motorola, called rival Bell Labs to inform them he was speaking via a mobile phone.[17]

Studying the timeline of cell phone development and mass consumer adoption gives you a feel for the global acceleration of change. After that initial call in 1973, the next ten years were full of research and development. Still, almost no consumer cell phone products or services were being produced for the average person on a budget. The price was too high and the need didn't exist—at least not in people's minds. To make a phone call while out, you'd just put a dime in a pay phone, which were absolutely everywhere. Government figures state there are only about 250,000 pay phones in service today, down from two million in 2000.[18]

In 1983, Motorola sold a big brick-like phone, the DynaTAC, which, again, was more for business callers, not everyday people. In 1993, when BellSouth sold the first smartphone, the average person was just starting to discover the benefits and novelty of pagers. But between 1990 and 2000, the worldwide number of cell phone subscribers escalated from 12 million to 1.5 billion. These 1990s phones weren't even "smart," of course, but with the release of the first BlackBerry phones in 2002, the demand for additional features began to escalate. In 2007, Apple released the first iPhone and has sold 2 billion units since—a number that doesn't include the whole host of other smartphones from competing companies.

With all these rapid advances in tech and consumer acceptance came an explosion in total global connection.

Year	# Cell Phone Subscribers
1990	12.5 million (0.25% of world population)
2000	1.5 billion (19% of world population)
2010	4 billion (68% of world population)
2020	4.78 billion (62% of world population)

That's an amazing escalation in the number of people across the planet who use cell phones (smartphones or not)—from 12.5 million to almost 5 billion people in only 30 years. And it's not like all those people went from landline telephones to cell phones as most of us did here in the United States. In many parts of the world, people went from having no access to any phone service to having a cell phone—and even a smartphone capable of accessing the internet. Likewise, some people went from having no home access to a personal computer to having an internet-connected cell phone.

Year	# Internet Users
1990	2.8 million (0.05% of world population)
2000	631 million (11% of world population)
2010	1.8 billion (26.6% of world population)
2020	4.5 billion (59% of world population)

* * *

Wait. Hold up. Did we even talk about the internet yet? In 1945—two years before the invention of the transistor—engineer Vannevar Bush wrote a prophetic article for *The Atlantic* titled "As We May Think." Bush's futurist vision described the "memex"—a collective memory machine connecting people and giving them access to all knowledge. Essentially, Bush foresaw what we now call the Information Age, predicting and hoping for the computers and internet that would make it possible.

"The *Encyclopedia Britannica* could be reduced to the volume of a matchbox," Bush wrote, predicting the mass digital storage of information we now take for granted. "A library of a million volumes could be compressed into one end of a desk."[19]

Indeed, the encyclopedia on CD became a bestselling commercial product of the 1990s. People were amazed that one disc could hold the contents of an entire physical set and was priced less than the cost of one physical volume. As we know, Bush's prediction didn't even go far enough. *Encyclopedia Britannica* stopped printing sets altogether in 2010 because this new thing called Wikipedia could be accessed online anywhere in the world—for free.

Bush correctly predicted that interpersonal communication would take place digitally. In 1969, the Department of Defense began ARPANET so the military could communicate more efficiently nationwide. In 1974, the first *commercial* version of ARPANET began, becoming the first internet service provider (ISP)—and remember, this came *before* the advent of the personal computer. But in 1985—little more than one decade later—Steve Jobs was able to say, "The most compelling reason for most people to buy a computer for the home will be to link it into a nationwide communications network. We're just in the beginning stages of what will be a truly remarkable breakthrough for most people—as remarkable as the telephone."[20]

And so, commercial providers for the masses launched in 1989, as Tim Berners-Lee invented the World Wide Web. By 1995, the US government decommissioned ARPANET, and internet service came into our homes entirely through commercial service providers. In 2000, less than 1% of Americans had broadband in their home; by 2021, that number had risen to 77%.

THE FUTURE OF WORK VS. THE STATUS QUO

All of these facts from the history of tech illustrate the accelerated rate of change, of course, but here's the connection to the broader theme of this book: the rise of the independent workforce would have been impossible apart from the creation and widespread adoption of cell phones and the internet.

Okay, so that's obvious. But let's go one step further. I would argue that once these technologies became common, the birth and growth of the independent workforce was a natural consequence. The future of work is independent because the tech creates an option that people organically desire. Online shopping or streaming video was an inevitable, foregone conclusion to the creation of the internet.

Likewise, the independent workforce is an inherent, organic fruit that emerged on the tree of these technologies. Whatever road bumps and potholes we discover and need to fix about the "gig economy" and independent professional work, the fact remains: people want the freedom to drive down this road.

Therefore, barring a global, catastrophic-apocalyptic event that destroys our technological infrastructure, the digital revolution will be both permanent and ongoing. And these changes impact every area of our lives, including how, where, and when we can work. This trendline will not stop, it will not reverse, and it will not slow down.

The window of time for new technology to transform society has shrunk. Technology moves from one phase to another quicker than ever before. Moving from seed to tree, from being misunderstood by the masses to mass adoption, from living at the edge of society to inhabiting the core—the timeline has hit warp speed. "Edges have always been engines of transformation," John Hagel, John Seely Brown, and Lang Davison wrote, "but, until recently, one could notice something emerging on the edge and—because it would take so long for its effect to be felt in the core—safely ignore it. There was comfort in the knowledge that one could lead a long and productive life without having to master the practices emerging on the edge. We are now in a different era, one where edges emerge and rise up with astonishing speed to catalyze changes on a global basis in less time than ever before."[21]

Several of the innovations we have been discussing *converged simultaneously* to make independent work possible and profitable. For instance, online marketplaces allow for near-frictionless talent engagement, regardless of geography. For the first time, these marketplaces empower forward-thinking organizations to access the best talent wherever they may be. The rise of the "digital nomad" is the starkest example of this trend, with workers who live remotely and earn their living while not being tied to a specific location. Adopting technologies such as Zoom, Slack, and Basecamp made the virtual office a reality, especially as organizations turned to remote work to keep businesses open during the COVID-19 pandemic. This accelerated the acceptance of remote work. As technology continues to evolve and the cultural acceptance of remote work grows, we will see even greater adoption and further innovation that makes it technologically and logistically simpler for organizations to source, engage, and manage independent workers.[22]

The impediment to change is the stubborn clinging to the status quo—the comfort that too many people find in *not* accepting change. It takes more than fancy new tech to change the mind and move the actions of a risk-averse institution like a business. At the company I lead, MBO Partners, we have tracked the size, sentiments, and demographics of the external workforce for twelve years—longer than anyone else—for our influential annual report, "The State of Independence" (I'll discuss this further in chapter 6). We know there has been *for more than a decade* a surging wave of independent-minded people who have entered the independent workforce. I emphasize "more than a decade" because some pundits think the gig economy and remote work surge only came about because of the pandemic. But that's not correct. The pandemic *did* accelerate change—breaking many people and companies out of their status quo mindset about independent work. But the pandemic did not birth the move toward independent work.

A similar catalyst arose during the 2007–2008 financial crisis. When masses of people were thrown out of work, losing jobs that had seemed impregnable and secure, many took the plunge into the freelance and independent contractor work they had been dreaming of for years. It often takes a kick in the seat of the pants to get us to do what we want or need to do.

Did you know the gas crisis throughout the 1970s also led people to dream and discuss how to make possible what we now call "remote work" or "work from home"? Fewer people traveling on roads would mean less gas consumption, pollution, and traffic. That crisis led to people trading in their gas-guzzling, robust engines in favor of small, lightweight, fuel-efficient cars. I got my driver's license in 1980. My first car was a Gran Torino Elite (yes, like the Clint Eastwood movie). But my second car was a Honda Civic.

So, researchers studied the idea and coined the word *telecommute* in 1973.[23] The necessary tech wasn't ready yet at the time, but by 1979 a *Washington Post* article reviewed the new technologies of the decade and concluded that "Working at Home Can Save Gasoline":

> Even more far-reaching have been the changes in the nature of the "machinery." Some of the most dramatic have emerged within the past decade through the rapid advances in computerization and electronic chip-technology. Revolution in reverse. Future historians may well view this period as an Industrial Revolution in reverse, since it is providing the working tools that make it possible to move a growing number of employees out of centralized workplaces into new types of "cottage" industries.[24]

The author was correct to note just how dramatic the changes in technology would be as they brought about a revolution in work. And here's another fun fact to illustrate how fast things change: When the *Washington Post* published that article in 1979, its current owner (Jeff Bezos) wasn't yet old enough to earn his driver's license and was still a year away from getting his first job—at McDonald's. Bezos and I were born the very same week in 1964, and it's amazing to consider just how much technological change has come to the workplace and the workforce since even those late 1970s days when we were young teens doing manual jobs.

TYPEWRITERS ARE *NOT* BICYCLES FOR THE MIND

And speaking of 1979, Steve Jobs attracted national media attention to Apple and himself with the debut issue of *Inc.* magazine in April of that year, containing a story about Jobs and his company. Then, in November 1979, *Time* profiled them both in glowing words, talking about "personal computers"—and yes, they put those words in quotes. Jobs, still just twenty-three, bragged that "We will sell more computers this year than IBM has in five." These early articles had to carry a lot of weight in explaining how and why a computer might one day be both cheap and useful enough to be purchased for home use.

Inc. again profiled Apple in October 1981, this time putting Jobs on the cover of a national magazine for the first time. This came after Apple's IPO, so the article framed the company not so much as the scrappy upstart it had been but as an industry leader. The article opened the hood of corporate Apple to see what other revolutions might be found, and what they found was transforming how their own employees worked. As evidence, *Inc.* noted that Apple CEO Mike Scott had sent a memo the year before with this ultimatum:

> EFFECTIVE IMMEDIATELY!! NO MORE TYPEWRITERS ARE TO BE PURCHASED, LEASED, etc., etc. Apple is an innovative company. We must believe and lead in all areas. If word processing is so neat, then let's all use it! Goal: by 1-1-81, NO typewriters at Apple ... We believe the typewriter is obsolete. Let's prove it inside before we try and convince our customers.[25]

This doesn't sound revolutionary by today's standards, but remember this was 1980, so how *would* typewriter-less correspondence be done? Letters, reports, memos—analog, analog, analog. And keep in mind that electronic typewriters were introduced in 1978, containing microchips, a viewing panel, and memory capacity; these machines were actually as advanced as they ever had been.[26] But an *advanced* analog machine is still just an analog machine.

That a company with over 2,000 employees and $100M in sales could throw typewriters out the door said a lot about how far the personal computer had come in less than five years. But to the point of our book: The new tech also got Apple (and everyone paying attention to these kind of magazine stories) thinking about what type of work their employees were doing. How would the tech transform the future of work?

Ann Bowers, Apple's VP of human resources, told *Inc.*, "We may have saved on personnel in some areas, but what's more important is that we're using a higher level of people's talents. Instead of efficiency, I like to talk of effectiveness."

That sounds great, but wouldn't people be displaced? *Inc.* explained: "Five months after the decision was made to do away with typewriters at Apple Computer, the term 'secretary' was abolished and replaced by 'area associate' to reflect the more varied responsibilities made possible by personal computers."

"We felt we needed a different term," Bowers said, "because 'secretary' was so loaded with connotations of typist, errand-runner, and phone answerer. We wanted to expand the area 'associates' functions so they could use their brains, in addition to their clerical skills."

That's not tossing people to the side. Yes, the job title and responsibilities changed, but the new tech and mindset provided employees with opportunities for upskilling and more meaningful work. "Not only do our area associates have the *freedom* to do more rewarding, enriching tasks," Jobs said, "they have the chance to get involved in solving problems that can ultimately affect the success of the entire company."

Jobs pointed out an employee sitting nearby, "a young woman with no previous computer experience." She was supplied with an Apple II and told to familiarize herself with the machine. Again, it's not a revolutionary concept by today's standards, but this "innovation"—supplying employees with a personal computer and expecting its use to transform how work got done—is a major point of the *Inc.* article and Steve Jobs's vision for how technology would enhance work. "In another month, she should be able to take on other functions within the company," Jobs said. "There's a special relationship that develops between one person and one computer that improves productivity on a personal level."

So it was the technological advances (in this case, advances ushered in by Apple itself) that catalyzed the "the future of work" at Apple.[27] Likewise, it was the tech advances of the digital revolution that led to the rise of the independent workforce—and with similar results: expanded and enhanced work.

CONVERGENCE, CONVIVIALITY, AND DECENTRALIZED COMMUNITY

Apple's success pushed IBM to enter the PC market in 1981, followed by endless IBM clones. That's why in 1982, the year I graduated from high school, *Time* magazine's editors chose the personal computer for their "Person of the Year" issue—changing the title to "Machine of the Year."

> There are some occasions, though, when the most significant force in a year's news is not a single individual but a process, and a widespread recognition by a whole society that *this process is changing the course of all other processes* . . . The "information revolution" that futurists have long predicted has arrived, bringing with it the promise of dramatic changes in the way people live and work, perhaps even in the way they think. *America will never be the same.*[28]

Notice that description? The accelerated changes and the convergence of those changes would transform all society—not just the society of tech geeks. *Time*'s focus was, of course, on America, but as we know, the information revolution went global.

Historians of the computer revolution have shown that the 1970s "Homebrew Computer Club" hobbyists and hackers in Silicon Valley were significantly influenced by the writing of philosopher Ivan Illich, especially his landmark 1973 book *Tools of Conviviality*, advocating for the proper use of technology. Illich argued that we should "give people tools that guarantee their right to work with independent efficiency."

For Jobs and Wozniak, this meant lowering the cost and complexity of computing in order to decentralize and democratize computing. As Jobs said as early as 1981, "There is a common conception that people have of computers, which is more along the lines of [George Orwell's] *1984*—very large, very centralized computers . . . When people actually see what a personal computer is, they see something they can hold in their hands . . . It is very decentralized. It's very democratic . . . It is enriching people's lives. It is freeing people to do things that we think people do best."[29] By 1983, the Apple II became the first personal computer to have sold a million total units.

WOZ'S US FESTIVAL

Speaking of "enriching people's lives"—Apple's IPO made many millionaires within its executive suite, and its two founders each found himself worth several hundred million dollars. New cars and houses followed, of course, but Wozniak then did something unique with his wealth. He spent a total of about $22M ($67M in today's dollars) of his own money to sponsor "US Festivals"—two huge music festivals in Southern California that drew 400,000 people in 1982 and 670,000 people in 1983 (setting a Guinness World Record).[30] The festivals also included huge pavilions to showcase amazing new electronics and technology. Music historians now rank these in the top 10 of such events for the decade, calling it the "Woodstock of the Eighties." The "US" didn't mean U.S. or United States. The name played off Tom Wolfe's description of the 1970s as the "Me Generation." Instead, Wozniak wanted his generation and the 1980s to be known as the US generation—to come together for the common good.

Wozniak even attempted some international peacemaking with the USSR, creating a live satellite linkup with music lovers in Moscow. Eddie Money was beamed to the Soviet Union, right there in 1982, with the Cold War still in full swing. As Steve Jobs would famously declare years later, "The people who are crazy enough to think they can change the world are the ones who do."

Bill Graham, the same legendary concert producer we spoke about in the introduction, partnered with Wozniak to produce the festival. What a difference five years had made, as Wozniak didn't have an extra dollar or hour to spend in 1977, but then teamed up with the best producer and hottest bands on earth in 1982. Talk about "the rate of change is accelerating"! Not bad for a guy who was barely into his thirties at the time of the festivals.

"I'd do it again in a minute, I really would," Wozniak wrote in his autobiography. "Everyone had fun! Smiles everywhere . . . One of the most memorable moments for me was when concert promoter Bill Graham came up to me near the end of the concert the first year. There was a huge full moon, and Sting and the Police were onstage. And Bill put his arm around me and said, 'Look at this, Steve, just look at it. You're not going to see this but once in a decade. This is so rare.'"[31]

◆ ◆ ◆

As I bring this chapter to a close, let me ask a rhetorical question: Except for sentimentality or nostalgia about "simpler times," would you roll back the clock and return to the tech of 1970? 1980? How about 1990? Or even 2000? Nobody would, because the accelerated change revolution of one decade becomes the status quo and expectation of the next. And that's why I know that the movement of people out of full-time employment and into the independent workforce will not reverse itself.

While in Walmart recently I saw they had a laptop for sale, priced at $200. Though these models wouldn't perform at the level I need, I looked at its spec sheet and realized that this humble device sitting unguarded on a shelf right next to bins full of $5 DVDs and $10 BVD underwear had more computing power than was available to the US government in its fight against Hitler. That's because the rate of change is accelerating, those changes are converging, *and* the progress is deflationary—which is the theme of the next chapter.

2

GET YOUR MEMORY FOR NOTHING AND YOUR CHIPS FOR FREE

Force #2: Progress Is Deflationary

We shape our tools and then our tools shape us.
—Marshall McLuhan

As Bill Graham wrapped his arm around Steve Wozniak and congratulated him on his 1982 US Festival, the Police gave everyone their money's worth with a set of twenty songs.[1] Considered one of the hottest bands on the planet and led by their front man Gordon Sumner—better known as "Sting"—the Police played "Message in a Bottle," their 1979 song, which became their first #1 on the UK charts.[2]

A lonely man on the island threw into the ocean a bottle with a message, hoping someone somewhere might get it and send a message back. But a year passed with no response, deepening his despair. Then, he awoke one morning to find "one hundred billion bottles washed up on the shore."

Don't get hung up on figuring out how he threw one bottle into the ocean and got 100 billion in return. It's metaphor, okay? It means that lonely and alienated people sometimes discover they're "not alone in being alone." This man didn't have Tom Hanks's *Cast Away* volleyball named "Wilson" to keep him company, so he turned to the bottle instead.

Sting says "Message in a Bottle" is one of his favorite songs. "I like the idea that while it's about loneliness and alienation, it's also about finding solace and other people going through the same thing. The guy's on a desert island and throws a bottle out to sea, saying he's alone, and all these millions of bottles come back saying, So what? So am I!"[3]

Now, let's take these lyrics literally and have some fun here, to illustrate this chapter's theme: "Progress Is Deflationary." The man received one hundred billion messages in one hundred billion bottles. Soda bottles were worth a nickel each in 1982, because that's how much deposit you'd get when you returned them to the grocery. So collectively, all those bottle senders tossed $5 billion (1982 dollars) of glass into the ocean—that's $16 billion in today's dollars.

But now, fast-forward to 1989 and watch as the man signs up for an AOL account with this newfangled thing called email. He awakes one morning to 100 billion messages in his inbox. (Yes. He receives email on the island. Don't ask me how that works and roll with me here.) Tech historians estimate that even in the year 2000, the total *worldwide* number of emails *sent* was less than 600 billion—*for the entire year.* By contrast, almost 350 billion emails are now sent every day.[4]

How much did it cost for the man to receive all these messages? You may think it was free—but that's not exactly right because AOL charged $2.95 per hour at that time. If the man read one email every five seconds, he'd spend $407 million ($842 million today) for the 138 million hours needed to read all those messages. Even when AOL switched to a flat monthly rate of $19.95 in 1996, it would take him 191,000 months to read the emails, costing the man $3.8 million ($7.8 million today) in AOL fees.

Fast-forward once more to the present day and give the man access to a smartphone with unlimited messaging. That service would cost less than $100 per month, providing the man with all the apps and computing power we now take for granted. He could even use an "Uber for boats" app and have someone rescue him off the island.

And if 100 billion people *did* text him, the cost to him would remain the same because *receiving* one hundred billion texts costs the same as receiving one. (Some exclusions apply. See store for more details. Offer not valid in North Korea or Iran.)

And here's the kicker. He actually wouldn't even need email or SMS to keep up with friends and family because their daily social media would suffice. He could Facebook his blues away or Instagram beach pics at sunset—with the tag "no filter." Or he could post videos on his TikTok, allowing members of the CCP in China to know his precise location at any moment—and maybe even rescue him?

Ironically enough, if the man was on the island today, he might discover the paradox of social media: it can increase loneliness—more blues, not less. Being connected to everyone feels about the same as being connected to no one. That being the case, our island man wouldn't even attempt to keep up with his 100 billion Twitter followers and Facebook friends. If they all private messaged him, he'd just set up filters to mute all except his Dunbar 150 ("Dunbar's number" is the idea that we all have a cognitive limit of about 150 for the number of people we can actively relate to in our social group[5]). The point here being that the rapid tech changes have also transformed our social structures and relationships—for better or worse. The deflated *cost* to connect increases the *value* of connecting with people we truly want to relate to (our unique Dunbar number). But the flip side is that cheap connectivity costs have radically devalued our so-called connections with everyone else. In chapter 14, we will talk about how independents aren't loners—knowing that their lives are better "with a little help" from their friends.

To summarize, ending this man's island loneliness would cost either the sender or receiver the following amounts (in today's dollars):

1982	Glass bottles	$32 billion
1993	AOL/per hour	$842 million
1996	AOL/flat fee	$7.8 million
2007	iPhone & apps	$100/month

That's a fantastic increase of efficiency and deflation in price in a span of only 25 years, to say nothing about the incredible decrease in environmental impact: 100 billion emails or DMs versus 100 billion pieces of glassware washing up on a lovely beach.

And don't forget about speed. People complain about the slowness of email because it lacks synchronicity.[6] But leaving aside the human inefficiency factors, digital communication moves at the speed of electrical waves and light pulses traveling on fiber optic glass, not the speed of glass bottles traveling on ocean waves.

I'm just being cheeky with all this talk of "messages in bottles." Still, even if I switched out the analogy and compared digital comms with postage stamps and letters, the same basic principle applies: *progress is deflationary*. When communication technology morphed from analog to digital, the world gained a far superior product, as judged by cost, speed, reliability, and environmental impact. That's why, in 1996, more emails were sent for the first time in the United States than postal mail letters. The USPS delivered 128 billion pieces of physical mail in 2021; every single day that same year, the world sent 320 billion emails.[7] Our means of communication progressed beyond what anyone could have ever believed in the 1700s (horse and foot delivery), 1800s (steam engine locomotives and ships), or even 1900s (automobile and air transport). The speed *and* quality increased even as the cost decreased exponentially.

✦ ✦ ✦

Deflation is a general reduction in the price level of goods and services in an economy over time. Technological progress increases production efficiency and escalates competition (i.e., drops barriers to entry). The convergence of technologies creates this downward pressure—and so that's why we say that progress is deflationary. In the absence of a monopoly, as companies find ways to produce goods and services more efficiently and at lower costs, they lower prices and attract more customers. This, in turn, puts pressure on other companies in the industry to lower their prices as well, leading to a general decrease in prices across the sector.

Converging innovations not only change societal norms, they also can disrupt existing industry value chains. Taking advantage of these supply chain and distribution changes, innovative companies can beat out well-established incumbents faster than ever by improving the quality, speed, or price at which value is delivered. Higher value = higher speed + better quality + lower price. This force is known as deflationary progress.[8]

Do you tend to view tech-driven progress positively, negatively, or mixed? The answer to that question typically depends on what was disrupted. When new tech disrupts by making some aspect of our lives easier, cheaper, or more efficient, we sing its praises. But if the new tech takes away your job, you're not so happy. Though the accelerating rate of change will be both disruptive and beneficial overall, it will cause some people (and enterprises) to be left behind. "Entrepreneurial Darwinism" means adapting your business or career to survive and thrive in response to new tech—the fittest will survive. I don't say that cavalierly but simply as a matter of fact.

Progress is deflationary. That's the theme of this chapter and the second of the "Six Forces Shaping the Future of Work." Like the previous chapter, our examples will come primarily from tech—hardware, software, AI, and the internet of everything—all these progressions that impact every aspect of our lives, including our work. And I will make the case that the rise of the independent workforce came as a direct result—an inevitable and irreversible consequence of progress being deflationary.

MOVE BITS, NOT ATOMS

Although the cell phone in your hands wasn't even technically possible 40 years ago, the sum total of its components would theoretically have cost billions of dollars. Even in the early 1990s, the technology powering today's smartphone would have cost $100 million.[9] But now, even advanced smartphones cost less than $1,500. Hence, the total global number of cell phone and smartphone users now approaches seven billion people.[10] The ubiquity of these devices means we've arrived at the point in history where we don't even think about them in terms of what they are: supercomputers.

This fulfills the prophetic vision of Adam Osborne, the founder of Osborne Computer Corporation—a pioneer of portable computing—who said in 1982, "The future lies in designing and selling computers that people don't realize are computers at all."[11]

I used my first portable computer around 1987, a company-owned Compaq Portable 386, which weighed eleven pounds, had less than 10 MB of RAM, and cost $8,000 ($19,000 in today's dollars).[12] This machine was *powerful* (by the standards of that day) and as *portable* as a sewing machine (that would have been a bragging point in 1987). But today I could buy a dozen iPhones for the same price as my Compaq 386. And I could *carry* two dozen iPhones for the same weight as that first "portable" I was so proud of.

That's deflationary progress: Smaller tech. More powerful tech. Cheaper tech.

This also illustrates Nicholas Negroponte's "Move bits, not atoms" principle for success in the digital age. The latest iPhone *does* have atoms (around 200 grams' worth), but we can measure progress by all the atoms' worth of physical tools our smartphones have replaced. When cell phones first launched, they were only that: phones. People didn't expect them to be high-tech Swiss Army Knives, replacing a toolbox worth of equipment—but that's exactly what's happened.

A column posted online in 2014 made this point remarkably well by reprinting a 1991 Radio Shack advertisement published in the *Buffalo News* to market the must-have technology.[13]

Analyzing the ad, the author listed every item he had replaced with his iPhone and concluded: "You'd have spent $3,054.82 in 1991 to buy all the stuff in this ad that you can now do with your phone ... the technology of only two decades ago now replaced by the 3.95-ounce bundle of plastic, glass, and processors in our pockets."[14]

The bits replaced the atoms, and the *apps* eliminated the *appliances*. That's deflationary progress. Like *Time* magazine predicted in 1983, "Perhaps the revolution will fulfill itself only when people no longer see anything unusual in the brave New World, when they see their computer not as a fearsome challenger to their intelligence but as a useful linkup of some everyday gadgets: the calculator, the TV, and the typewriter."[15]

It's worth noting that when this column was published in 2014, Radio Shack operated 4,100 stores in the United States and 7,000+ worldwide. But being unable to transform itself to compete with online retail, the company filed for Chapter 11 bankruptcy the very next year; fewer than 400 stores remain today.[16] Simply put, their business model involved owning way too many atoms—all those sunk costs from brick-and-mortar stores, overhead, and warehoused inventory.

Breakout

To illustrate this principle further, let's return to Steve Wozniak and 1977, this time peering over his shoulder as he experimented with the BASIC software to see if he could get his new machine to do fun stuff—video games. He wanted to program *Breakout*, the Atari game he had engineered with chips a few years earlier as a favor to his friend Steve Jobs, who worked for Atari. And that's when Woz experienced "the biggest earthshaking Eureka moment ever."

> I sat down and started typing in BASIC the commands I needed to make one row of bricks—just like the ones in Atari's arcade game—and it worked . . . And then I played with all these parameters and it only took a half hour total. I tried dozens and dozens of different variations of things until, finally, I had the game of Breakout completely working on the Apple II, showing the score and everything. I called Steve Jobs over. I couldn't believe I'd been able to do it, it was amazing.[17]

Because kids today can code a simple game in minutes, it's difficult to understand how this was "amazing" or revolutionary. Still, before Woz's eureka moment, the few video games in existence were built with hardware, not software. If you looked "under the hood" of even the simplest video game in 1976, you would see wires and chips going everywhere: hardware. But building the game in software? Wozniak explained this to Jobs: "I said, 'If I had done all these varieties of options in hardware the way it was always done, it would've taken me ten years to do. Now that games are in software, the whole world is going to change.' That was the exact moment it sank in."

Building a game in thirty minutes instead of a decade is also revolutionary progress because creators could do *more* with less. All games after that point could reinvest the saved time and resources, causing games to be created quicker, cheaper, and better. Wozniak later explained:

> Software games were going to be incredibly advanced compared to hardware games—games that were hardwired into arcades and systems like that. These days, the graphics are so great in games. They have gotten incredibly complicated and huge in size. If they had to be in hardware, there wouldn't be enough time in the universe to design them.[18]

This is crucial to understand because it will impact our later discussion about the independent workforce (and its relationship to tech). Woz is saying that the new, advanced way of doing the work didn't just save time; it made the impossible possible. And as a corollary, the "software, not hardware" approach to game design raised the bar on all games and game makers—a reality that continues today. Each decade raises and fulfills consumer expectations for the games to be better and to do so without any dramatic price increase—or even, with a price decrease. In 1976, Atari's home console of *Pong*, with its *one* built-in table tennis game, cost consumers about $100 ($525 today)—roughly the same price as the latest Xbox.[19] That's deflationary progress.

The principle of "build *Breakout* with software, not hardware" was Woz's pioneering application of the "move bits, not atoms" principle. All software-driven strategies within the digital economy flow from that same fundamental mindset, as we will see below. And though I'm getting ahead of myself here, the independent workforce and remote work also flow from this revolution. People (atoms) can do their work digitally (bits) from any location and at any time. And once this happens, the bar of expectations is raised even as the price decreases. The workforce—independents and employees alike—produce more and better goods and services digitally than they could in an analog world.

• • •

In 2022, when Apple became the first company to hit $3 trillion in market value, Wozniak waxed nostalgic about the company: "When we started, we thought it would be a successful company that would go forever. But you don't really envision *this*. At the time, the amount of memory that would hold one song cost $1 million."[20]

The figure Woz quoted sounded crazy, so I looked up the historical price for computer disk memory—and Woz was right:[21]

Year	$ Cost per Megabyte (2023 USD)
1957	$411,041,792
1959	$67,947,725
1960	$5,252,880
1965	$2,642,412
1970	$734,003
1973	$399,360
1975	$67,584
1976	$48,960
1977	$36,000
1979	$6,704
1981	$4,479
1991	$39.80
2001	$0.148
2011	$0.005
2021	$0.003

Of course, in 1976, nobody played songs stored on a computer or other digital device—that wouldn't arrive for three decades, most notably with the iPod and the iTunes store. But Woz's point is true—truer than I could almost believe when I saw these prices. Today, you can essentially get your memory for nothing and your chips for free. If technological progress *wasn't* deflationary, we'd be in dire straits.[22]

THERE'S MOORE TO THE STORY

The point isn't technology history—I'm not a historian and this isn't a history book. But knowing what got us to where we're at is important if we're going to see what lies ahead, and the rise of the independent workforce could not have taken place in my dad's generation—the tech foundation simply didn't exist. And a corollary principle is that, barring a meltdown that returns us to pre-1947 technology (i.e., before the transistor), the global, independent workforce will continue to grow in size and influence. You might say it's a "law" now in place.

As the Information Age progressed, people noted various "laws" that seemed to govern the digital world, impacting our lives even if we've never heard of them. There's a twofold reason for my mentioning three of these laws (Moore, Metcalfe, and Gilder): First, each law illustrates the theme of this chapter—that progress is deflationary. Second—and to the point of the overall book—the end products of each law being true are the myriad technological breakthroughs that gave birth to and grew remote work and independent work.

Moore's Law

In the early 1960s, Intel cofounder Gordon Moore noticed that with each passing year, his company could place a larger number of transistors on each microchip. In 1965, he wrote an article in *Electronics* magazine predicting the future of semiconductor production, power, and pricing. Now known as "Moore's law," he said that the number of components in a dense integrated circuit would continue to double each year for the next ten years. A 1965 microchip held 64 transistors, but Moore predicted that 1975 chips would hold 65,000. As a result, the price of microchips would decrease even as their quality and power would increase.[23]

Moore's law proved true, though he later claimed that his prophecy ended up being something that *drove* the industry forward to greater accomplishments rather than predicting it. Either way, as we have seen with the Altair of 1975, the "cheap chips" reality ushered in the personal computer revolution. Hobbyists could finally afford the microprocessors and component parts needed to build themselves a computer. And Moore's law also explains why computers and consumer electronic products feel obsolete within a few years of purchase. Better, faster, cheaper: that's the accelerated rate of change.

"We rarely think about chips, yet they've created the modern world," wrote Chris Miller, author of *Chip War: The Fight for the World's Most Critical Technology*. Miller said the chip industry annually produces "more transistors than the combined quantity of all goods produced by all other companies, in all other industries, in all human history. Nothing else comes close." And what is the societal and economic impact of all those chips? Miller writes, "Most of the world's GDP is produced with devices that rely on semiconductors. For a product that didn't exist seventy-five years ago, this is extraordinary."[24]

And to use that fact as an analogy, I believe the following is true: independent-minded innovators produce most of the world's GDP.

Metcalfe's Law

Robert Metcalfe, the engineer who first set up a functioning Ethernet system in 1973, talked about how networks are valuable in proportion to how many "nodes"—people, accounts, machines—there are within the network.

Metcalfe was dealing with the problem of how to get all the computers at his work set up to use the new laser printer they were developing. But the "law" goes beyond printers, explaining how the "network effects" shape the digital business models we now take for granted.

Suppose a digital platform doesn't quickly accelerate—the number of people who join and use it regularly builds, but the growth comes too slowly. In that case, others won't jump in at all because nobody wants to sit there wondering if they're typing content into a black void with no audience. Nobody depends on Uber in towns where only a few drivers have signed up. In the 1990s, fax machines were powerful business tools only because everyone had one. If your business had the only fax machine, what good would that do? Likewise, in the early days of electric cars, users had difficulty finding charging stations because the demand had not yet reached a critical mass. But as charging stations were built and became ubiquitous (at least in urban areas), more people considered buying an electric vehicle. Seeing charging stations all over the place normalized electric cars for otherwise skeptical consumers. Also FOMO kicks in: fear of missing out.

For our purposes in thinking about the future of work, the point is that the exponential growth of a network leads to ubiquity—the mass adoption of the new thing. As recently as the 1990s, people weren't sure what to think about the security risks of banks having a website that account holders could log in to. Now Gen Z will be the generation that banks without having ever set foot inside an actual bank building. From seed to sapling to tree, new technologies create the networks that become the fully mature, accepted realities for everyone.

When the gig economy was a baby, it seemed exotic. Now venture capitalists hear pitches every day for new businesses described as "the Uber of *X*." Not only did Uber itself grow exponentially over the past decade, but the Uber business model spread across all industries. The accelerated growth of the independent workforce has now established network effects of such scale that I would argue it has reached critical mass. And because there's a critical mass, there will be accelerated knowledge flow and the lowering of barriers to entry. If you've never met an independent entrepreneur, the whole thing might seem scary. If half the people you drink a beer with are independent entrepreneurs, the know-how for working independently has become ubiquitous.

That's network effects. That's the accelerated rate of growth.

Gilder's Law

And speaking of growth, the third example of a law that governs the spread of technology in the digital era is "Gilder's law," the idea that "bandwidth grows at least three times faster than computer power."[25]

Suppose you're old enough to remember the "dial-up" days of the internet. In that case, you also remember the cost and concerns about bandwidth.

Parents kept track of bandwidth burn rate, lest their teens use up a month's supply in the first few days. In 1995, one could hardly imagine a future of "streaming video" because even downloading a picture of your cousin's cat would take several seconds or longer, depending on the size of the image and the speed of your bandwidth. It wasn't just that your computer that was slow; it was the bandwidth.

Thankfully, Gilder's law has proven true, as evidenced by the immense flow of digital data we receive daily. Bandwidth flows so fast and freely now that most of us don't even think about it. You can even use the "Free Wi-Fi" while eating a cheeseburger at McDonald's—and the speed is unbelievably fast compared to the turtle-like bandwidth we paid for back in the 1990s. And remember, the escalation of bandwidth capacity affected all devices that use it, not just computers sitting on a desk. Since the introduction of 1G in the 1980s, there has been a remarkable increase in the bandwidth available on cellular networks. With each new generation, from 2G to the current 5G, data rate speeds have escalated even as costs plummeted.[26]

＊ ＊ ＊

In the past two or three centuries, there has come a point when prognosticators have begun to declare that "we've done it all"—that innovation and invention will plateau, and progress will slow. Is that where we are today? Do we see signs of diminished acceleration of change? Not hardly. "There's still so much you can do with technology to improve the customer experience," Jeff Bezos wrote to Amazon employees and shareholders in 1997—and he continues to repeat this theme almost three decades later. "And that's the sense in which I believe it's still Day One and that it's early in the day. If anything, the rate of change is accelerating."[27]

These three laws—Moore, Metcalfe, and Gilder—relate to the three building blocks of technology: processing, storage, and transport. These laws have all proven accurate, and each of their accelerated rates of change converged with the other, producing demonstrable change within society.[28] But will they continue to improve?

DEFLATIONARY PROGRESS AND
THE 30% EXTERNAL WORKFORCE

Yes, the continued acceleration of change in technology will continue to deflate its price—which will further lower the capital costs necessary for entrepreneurs to do their work. As a result, the external workforce will continue to grow in size and influence with every wave of cheaper, advanced technology. And as this happens, enterprises that utilize independents will also experience a deflation in labor costs and an uptick in agility and innovation. Why? I'll explain this further in later chapters, but here's the short answer.

Digital work can be done anywhere at any time by anyone a business chooses to compensate for that work—including the independent workforce. But specifically using external talent will increase business flexibility and agility for businesses and lower the costs of labor. From my own business experience and common sense about how much extra costs are incurred with full-time employees (FICA, benefits, onboarding, etc.), I believe that when businesses leverage the external workforce they will see a 15% to 35% reduction in employment expenses. Anecdotally, such numbers don't even tell the whole picture, as successfully implementing independent workforce programs also leads to greater client satisfaction and improved processes. A more efficient use of resources leads to a more efficient way of working.[29]

Since the pandemic, companies have been flopping back and forth on the topic of remote work and hybrid work—even "Big Tech" companies with the sophisticated knowledge and resources to know better. Mark Zuckerberg, CEO of Meta, predicted in 2020 that half of the company's employees could be working from home within five to ten years.[30]

I don't want to conflate "remote work" with "independent work"—or to suggest that remote work for *employees* isn't also a significant component of the future of work. But I want business leaders like Zuckerberg to understand that supporting remote work for employees is great—but it's just the first shift of mindset that needs to happen. Supporting remote work for employees is a great start, I would encourage Zuckerberg—and anyone in business—to consider going further down the "working from home" path by simply utilizing independent professionals for at least 30% of their workforce spend. That is, allocate 30% of the dollars spent on your work-force (not 30% of the total numbers of noses) on independents.

Utilizing the independent workforce also makes a company more agile as the economy heats up and cools off. In the final quarter of 2022 and the beginning of 2023, we saw massive layoffs throughout Big Tech companies, even as profits continued to soar. Overall, the tech industry employed more people than ever (25 straight months of net employment growth as of December 2022). There were 100,000 layoffs in tech alone; Alphabet (Google's parent company) terminated 12,000 employees in January, and Microsoft cut 10,000.

There are many causes for this, but executives have admitted that over-hiring in 2020 and 2021 is chiefly to blame. Consider how much better it would have been if companies had utilized independents during those years, putting them to work on projects and ongoing work but not onboarding them as full-time employees.

Journalists noted that many laid-off tech workers felt like they were experiencing "the Great Betrayal," and many of those decided to ditch full-time employment and join the independent workforce. In one survey of 4,188 laid-off employees, 1,007 reported they had started their own business since being terminated.[31] In a separate survey of 500 knowledge workers, 66% said they were ready to "break up with full-time employment" because "the recent waves of layoffs have made them lose trust in the stability and security of full-time employment." And 62% said the recent layoffs "made them feel less secure about committing to one employer."[32]

Here's a free piece of advice to corporate execs: When CEOs are prepping for mass layoffs caused by their company's fragility, I hope they'll think twice about the awful optics of simultaneously lavishing their C-suite with costly perks. The night before Microsoft announced their 10,000 layoffs in January 2023, top executives were across the ocean at the World Economic Forum in Davos, Switzerland, getting serenaded by Sting at a private event for fifty people. "Doesn't get much more Marie Antoinette than that," said a pundit on cable news. The *Wall Street Journal* reported that the timing was "a sour note to some [Microsoft] employees." Sour indeed. As someone tweeted: "The message in a bottle was: You're fired."

Okay, so here at the end of this chapter, let me make explicit the connection between the importance of the external workforce and the central thrust of this chapter—that "progress is deflationary." I hope we can all agree that yo-yo hiring and firing diminishes morale. But thanks to the digital revolution and all of its converging technologies, there's no excuse for failing to utilize the external workforce to build into your company greater agility for the changing economic cycles.

Progress has deflated the tech to the point that there's no excuse that can be made about the cost of the tech infrastructure—especially when compared to the exorbitant costs of physically officing an entire workforce. Companies that ignore the external workforce will increase the likelihood of dramatic and unnecessary hiring and firing with each surge and contraction of their industry or the economy.

In sum, the deflated technology allows a company to increase agility by fractionalizing its workforce. Whether you want to admit it or not, the reality is that the digital revolution has already fractionalized *everything*—and most certainly it has fractionalized the workforce. And that is the theme of the next chapter.

3

WE ARE NEVER EVER GETTING BACK TOGETHER

Force #3: The Fractionalization of Everything

> There are only two ways to make money in business: bundling and unbundling.
>
> —Jim Barksdale, former Netscape CEO[1]

uick. What do all these fictional people have in common? Sherlock Holmes, Lisbeth Salander (*The Girl with the Dragon Tattoo*), Katniss Everdeen (*The Hunger Games*), Mike Ehrmantraut (*Breaking Bad*), Peter Parker (*Spider-Man*), and *Star Wars* characters Han Solo, Boba Fett, and Lando Calrissian. Hint: It has something to do with their work life. I'll give you a minute to figure it out.

THE BEST/WORST OF TIMES (CHOOSE ONE)

When I talk about the fractionalization of everything, I'm referring to the increased fragmentation and specialization within modern life. From the economy to culture, technology to politics, we see this macro trend—this third "Everson Evolution"—in nearly everything, everywhere, and all at once.

We see fragmentation and specialization in the cultural and political spheres. With the rise of social media and other digital platforms, people connect directly with others who share their interests and beliefs, creating a multitude of microcommunities that cater to every possible taste and preference. Political parties and interest groups cater to ever-more specialized and specific population segments, leading to polarization and tribalism. With a wider variety of niche subcultures and communities available in the palm of our hands, culture fractionalizes. As a result, it takes intentional behavior and thinking to find common ground and work toward shared goals in business and culture.

In the 1980s, we fractionalized homeownership with mortgage-backed securities. In 2022, only about 40% of homeowners actually owned their home outright with a paid off mortgage.[2] But for anyone who has a retirement account invested in a balanced fund, they actually own a tiny fraction of other people's homes through these mortgage-backed securities.

If you've stayed at an Airbnb, that's fractionalized lodging. When you jump into a ride-sharing vehicle like Uber or Lyft, that's fractionalized transportation.

Fractionalized real estate investments allow you to own a small percentage of a property—like an apartment building or office space—earning a share of the rental income and sharing in potential appreciation of the property's value. Fractional art or collectibles (rare stamps, coins, sports memorabilia) make you the partial owner of a piece of art you couldn't afford to buy outright. Cryptocurrency investing follows the same logic, allowing investors to buy into a small ("fractional") amount of the currency (i.e., Bitcoin or Ethereum). Fractional stock investing? Same principle.

The next significant asset to be fractionalized is the most valuable asset of any company: its workforce and people. Companies will increasingly fractionalize their workforce to get the right people with the right skills at the right time and the right price. And workers are also taking advantage of this, fractionalizing their workday and careers in a way that has never before been possible. We see this trend in the rise of the gig economy and the growth of niche markets—the "long tail" applied to the workforce. Technological advances have made it easier than ever to connect buyers and sellers across the globe, driving this specialization of skills and project-based work for independents. By breaking down complex tasks into smaller and specialized components, fractionalization of work enables a distributed network of workers and technology to complete them.

Technological advancements drive this trend, beginning with the tech that makes it increasingly easier to perform digital tasks remotely and asynchronously by a distributed network of workers—or even by artificial intelligence. As a result, technology hastens *globalization*, as the barriers to entry for workers in different parts of the world are lowered each year.

And now, with the rise of the gig economy and independent work, technology has ushered in greater flexibility and freedom for the workforce. But if we're being honest, all this change has also created new forms of insecurity and instability. Like Charles Dickens's famous opening lines to *A Tale of Two Cities*: "It was the best of times, it was the worst of times . . . it was the spring of hope, it was the winter of despair, we had everything before us, we had nothing before us."[3]

When it comes to your career or your company's need for talent, you want to make sure you're on the "best of times" side of the fractionalization equation. How? By becoming an independent *or* utilizing independents.

FRACTIONALIZED LABOR

The term *fractionalized workforce* refers to the increasing number of workers in the United States who are engaged in nontraditional or nonstandard work arrangements. Workers who are fractionalized are not employed in full-time jobs with one company. They do not receive benefits such as health insurance, retirement plans, and paid time off, because those benefits (and income) form the traditional package of bundled incentives to attract and keep employees. But in addition to income and benefits, companies provide all of these "bundled services" to a traditional employee—in the sense that all of this work-related infrastructure would need to be replaced by an independent worker:

- Production
- Distribution
- Income
- Administration
- Benefits
- Team
- Learning
- Mentorship[4]

Before the digital economy, all of this infrastructure involved "moving atoms"—analog transactions burdened with friction and cost prohibitive. However, as author Li Jin has noted, "micropreneurs piece these components together on their own" through a variety of "software as a service" (SaaS) platforms.[5] As I always tell would-be solopreneurs: "The barriers to entry have never been lower."

In the past, jobs often required workers to perform a wide range of tasks and activities, which were bundled into a single job. If for no other reason, the employer sought to keep the employee continuously active—and there's nothing wrong with that goal. For example, a factory worker might be responsible for operating machinery, performing quality control checks, and packaging finished products. But, with the rise of automation and digital technologies, it has become possible to break down these tasks and activities into smaller components that can be performed by different workers, by remote or offshore workers, or even by machines.

BUNDLING AND UNBUNDLING

People interchangeably use the word *unbundling* for fractionalization. By definition, *bundling* is when one party, in most cases a company or business, decides the best option for the individual—the average, median individual.

When shopping for clothing for a young child or an infant, stores offer bundled outfits—a pair of pants, matching shirt, and clip-on bow tie—all together on a hanger. But adults buy their own clothes unbundled, picking and choosing to best meet their preferences.

Cable TV bundles packages of 50, 100, or 200 stations together for you, even if you only want a dozen. But then high-speed internet, smartphones, and all the other tech of the digital revolution came, and *presto*, consumers gained the ability to personalize their viewing selections with streaming subscriptions tailored to their exact tastes. As a result, people began to unbundle by "cutting the cord" of their cable, and many Gen Zers never subscribed to cable in the first place. Whereas 78% of Americans now subscribe to a streaming video service, only 56% percent take cable.[6]

And now, things are coming full circle as shrewd streaming video providers are partnering with content producers to increase the selections they can offer subscribers—leading to the *bundling* of content.

Bundling makes sense if you want the "Value Meal" because it's cheaper and easier to say "Give me a #2" than to select each item separately. But what if you're trying to lay off the carbs? Would you eat at McDonald's if they mandated that you buy Coke and fries with your burger? Of course not.

Choosing a gym? Bundling works great if you want to run on a treadmill, lift weights, drink a freshly made vegetable smoothie, meet friends for aerobics, work with a nutritionist, and steam in a sauna. But what if all you need is a 5 AM yoga class? Then, that boutique yoga studio—or even a live, online class—will meet your needs, get you in and out the door quicker, and probably cost you less.

You unbundle your insurance when you choose different companies for your auto, home, and life—if doing so provides superior value. But sometimes you'll get a discount and better overall value if you bundle all your policies together with the same company. The important thing is to have the freedom to make those decisions for oneself. Unbundling expands the freedom of choice for the individual. That's why workers are beginning to question the wisdom of employer-sponsored health insurance programs. Why should something as basic and essential as health insurance be "bundled" as a benefit of a specific job?[7]

In a similar manner to all these examples, unbundling work also makes companies more agile and innovative, enabling more specific skills for a specific outcome, rather than assigning an outcome to a predefined role within a company. Unbundling personalizes the work environment to each person rather than cohorts of people or functions. And for the company, unbundling increases options for the company—which leads to an increased agility.

Examples of fractionalized labor in the digital economy include online marketplaces like Amazon and eBay. They unbundled the traditional retail supply chain by directly connecting buyers (and laborers) and sellers, cutting out middlemen and lowering costs. We've already mentioned ridesharing, but similar "Uber of X" platforms for hiring talent include Taskrabbit, Postmates, and Freelancer. I would add my own company here, MBO Partners, though we are geared toward skilled independent professionals and are not part of the gig economy as commonly understood.

Crowdfunding platforms such as Kickstarter and Indiegogo have unbundled the traditional venture capital process by allowing individuals and small businesses to raise funds directly from many individual investors (we'll look at crowdsourcing in the next chapter). Social media platforms such as Facebook, Twitter, and Instagram have unbundled the traditional media industry by allowing anyone to create and share content with a large audience without needing a traditional publishing or broadcasting company. Cloud computing services like Amazon Web Services and Microsoft Azure have unbundled the traditional IT infrastructure by allowing businesses to outsource their computing needs to third-party providers, reducing the need for in-house IT staff and equipment. Dozens of publishing or educational platforms have sprung up to provide a direct bridge from writer to reader or instructor to student.

Critics who argue that fractionalization doesn't impact manufacturing or traditional "blue-collar" jobs forget that the digital economy touches every sector. Many manufacturers have unbundled their production processes by outsourcing specific tasks to domestic and international third-party suppliers. This can include components, assembly, and even entire production lines. Contract manufacturing has become increasingly common in recent years, allowing manufacturers to outsource the production of specific components or products to specialized contractors. And now 3D printing technology has the potential to unbundle the traditional manufacturing process by enabling the creation of custom parts and products on demand without the need for a conventional factory or supply chain. Advances in automation technology have allowed manufacturers to unbundle many production tasks and activities, reducing the need for human labor in some cases. And collaborative manufacturing models, such as open-source hardware and software development, allow manufacturers to collaborate with other companies and even individual users to create products and share knowledge and resources (we'll discuss open-source labor in the next chapter).

ROA AND THE 60/30/10 PRINCIPLE

Though many accountants deny that employees are assets—because they're unable to quantify talent into a line on a balance sheet—business leaders and management experts assert the opposite: "Our people are our most important asset" is a common claim in annual reports and CEO speeches. But until recently, "our people" always and only referred to employees who came into their office for a traditional workweek in order to receive a paycheck, perks, and benefits.

If you're a business leader, let me encourage you to consider shifting this language to "Skills are our most important asset." Thinking of "skills" rather than "employees" in the context of assets can help you change how you think of your workforce and make inclusion in return on assets (ROA) easier.

How readily can you tap skills as they are needed? I believe the faster you can accelerate progress toward business goals and the quicker you can pivot if external factors require it, the better your chances of succeeding, even in a down market. Access to the right skills at the right time can make a difference and provide the positive economic benefit that characterizes an "asset."

How can you ensure you have the right skills and assets in place when needed? Many companies have difficulty acquiring important skill sets through traditional employment. Some people with in-demand expertise are no longer willing to work within the 9-to-5 in-office structure that has been the norm for decades. Others, especially those with high-demand and hard-to-find capabilities, prefer to direct their own careers as independent professionals. Adding to the challenge, the needed skills may not require full-time attention or have a shelf life. For example, once the strategic initiative is finished, those skills may not be necessary, at least for a while.

Companies have previously addressed this specialized, short-term need for specific skills by "bolting on" contractors to their workforce. This often required working through a staffing agency with limited visibility into candidates and hefty fees to pay. In these scenarios, the acquired skills can be more liabilities than assets—the cost of the skills interferes with any positive economic benefit. But this is no longer necessary. Skills can now be moved entirely to the asset column by creating a fractional workforce.

During my years leading a global division of a premier consulting business, I pioneered a 60/30/10 work model. This fractional workforce—60% full-time employees, 30% independent contractors, and 10% offshore resources—is how the business now operates. There is a solid full-time-equivalent foundation, a talent pool that allows fast activation of independent professionals, and an offshore component with specific and cost-effective skills. This increased our enterprise flexibility and accelerated response time to changes in the market. In short, the skill-set portfolio resulting from the fractional workforce was a positive element of the company's ROA.

Firsthand experience with this work model made me a firm believer in the benefits of a fractional workforce. I believe it is the winning model today and will be in the future. It can support your business strategy by leveraging the best skill sets cost effectively, supporting enterprise flexibility and agility, and putting skills squarely in the asset column.

A fractional workforce can significantly impact ROA, which can help you and your business succeed as you navigate uncertain waters.[8] Understand the importance of fractionalizing your fixed cost structure—making that more variable—whether it's your leases, your computer stack, or your most valuable asset: your people. If you fractionalize, you improve your agility.

You can move fast in the areas that matter, plugging in and out. Companies that do so show a much greater valuation—to the tune of 1,400 basis points (for more on that see chapter 16, "Has Life Been Good to Me?").

IT'S ELEMENTARY, MY DEAR WATSON

So did you figure out what all the fictional characters I mentioned in the introduction to this chapter have in common? Answer: They all work fractionally. They're independents, dividing their labor among multiple employers and various projects.

Sherlock Holmes worked on cases as a consultant for the police or private clients. His services were hired on a case-by-case basis, and he would only work on each case until it was resolved.

Lisbeth, "The Girl with the Dragon Tattoo," is a top-notch hacker working for different clients—she is no one organization's employee.

In *The Hunger Games*, Katniss Everdeen uses her skills as a hunter and survivalist to survive and provide for her family, but governments and rich citizens also hire her for projects.

Breaking Bad's Mike Ehrmantraut is a fixer—mostly for one client, his "client of choice" being Gus Fring. But he also used his specialized skill set in service to Walter White and Jesse Pinkman. For a while, he even manned a toll booth at the county courthouse—exemplifying how many real-life independents do side hustles in addition to full-time employment.

The *Star Wars* characters Han Solo, Boba Fett, and Lando Calrissian worked independently as smugglers of goods and people, freelance pilots, bounty hunters, and casino operators.

Finally, Peter Parker worked as a freelance photographer for the *Daily Bugle* while also juggling school responsibilities and fighting crime as Spider-Man. In fact, because he began all the way back in 1962, Parker may have been the very first independent to combine freelance photography work with *web* design.

Bada boom.

4

YOU CAN'T TOUCH THIS

Force #4: From Knowledge Stocks to Knowledge Flows

Who would have imagined that Midwestern grandmothers
would be pirating needlepoint instructions over the Internet?
—Linus Torvalds[1]

Linus Torvalds. Either you know a lot about Linus Torvalds, or you've
never heard his name and have no idea that Torvalds's software is used
by hundreds of millions of people.

But were I to ask if you've heard the name Bill Gates or the company
Microsoft, you'd rightfully look at me like I'm an idiot for asking a dumb
question. Even if you don't know much about how computers work, you're
familiar with the term *operating system*, and you know the Microsoft product
called Windows, which runs about 90% of all personal computers worldwide, making Microsoft and Gates each among the wealthiest companies
and individuals on the planet. By comparison, Linux, Torvalds's software,
now powers only about 3% of personal computers, but 40% of websites with
known operating systems, 85% of smartphones, 100% of the world's top
500 supercomputers, and 90% of cloud infrastructure.[2]

Torvalds, though not a pauper, could be ultrawealthy (and could be just as famous), too, had he chosen a different business model for the product he engineered. But that would have meant an entirely different mindset for Torvalds—a different way of thinking about his work, money, and his life. Not better and not worse (in my opinion)—just different.

You see, Linus Torvalds wrote the Linux operating system and posted it online in 1991, giving it away for free and opening it up for development and improvement by anyone. That's crowdsourcing. That's open sourcing. That's open innovation. That's knowledge flow. And all those words describe the fourth of the six forces shaping the world today: "From Knowledge Stocks to Knowledge Flows."

As we saw in chapter 2, Gates and Paul Allen first adapted the software to run the Altair—that self-built personal computer that hobbyists went gaga over, including the Homebrew Club in Silicon Valley. Those guys (yes, almost all of them were guys) consciously embraced the "hacker" mindset at a time when that word didn't have any of the criminal computing overtones that were later attached to it. Hacking just meant bootstrapping, figuring things out, and sharing that knowledge with others. The idea of "life hacking" flows from this original definition of hacking.

As noted by journalist Steven Levy's 1984 book *Hackers*, a central tenet of the "Hacker Ethic" was "the free flow of information, particularly information that helped fellow hackers understand, explore, and build systems."[3] Levy chronicled how "hacker-formed companies would give out schematics of their products," and wouldn't worry about competition. "The proper hacker response to competitors was to give them your business plan and technical information, so they might make better products and the world in general might improve."[4]

But very early on, the "knowledge flow" mindset of the hardware hackers bumped up against the "knowledge stock" views of the software creators. The hobbyists started copying and distributing the "paper tape" containing Gates's version of the BASIC program, believing it was their right to copy it because the software belonged to everyone. Levy explained their mindset: "Why should there be a barrier of ownership standing between a hacker and a tool to explore, improve, and build systems?"[5] Indeed, the hacker ethic compelled them not just to use the BASIC software but also to actively make copies and give them away free—for the betterment of society. "No one seemed to object to a software author getting something for his work—but neither did the hackers want to let go of the idea that computer programs belonged to everybody. It was too much a part of the hacker dream to abandon."[6]

Gates, then 19, thought differently and wrote an open letter for publication in the newsletter read by the hobbyists. He said that while he appreciated the enthusiasm and feedback on his BASIC from the hobbyists, he had a complaint: "As the majority of hobbyists must be aware, most of you steal your software. Hardware must be paid for, but software is something to share. Who cares if the people who worked on it get paid? . . . Who can afford to do professional work for nothing? What hobbyist can put three man-years into programming, finding all the bugs, documenting his product, and distributing it for free?"[7]

Ironically, in the end, the hobbyists' "piracy" led to Microsoft's domination of the software industry. That is, the "knowledge flow"—albeit a flow that Gates challenged—helped Gates's Microsoft become the early leader in the field. As one of the founders of the Homebrew Club told Levy: "BASIC had spread all over the country, and all over the world. And it helped Gates— the fact that everybody had Altair BASIC and knew how it worked and how to fix it meant that when other computer companies came online and needed a BASIC, they went to Gates's company. It became a de facto standard."[8] Gates did not get what he wanted, but he got what he needed.

Both men were young at the time their products launched—Gates was 19 and Torvalds was 21—and both had ambition, intelligence, and normal human desires for material success. But Torvalds's net worth is estimated to be a mere $50–$150M compared to Gates's current net worth, reported by *Forbes* to be around $125B.[9] I suppose, based on the accumulated wealth of the founders, that you could make an argument that the open source and free knowledge flow will diminish one's earnings.

This isn't to praise or criticize anyone—not Gates, Torvalds, or those early software pirates. Instead, this story illustrates the difference between "knowledge stocks" and "knowledge flows." Whatever you think about the logic of Gates's 1975 "open letter" versus Torvalds's free distribution of Linux in 1991, we can agree that the world is now much different than it was when either of those operating systems first launched. And, under the leadership of Satya Nadella, Microsoft's CEO since 2014, the company has adopted a much more positive attitude toward open-source software.

THE SECRET FORMULA

Let me state up front that I'm not an intellectual property (IP) anarchist. I believe in patents. I believe in copyrights. The company I lead owns and protects proprietary information, and this book is copyrighted. There's nothing wrong with any of that.

Traditionally, companies have been built on an *ethos* of knowledge stocks; they develop a proprietary product or idea and then defend that innovative advantage against all rivals. If you're not inside the company as a full-time employee (and maybe even a longtime employee), then a company's knowledge stocks are off-limits, as if labeled: "Top Secret! You can't touch this!"

In today's business climate, however, the value of these breakthroughs is quickly eroded by rapid innovation and the unbridled power that comes from instant access to the best ideas and talent. As we learned from John Hagel and John Brown in an earlier chapter, modern businesses find innovation at the edge of their businesses instead of their proprietary core. They measure competitiveness not by the number of engineers on their payroll but by their degree of access to a global talent pool—knowledge flows instead of knowledge stocks.[10] That's not to diminish the need to patent and protect the "wealth of information" owned by a company. Indeed, such information is just that: wealth.

In the 1990s, DuPont developed a new process for making the synthetic fiber Kevlar, the material used in bulletproof vests. A former DuPont employee stole the process and sold it to a South Korean company, resulting in a prison sentence and hundreds of millions in fines and restitution.[11]

Coca-Cola's recipe for its signature soda is one of the most famous trade secrets in the world. The recipe has been kept secret for over 100 years and is known only to a small group of people. However, three individuals were arrested in 2006 for attempting to sell the recipe to rival Pepsi. Of course, if you consider the situation carefully, the notion of Pepsi changing its flavor to copy Coca-Cola is ridiculous. Marketing and promotion, production, and distribution: These are the primary factors determining the market share for sugary beverages—not blindly copying another company's product. If someone on the inside wanted to provide valuable intel to Coca-Cola's competitor, they would be slightly more successful by stealing all the advertising strategies for the upcoming years.

In 2016, Google accused Anthony Levandowski, a former engineer for the company, of stealing trade secrets related to self-driving car technology. Levandowski founded his own self-driving truck company, which was later acquired by Uber. Google sued Uber for stealing its trade secrets, and the two companies eventually settled the case for $245 million. The judge sentenced Levandowski to eighteen months in prison but called him "a 'brilliant, groundbreaking engineer that our country needs." On his last night in the White House, then president Trump pardoned Levandowski—at the urging of Peter Thiel and others—and called him "an American entrepreneur . . . [who] has paid a significant price for his actions and plans to devote his talents to advance the public good."[12]

In 2018, Tesla accused a former employee of stealing proprietary information about its Autopilot system and sharing it with a Chinese rival. The employee was later arrested and charged with trade-secret theft.

In 2019, Apple accused a former employee of stealing trade secrets related to its autonomous vehicle project. The employee allegedly downloaded confidential files before leaving the company to join a rival self-driving car startup.

These examples of corporate espionage do not disprove my point, however, because I'm not saying companies don't have a right to keep their intel to themselves and protect their research and development investments. That would be an absurd statement, so please don't misunderstand me.

But it's also a fact that opening a company's proprietary code base (knowledge) to others would have been heresy just twenty years ago. Yet today, even the biggest tech giants use open innovation, open sourcing, and crowdsourcing in search of innovation gold. They know that moving from the mindset of knowledge stocks to knowledge flows helps the industry innovate more quickly to create new products and better outcomes. Peter Drucker stated it this way: "Knowledge is power, which is why people who had it in the past often tried to make a secret of it. In post-capitalism, power comes from transmitting information to make it productive, not from hiding it."[13]

Let's apply this theme to the workforce. In the past, a typical work relationship consisted of a worker selling their skills to a company in the form of employment. This formed a binary transaction or knowledge stock. One problem with this relationship is its lack of liquidity or flow. The knowledge and the worker are all within—safe and sound, right? But this so-called security comes at the price of agility and innovation.

The second problem with this relationship is that it doesn't reflect the transitory nature of the employee-employer relationship. Gen Z and millennials will move from one company to another—staying, on average, less than three years. The knowledge they have in their soul and mind leaves with them even if all their laptops and memory sticks get turned into HR as they head out the door. Some of the knowledge flows whether you like it or not—and the flow is mostly ethical and legal (the above stories of espionage notwithstanding).

But though the traditional employer-employee binary marketplace gets stuck in knowledge stocks, selling skills on an open market creates a vitality of knowledge flow. The fast-growing independent professional workforce creates a market with liquidity where buyers and sellers can compete, ultimately creating more value for those who participate. Knowledge flows open up the movement of assets, giving enterprises access to the skills they need and providing contingent workers the control to do the work they love the way they want to do it.[14]

So we see that companies are migrating to more of a knowledge flow model because, by definition, no one company can ever hire the best and the brightest. You can hire great and excellent and fantastic people. Still, some of the best innovations, creative thinking, and capabilities come from *places* you could have never imagined and from *people* you could have never imagined. Businesses must broaden their aperture for what they define as "our talent." To see more high-performing people contribute to their company, they must include more than their full-time workforce.

The knowledge flow model says, "I want to tap into people for their knowledge of the exact things I need them for." By contrast, the knowledge stock mindset says, "I'm going to take that employee and try to monopolize their knowledge and the value that I can trade off of for that." Those two mindsets differ significantly and accomplish far different results.

But how does a business allow the independent workforce access to proprietary knowledge? I get asked this question a lot, so I'll address it here: When it comes to proprietary knowledge, do companies have reason to fear independents in their workforce?

Yes, and no.

Yes, because of human nature: people don't care about doing right if the reward for doing wrong is high enough.

No, because of human nature: people want to do what's right.

But also "no" for a second reason: The safeguards are already built into the system. There are contractual obligations not to share knowledge. And here's a little secret about the laws on the books in many states. If you run a business, you can contractually (i.e., "legally") tie up an independent contractor more tightly than you can an employee. That is, in many states there are laws that prevent you from obligating *employees* to sign noncompete clauses. Who an *employee* can go to work for after they work for you—those laws are getting more and more relaxed. Ethical loyalty may bind the conscience of an employee, but the law doesn't always do so. However, businesses *can* more easily prevent a *contractor* from working with a primary competitor—those laws are tighter. So, for employers worried about tying down their talent (which I would argue is not a good strategy anyway), you can get stronger contractual rights through the independent channels.

I should add that individual professionals also create IP, and companies should not be allowed to steal it from them. At the same time, independent contractors can protect the IP they created outside of a contract with a company—which is only fair. It goes both ways. Using independents and tapping into a platform with independents is a powerful mechanism for using knowledge flows for your human capital instead of knowledge stocks. Are you buying what I'm saying, or do mental models built on knowledge flow still dominate your company's thinking?

THE CROWD

To talk about the connection between knowledge flows and the power of the "crowd," let's read a Steve Jobs quote from 1989, when *Inc.* magazine interviewed him as their "entrepreneur of the decade" for the 1980s:

> I think humans are basically tool builders, and the computer is the most remarkable tool we've ever built. The big insight a lot of us had in the 1970s had to do with the importance of putting that tool in the hands of individuals. Let's say that—for the same amount of money it takes to build the most powerful computer in the world—you could make 1,000 computers with one-thousandth the power and put them in the hands of 1,000 creative people. You'll get more out of doing that than out of having one person use the most powerful computer in the world. Because people are inherently creative. They will use tools in ways the toolmakers never thought possible. And once a person figures out how to do something with that tool, he or she can share it with the other 999.[15]

Though Jobs mentions computers as a tool, he's focusing on something much broader: the power of the independent, autonomous tool users—the *crowd*—to drive innovation.

The crowd gets the tools, not just the chosen few. And because of this ubiquitous tech, here's what happens: Knowledge flows. Freedom, authenticity, innovation, improved lives, and more creativity—these all come from the decentralized tech creating knowledge flow to and from the crowd.

Then Jobs finished his answer with words that I could have just as easily placed in chapter 2's discussion on the accelerated rate of change. This just goes to show how interconnected all six of these trends discussed here in part 1 are.

The technological advances are coming at a rate that is far more ferocious than ever. To me, it's staggering to contemplate the tools we're going to be able to put in people's hands in the next few years—and I don't get impressed by this stuff so easily anymore.

So what we're doing here is driven by a fairly strong faith that people are going to continue to be as creative and as ingenious and as sharing with their results as they have been over the past 15 years. That sharing gives us a kind of leverage. For every improvement we can make in the tools we give people, we can improve the ultimate results even more, thanks to this leverage. That's what gets us so excited.[16]

Sharing. Do you hear that? That's the *sharing* economy. It's the sound of the *crowd* joining in to use their genius and creativity to build a business and make a life. That's knowledge flow, driven by the rapid advances in tech that now make it absurd to think of going back to a business model dominated by knowledge stock thinking.

That's *crowdsourcing*—open innovation that involves outside sources of knowledge and expertise to resolve issues and come up with fresh ideas. Crowd*funding* works the same way, except the goal is . . . funding. These open-source strategies enable the flow of knowledge, as organizations tap into the collective intelligence of a large group of people to solve problems and generate new ideas. Organizations can tap into a broader range of knowledge and expertise than they would be able to access on their own.

Moreover, the information generated through crowdsourcing can be shared and disseminated across multiple channels, allowing for the spread of knowledge and expertise beyond the initial participants. This can lead to further innovation and creativity as individuals build upon and improve upon the ideas generated through crowdsourcing.

Another crowdsourced knowledge flow is behavioral capital—the collection, aggregation, and modeling of data in a way that yields valuable insights.[17] Data sources have proliferated with the Internet of Things (IoT), and the technology infrastructure is now embedded everywhere via sensors and other data-gathering devices. The assets generated from this data can create digital models of real-world activity, revealing how people, machines, and systems have behaved in the past, how they are likely to act in the future, and how that behavior can be influenced.

Behavior capital gives companies visibility into their systems that they otherwise wouldn't have. It reduces error and risk: A decision-maker can take chances in the virtual world that would be unbearable in real life. For example, automotive and aerospace industries can design, test, and evaluate prototypes—including the human interaction with these prototypes—without risking human life or massive commitments to physical manufacturing. The same applies to architecture, construction, transportation systems, and urban planning.[18] Decision-makers in finance can simulate outcomes to proposed strategies without the risk of real-world consequences. Surgeons now routinely rehearse their techniques virtually. Marketers can do "A/B" testing virtually to gauge the effectiveness of their advertisements before committing huge sums on ad buys. Bottom line, behavior capital raises the ability of companies to control their operations more effectively and substitute new products for old ones more easily and rapidly as circumstances change.

One of the most successful generators of behavior capital is the Waze navigation app (acquired by Google in 2013). Initially developed in Israel, it found early use in restricted zones, where maps are unreliable and dangerous situations may develop. It ultimately found a passionate audience among commuters and others seeking to avoid traffic delays. The information that Waze provides is partly generated from machine learning; it knows the traffic patterns and how they might change. It also incorporates data from its users' speed and behavior; when they slow down in a traffic jam, that information instantly becomes part of the Waze model. Waze users can also report on road conditions, increasing real-time accuracy. Waze's "behavior" and users' behavior interact because it's a knowledge flow—not simply a knowledge stock (i.e., a paper map).

The concepts of crowdsourcing and open sourcing overlap to some extent, but they do not necessarily denote the same thing. Open sourcing refers specifically to the practice of making source code or other knowledge assets freely available to others so they can collaborate and innovate with greater speed. Crowdsourcing, on the other hand, refers to the practice of obtaining information or services by soliciting contributions from a large group of people, often through online platforms. While crowdsourcing *can involve* open sourcing, in that the contributions solicited from the crowd may involve sharing knowledge or expertise, it can also involve other forms of contributions, such as labor, funding, or data. Additionally, not all open-source projects involve crowdsourcing.

But here's the important thing for our thinking about how all this applies to the future of work: don't get hung up on the semantic lines between all these terms and don't get trapped into believing this is mostly about coding, software, or IT. Instead, apply these ideas—the essential philosophy of open-/crowdsourcing—to the war for talent. Think of open sourcing and crowdsourcing almost as a metaphor, an analogy to move your thinking toward greater utilization of independents. Think in terms of a Venn diagram with two circles: (1) your company's traditional HR strategy for talent acquisition and (2) open-/crowdsourcing *philosophy*. Where those two circles overlap, you will find the independent workforce working for enterprises—either your business or your competitors.

As noted earlier, every CEO will say that their most important asset is their people. But it's time they expand the definition of "people" to include external workers because many of the most talented professionals in the workforce choose to be independent. As author Jeff Howe wrote back in the mid-2000s: "Remember outsourcing? Sending jobs to India and China is so 2003." Howe predicted "the new pool of cheap labor" will be "everyday people using their spare cycles to create content, solve problems, even do corporate R&D."[19] Not to beat a dead horse here about changes in technology, but Howe wrote those words before the introduction and ubiquity of the iPhone and before Uber or any of the "Uber of *X*" companies started. The idea that your company can find valuable talent by looking for "everyday people" who use "their spare cycles"—this shouldn't even be debated nowadays.

And don't forget how all these macro trends here in part 1 are like the interconnected threads of a spider's web. Talk about one and you'll soon be talking about the other. The open-/crowdsourcing themes could have been discussed in the previous chapter on fractionalization because open sourcing involves aspects of knowledge stocks/flows *and* the fractionalization of labor.

From the perspective of knowledge stocks and flows, open sourcing can be seen as a means of increasing the flow of knowledge across organizational boundaries. By finding source code or other knowledge assets from independent entities not directly controlled by your company (e.g., employees), the exchange of ideas will improve overall innovation and efficiency in your business.

From the perspective of the fractionalization of labor, open sourcing can be seen as a way of leveraging the skills and contributions of a distributed network of contributors. By allowing anyone to contribute to a project, open sourcing (i.e., using independents) can create a more diverse and geographically dispersed workforce, leading to greater specialization and efficiency in the work being done.

THE CATHEDRAL AND THE BAZAAR

Software developer and open-source advocate Eric Raymond wrote an influential essay in 1998, later turned into a book, titled *The Cathedral & the Bazaar: Musing on Linux and Open Source by an Accidental Revolutionary*. It's considered influential because it led Netscape to release its source code and to begin the Mozilla project. And Jimmy Wales, the cofounder of Wikipedia, credits the article as being the thing that "opened my eyes to the possibility of mass collaboration."[20]

As you can guess, "Cathedral" and "Bazaar" are part of an extended metaphor. The Cathedral approach to software development involves experts working in isolation, designing the product in a hierarchical and closed environment. Before they begin, a clear set of requirements and processes are established—much like the blueprint for a physical cathedral.

By contrast, the "Bazaar" approach takes its analogy from a bustling, public marketplace. In a bazaar, people show up—people you wouldn't have even known within the Cathedral model. And because of digital technology, they "show up" from time zones across the globe. They bring their ideas and expertise to the development process, resulting in the process becoming iterative. The software evolves over time because of the contributions of a diverse set of developers.

Don't get stuck on this being an analogy that only applies to software. I'm adopting Raymond's Bazaar analogy for our thinking about the future of work and the independent workforce. Raymond argued that the open-source Bazaar model leads to a better product—quicker to "finish" (and even that word is redefined) and cheaper. It's also better because of the diversity of thought that went into its creation.

Torvalds chronicled the Linux story in his own book, evangelizing for the knowledge flow way of thinking:

> From a party of one it [Linux] now counted millions of users on every continent... Not only was it the most common operating system running server computers dishing out all the content on the World Wide Web, but its very development model—an intricate web of its own, encompassing hundreds of thousands of volunteer computer programmers—had grown to become the largest collaborative project in the history of the world.
>
> The open source philosophy behind it all was simple: *Information, in this case the source code or basic instructions behind the operating system, should be free and freely shared for anyone interested in improving upon it.* But those improvements should also be freely shared. The same concept had supported centuries of scientific discovery. Now it was finding a home in the corporate sphere, and it was possible to imagine its potential as a framework for creating the best of anything: a legal strategy, an opera.[21]

That's right! Knowledge flows are "a framework for creating the best of anything." Now, apply that same thinking to your company's talent acquisition strategy. You say you want the best talent available, but you're also leery of losing your lockdown on your stock of knowledge. I'm here to say: You've got to let that fear go. You only get what you give. You only find the talent you need when your company thinks "open," not "closed." You must abandon the idea of knowledge stocks and embrace the belief in knowledge flows.[22]

To do so might mean going against the status quo of your company's HR culture. Torvalds wrote that the argument for maintaining the status quo in a company is actually a convincing argument because "people are frightened of change" and "they don't know how it is going to turn out." I would add that these same arguments often keep a company from opening its talent acquisition strategy to the external workforce. "By sticking to the status quo," Torvalds wrote, "a company can make a better judgment of where it will go, and sometimes that seems more important than being hugely successful."[23]

Is that true of your enterprise? Torvalds predicted that companies who fear open sourcing "will be predictably successful instead of being unpredictably really, really, really successful."[24]

Ultimately, you have to lead your business in the direction of freedom, openness, and authenticity. "It's a difficult stance at first," Torvalds wrote, "but it creates more stability in the end."[25]

Finally, to connect to the main theme of this book—the presence of the external workforce—Torvalds had this to say:

> One question has to do with how people inside the company would feel about the possibility of having an *outsider* produce work that is better than their own—and having that so publicly noticeable. I think they should feel great about it, and great that they are getting paid for not even doing most of the work. In that regard, open source—or open anything, for that matter—is unforgiving. *It shows who can get the job done, who is better.* You can't hide behind managers. Open source is the best way of leveraging *outside talent.*[26]

That's exactly right. And that's the mindset you need if you're going to win the war for talent.

5

WE ARE THE CHAMPIONS

Force #5: Winning the War for Talent

The war for talent is over. Talent won.
—Tim Ryan, PwC US chairman, 2022[1]

Over the course of three consecutive days in May 1977, three British bands each made a unique move that not only shaped their own future but also left an indelible mark on the world of rock music. The spirited competition for the attention of young music lovers was fierce and genuine. Who would win?

May 27, 1977: The Sex Pistols—the group who launched punk rock—released their highly controversial version of "God Save the Queen," describing the British monarchy as a "fascist regime." The group's lead singer, Johnny Rotten, said, "You write a song like that because you love them [the working class Englishman], and you're fed up with them being mistreated."[2] The *Guardian* called the group "insolent and violent" and described punk as "the anarchic rock of the young and doleful."[3] Another described punk as "a polarizing force, a groundswell revolt against the old order, pitting one generation against the next."[4] In early 1978, the Sex Pistols disbanded, after just two and a half years together; the next year their 21-year-old bassist, Sid Vicious, overdosed on heroin.

May 28, 1977: Four then unknown musicians publicly played a gig together for the first time, and they saw their future. By mid-August, they had whittled themselves down to a trio built with the two Brits and the American, branding themselves as "the Police."[5] And though they had formed their band with the idea of fitting into and capitalizing on the popularity of punk rock, they instead emerged as leaders of the New Wave musical scene. In early 1978, they broke out with their signature song, "Roxanne." By 1983, music journalists and fans considered the Police one of the world's biggest rock bands.[6]

May 29, 1977: Queen finished that night's concert with a cover of Elvis's "Jailhouse Rock" and then "God Save the Queen"[7]—a loud but noncontroversial version. Though their 1975 album, *A Night at the Opera*, had established them as international superstars, with its "Bohemian Rhapsody" leading the way, by 1977, critics wondered if the fresh musical sounds coming out of London would displace Queen. Rock historian Mick Hall explained the 1977 landscape:

> At a time when punk rock was considered the new critical yardstick, Queen suddenly epitomized everything about the old rock aristocracy that was now held in contempt . . . The vast gulf between what was now regarded as the spiky, blades-drawn future and the flatulent, fairy-dust past was thrown into sharper relief when one compared Johnny Rotten's "God Save the Queen" with Queen's own bombastic version of the national anthem which still closed their shows.[8]

Clearly, the times they were a-changin', and the fierce competition between musical groups and styles had become intense.

But as guitarist Brian May walked off that stage that night in Bingley Hall in Stafford, England—a venue with thunderous acoustics, often used for cattle shows and agricultural exhibitions—he turned and listened to eight thousand sweaty fans singing spontaneously the chorus to Rodgers and Hammerstein's "You'll Never Walk Alone."

May was mesmerized and inspired. Fans had been doing more and more of this kind of thing lately, often prompted by Queen's charismatic frontman, Freddie Mercury.

"The audience were just responding hugely. And they were singing along with everything we did," May later recalled. "Now, in the beginning, we didn't relate to that. We were the kind of band who like to be listened to and taken seriously. So people singing along wasn't part of our agenda."[9]

But May kept thinking about the crowd and their energy.

"We can no longer fight this," May said to Mercury. "This has to be something which is part of our show, and we have to embrace it, the fact that people want to participate—and, in fact, everything becomes a two-way process now."[10]

May said he "woke up the next morning" with an idea for a bit of audience participation percussion: stomp-stomp-clap. Stomp-stomp-clap.

"You remember our last concert?" May said to the band (as portrayed in the 2018 film *Bohemian Rhapsody*). "The crowds were singing our songs back to us. I mean, it was deafening, but it was wonderful. They're becoming a part of our show. I want to encourage that, so I've got an idea to involve them a little bit more . . . I want to give the audience a song that they can perform. All right? Let them be part of the band. So, what can they do? [Stomp-stomp-clap] Imagine. Thousands of people. Doing *this* in unison."[11]

May wrote the "We Will Rock You" lyrics, closing the song with his wailing guitar solo. Queen recorded and released the song together with Mercury's "We Are the Champions," and radio stations have played the songs back-to-back ever since. In fact, most people probably consider the two songs as one song with two parts.

The songs were released on October 7, 1977, and soared to #2 on both the US and UK charts. Undoubtedly, one of the most renowned stadium anthems worldwide, these two songs are a staple at sporting events across every continent. The Grammys inducted the tunes into their Hall of Fame in 2008, and *Rolling Stone* ranks it as one of the "500 Greatest Songs of All Time."[12] And in 2011, scientists quantified "We Are the Champions" as the "catchiest song" in this history of pop music: "[There is] a special combination of neuroscience, math, and cognitive psychology that can produce the elusive elixir of the perfect sing-along song."[13]

Initially, May bristled against Mercury's "losers" and "champions" lyrics. "The first time I heard that 'no time for losers' line, I said, 'You can't do this, Fred. You'll get killed,'" May said, thinking that Mercury was describing the band as pompous victors. "But it wasn't saying that *Queen* are the champions. It was saying, 'We, *everybody*, are the champions.'"[14]

* * *

In the future of work, we can *all* be champions in the war for talent. Now, hear me out when I say we can all win because I don't mean that we'll all get trophies for participation or that workers and enterprises will go from one success to another. Nope. That's not how the real world works. A free market economy like ours certainly has winners and losers, and you don't want to be on the wrong side of that line. I can point out a path for you—and that's what I hope to do in this book—but nobody can make you follow it.

Competition and rivalry are inherent within capitalism because individuals, businesses, and organizations compete against each other in the marketplace to attract customers, sell products or services, and generate profits. So, whether we use the term *compete* (and draw on sports analogies) or talk about *conflict* (and use military metaphors as I am doing here), the principle is the same: participants vie for success and strive to outperform the other side in order to win.

ENTERPRISE VS. ENTERPRISE

Enterprises battle each other for more employees. Every business needs more workers—more in quantity and more in quality. Even though in some industries and low-skill lines of work, the HR department hardly needs more than a warm body, even those positions are getting hard to fill. However, enterprises are *really* feeling the pinch when it comes to acquiring and retaining *skilled* workers for full-time employment.

CFOs regularly report that "hiring and retaining staff" is "the most difficult task" facing them. Fifty-four percent placed this concern at the top, far ahead of "forecasting" (36%) and "cutting costs" (35%).[15] "The data from CFOs align with what we are hearing from H.R. leaders," reports a Gartner survey, "namely that competition for talent is expected to become fiercer over the medium term, and retaining that talent will become more challenging."[16]

Business leaders know their employees are not a permanent workforce because loyalty is dead, and their competition must also find and hire talent. When the siren song of a job with increased pay and benefits rings in an employee's ears, will they jump ship? If they do, then how will the business fill the vacancy? Will they repeat the cycle by pilfering a full-time employee from another company, or are they willing to think afresh about their talent acquisition strategy?

The problem is that the labor force—defined as "all people age 16 and older who are classified as either employed and unemployed"[17]—is shrinking. Hence, businesses now compete against each other for access to this ever-shrinking labor force. Simply put, there are too few people to do the jobs to be done. But *why* is the labor force shrinking? Two reasons top the list of explanations.

First, we face an ongoing decline in the total number of working-age people (people aged 18–65). I know that such a statement stands in opposition to all the breathless reporting about overpopulation—written by people whose primary life experience must be living in a Manhattan-dense urban area. Let me be clear and contrarian to a prevailing myth: the United States actually faces a *scarcity* of human capital, not a surplus. We're short on people and getting shorter by the year. We are in a talent shortage, not a talent surplus. This reality doesn't change with the monthly jobs report, because low unemployment doesn't birth more babies or allow for greater numbers of skilled immigrants. As the title of an opinion piece in *Forbes* stated, "Unemployment Is Low, but So Is the Labor Force Participation Rate."[18] We must understand that no matter if the job market is tight or loose, the demographics won't change.

This ongoing decline in the total number of working-age people has come about because of at least three factors:

- Retirement: Over three million baby boomers exited the US work-force in 2020 alone. That's more than 10,000 retirements per day, a number that will continue unabated until 2030—the year all boomers are at least 65. As a nation, we have not and are not re-placing the retirees in sufficient quantities with new workers from the next generation. Why? Because . . .

- Birth rate: We're now 50 years into a downward trend in the US birth rate, which needs to be 2.1 per woman in order to have a growing population. The current birth rate in the United States is 1.6 per woman, and the last time the US birth rate was 2.1 was in 2007. By 2034, we will see a demographic statistic that has never taken place in our nation's history: children will be outnumbered by adults.[19]

- Immigration: There are fewer immigrants yearly due to domestic policy changes and regional and worldwide megatrends. I know that immigration is a hot-button political issue, and it's wrapped up in other matters like how we control our borders, process work visas, and vet the people entering our nations. That being said, it's simply a fact that our labor force has shrunk as the number of im-migrants has declined.[20]

Second, not only do we see a decline in the total number of working-age people, but we also have witnessed a decline in the labor force participation rate (LFPR) over the past twenty years. The Bureau of Labor Statistics, us-ing information collected by the US Census Bureau, measures the LFPR—defined as "the number of people in the labor force as a percentage of the civilian noninstitutional population . . . the participation rate is the percent-age of the population that is either working or actively looking for work." In 2000, the LRPR was 67.1%, in 2019 (pre-pandemic) the rate was 63%, and it still held above 63% even as late as February 2020. But the pandemic and post-pandemic effects brought the participation rate down as low as 60.1%. The average rate in 2023–2024 hovered around 63%.[21]

So the first decline showed the size of the pool of potential workers, but the LFPR shows the declining percentage of people within that pool who are (or are trying to be) participants in the workforce. Even if the LFPR holds fast, the same percentage of a smaller pool of workers means a smaller total workforce. But with a decline in both the pool *and* the participation rate, it's little wonder that the entire labor force has shrunk.

THE PANDEMIC, THE GREAT REALIZATION, AND GREAT RESIGNATION

Economists and historians are now analyzing labor data from the past five years to determine the causes of the declining LFPR. When the pandemic hit, it shifted everything we understand about the labor force through the shutdown of businesses and the explosion of remote work. The pandemic showed people that they can work comfortably from pretty much anywhere. So they did.

Employees' eyes opened to the benefits of flexibility regarding *where* and *when* they worked. I call this "the Great Realization"—a shift in perspective and mindset. As a result, workers decided they wouldn't return to the old system, even if it meant quitting their jobs—and that's precisely what they did. Millions of people chose to leave their jobs every single month. In both November 2021 and April 2022, over 4.5 million people walked away from their current positions (i.e., 3% of the total workforce voluntarily resigned). These months marked the peak of the "quits" phenomenon now labeled "the Great Resignation."[22] In fact, according to the US Bureau of Labor Statistics, this was the highest percentage the quits rate has ever been in the Bureau's 21-year history of keeping such records.[23]

Even as the quits rate is on a trajectory to return to pre-pandemic levels, here's what we learned from the Great Resignation: people were leaving the workplace in droves, but they were *not* "not working." Many were just going independent, working for themselves on their own terms instead of for their former employer. The stats since 2020 reveal this point: There were 72 million independent workers in 2023, up 41% over 2021 (51.1M) and up 88% over 2020 (38.2M).[24]

People are realizing the possibilities of change and are taking control of their lives and careers. We're seeing the largest and fastest scope of global evolution ever known. We're at a point of the merger between technology, international trade, rising independence, skyrocketing demand for skills, and the relentless search for efficiency. So how can employers retain workers to get work done in the face of this tidal wave of resignations? The answer: you must look at independent workers as an essential consideration in your workforce planning.

LABOR FORCE HEADLINES

Before we go further, let's use the daily newspaper to test the premise of this chapter. That is:

- the labor force will continue to shrink;
- therefore, the war for talent is only going to accelerate;
- therefore, independent workers must become core to an enterprise's workforce planning.

So go ahead and look at a few issues of the *Wall Street Journal* or business headlines from any news source during the past month. The five themes I list below are not exhaustive, and the details are sure to change over time, but today and in the future, you'll see headlines about:

1. the battle over return-to-office initiatives
2. the fear of AI and automation
3. the insane shortage of workers in skilled trades and manufacturing
4. the changing nature of credentialing for jobs and related discussion about the function of higher education
5. expansion and contraction in specific sectors (i.e., "layoff stories")

I'm confident this will hold up even if you're reading this book five years from its publication because the shrinking of the labor force in America will only accelerate. On the making of predictions, Linus Torvalds once asked,

"Is there anything more obnoxious than business prognosticators? Those self-important types who pretend to know where the insane technology amusement ride will take us?"[25] Look, I get it and want to be humble with my prediction-making—but here's why I believe in what I'm writing about the future of the labor force.

First, the battle over "return to office" initiatives shows just how much the pandemic accelerated trends already in place before 2020. We will look at this in depth later, but here's the summary: The workforce wants location and schedule flexibility. If you can't make a valid case as to why you can't offer that to them, they will find work elsewhere.

Sure, some jobs, by their very nature, are location specific—nobody can deny that. But technological changes are accelerating at such a rate that only a fool would definitively state that "such and such job can never be remote"—because, honestly, it probably can and will be done remotely at some point soon. The point is that if you're an enterprise, you'd better have a strong justification for demanding that your workforce be in a specific place and at a particular time.

And to the larger point of this book, once you agree that certain positions can be done remotely, it's easy to take the next logical step: an independent can do this job. That's why, in a recent survey of HR leaders, almost half of them believe that a policy forcing "a return to the office would hurt their ability to attract and retain talent." And "As a result, there's an increased demand for independent workers." Fifty percent of HR leaders report they are using independents more now than in the past and are more likely to do so in the future.[26]

Second, year in and year out, you will find multiple stories per week about the alleged threat to jobs that AI or automation poses. Let me state up front my thought about this particular fear: it's bonkers. In the United States alone, we know there are twice as many job openings as there are unemployed. Despite all the concerns around AI or automation eliminating everybody's job, we have a capital scarcity issue, not an abundance of human capital.

Yes, automation and AI will most definitely eliminate certain jobs, the same way innovation always disrupts the workforce. In 1894, New York

City had a population of 100,000 horses, producing 2.5 million pounds of manure daily. The city employed a lot of people to clean up the crap, literally, and those jobs were almost entirely eliminated within fifty years.[27] But in 1950, would you rather be a manure scooper or a mechanic at an auto shop (or one of the thousands of other types of jobs made possible by the combustion engine)? So it goes with AI or automation: It gives and it takes away. The historical record indicates that AI and automation give a lot more than they take.[28] So winning the war for talent will involve utilizing both AI and the independent workforce together.

Third, the labor shortage affects blue-collar and white-collar jobs alike. People think there aren't many open manufacturing jobs in the United States, but across the nation, that's just not true. The manufacturing industry, which hires 13 million people (10% of the private sector), says they need 800,000 more workers just to fill all available positions.[29] And skilled tradesmen—electricians, carpenters, plumbers, and welders—now walk out of training school and into their first jobs with salaries starting at $50–$90K a year. That's the law of supply and demand at work.

Think about this as the "Mike Rowe thesis"—that people who do "dirty jobs" will always be in demand. And when those "dirty jobs" also take skill and hard physical labor, the compensation will reflect that fact. Hence, you see articles with titles like "You might want to ditch your desk job to become an electrician."[30] And to the point of this book: When was the last time you called a plumber or electrician who didn't work for themselves or for a small business? If someone cuts your grass, I'd wager that you hire an independent—a small business owner with fewer than 25 employees, right? The barriers to entry into entrepreneurship have never been lower, and the need for labor in physical occupations has never been greater.

This leads to a fourth headline I see all the time: the changing nature of credentialing for jobs and the related discourse about the value of higher education. Smart governors from both sides of the political aisle have been choosing to "scrap degree requirements for most state jobs" because of "staff shortages" and to "expand opportunities for workers." For example, Virginia governor Glenn Youngkin, a Republican, mandated in July 2023 that "state agencies will no longer require degrees or give preference to job candidates who have them for 90 percent of state jobs."[31] Ninety percent! In one stroke of the pen!

The *Washington Post* noted that "critics warned that he [Youngkin] was lowering standards and devaluing higher education." But former president Obama praised these types of policies earlier when other states put them into place, saying: "Here's an example of a smart policy that gets rid of unnecessary college degree requirements and reduces barriers to good paying jobs."[32]

Yes, credentials are needed for jobs. But the days of mandating a college education seem to be coming to an end in many sectors, in favor of job-specific and skill-specific credentials. Young people might want to rethink borrowing tens of thousands of dollars for an undergraduate degree leading to a field of employment that pays $40,000 a year, if they're lucky enough to even find work.[33] And to the point of this book, if your business is smart enough to hire an independent to accomplish the work you need done, do you really care about the degree they earned or where they earned it?

Fifth, let's pick a news story about layoffs—the downside of the "boom and bust" employment cycle. One might argue that layoffs prove we have too many people for too few jobs. Not so, because layoffs and hirings actually happen to specific companies as a result of cyclical turns in the economy. And even when you read many stories about layoffs in a particular industry (in early 2023, it was tech companies like Google, Meta/Facebook, and Microsoft), the underlying data for the industry often shows an uptick in job creation. The layoffs were company specific due to their previous overhiring—not a sector-wide malaise.

That brings me once again to intersect with the independent workforce. Companies need agility in hiring and the ability to expand and contract their workforce quickly and with as little disruption as possible. But how?

Answer: independents! And lest you think I see a nail everywhere because I only have hammers in my toolbox, please explain to me how your company—apart from increased utilization of independents—can both win the war for talent *and* stay agile through economic fluctuations?

Oh, and I hate to tell you, but there's one more overlap between independents and layoffs—and if you're a business owner, you may not like to hear this. When you lay off employees these days, more and more them are opting to start their own business. *PCMag* reported on a survey of over 4,000 respondents of people who had been laid off, finding that over 1,000 of them "reported starting their own company post-layoff." Which is to say, laid-off employees can become your latest competition for business. And to add insult to injury, "84% of new founders tapped connections from their former companies for funding."[34] And often, they use their severance package money to kick-start the solopreneur or micropreneur ventures! So, these new independents *are* available for your workforce—but only as independents. Once bitten, twice shy: they're simply not available to be one of your full-time employees.

THE SHIFTED BALANCE OF POWER

As I work alongside independents and the enterprises that increasingly use the external workforce, I am convinced that the "labor vs. management" warfare can become a thing of the past. In the battle for talent between enterprises, we can all win. But you must expand the "we" to include *all* the workforce, not just your full-time employees.

The independent workforce puts the balance of power in the hands of labor. With all the human capital scarcity challenge, the balance of power has shifted away from the employer and to the worker. As a result, traditional employees realize they can work for multiple companies independently. There is such a demand for highly skilled people that they choose to work independently. The pandemic accelerated this trend, but it isn't the root cause.

As a business leader, should you worry about the independent workforce shifting the balance of power to labor? I argue "no" and here's why: Utilizing independents *correlates* to a quantifiable surge in a company's profit, agility, productivity, and innovation (see chapter 16, "Has Life Been Good to Me?"). So, not to be flippant, but if you're an enterprise, then ask yourself this question: If defining "workforce" to include independents correlates to a surge in your company's basis points, do you honestly give a rip that the "balance of power" has shifted to the workforce?

* * *

As a business leader, a first step to take for better positioning your company in the war for talent is to find out how your company *defines* who its workforce is. Chances are, they define their workforce as their employees—and that's all. Instead, they need to explain it with a broader aperture because, by definition, you want to have access to all the available assets possible. They must inform their HR department: "Our workforce is *anyone* who can add value and get work done at this company. Our workforce is not just my full-time employee base."

Ask any CEO what their most important asset is and they'll say it's their talent. If you lead a company and want to access the best talent on the planet, you cannot ignore those who have chosen to be independent professionals because so many great people will never choose to be a full-time employee for your company. Don't take it personally.

Broader recruitment, targeted and ongoing skills training, and better plans for talent retention regardless of employee status—these strategies can keep companies fresh and free from so-called "talent droughts." Here's why. In 2023, more than 72 million people in the US workforce worked independently in some capacity. So, by definition, if you don't have a workforce deployment strategy that includes those 72 million people, there's no way you're accessing the best talent on the planet.

Independent work isn't a fading trend. By 2025, over half of all Americans will have worked independently. So how do you possibly deal with this if you're an enterprise? You can't ignore it. Every company I talk to tells me, "I don't have enough of the right people." Nobody can get enough of the right people, and it's because they're fishing in the wrong pond. Enterprises think *people* means *employees*.

With the expected "Great Return" on the horizon (when companies expect people to reenter the workforce), many workers *will* return to work, but as consultants or freelancers. So, it's time to consider how you'll engage these independents. One way to plan for the boom of independents is to start building out your talent pools for projects on your road map. Talent pools (groups of independent workers who are queued up, compliant, and ready to work with you) can help you hit the ground running on your up-coming projects as soon as they get the green light.

C-SUITE LEADERS HOLD THE KEY TO UNLOCKING A FUTURE OF WORK PARADIGM SHIFT

The US technology and professional service industries laid off thousands of workers in 2023. Corporations grappled with many accelerating changes, making the workforce model even more challenging than before, including evolving technologies, economic uncertainties, and marked shifts in consumer behavior.

To enterprise leaders, a playbook for managing these changes may seem to be noticeably absent. But I take a more positive spin. The playbook depends on how you allocate and deploy your human capital strategy—and it's sitting right under your nose.

Any leader worth their salt acknowledges that their people are their most important asset. However, too many leaders delegate their people strategy to those who aren't also responsible for the organization's P&L functions.

Before coming to MBO, I spent two decades at PwC, including time as the pricing and profitability leader. While I may be biased to say the firm has done better than many in recent months (and admirably committed to not laying off any staff), they do so in part because they clearly understand and articulate their workforce mix to strategically leverage their best assets—people.

What does this mean? It means that operating leaders (I include partners in professional services firms as a part of this) are accountable for achieving a strategic mix of talent combining full-time workers, contingent labor (independent contractors), and offshore talent to bring the right skills to their projects, quickly, while appropriately allocating operating capital. It enables discipline without disruption in harsh economic climates and agility in growth areas without bloat.

But what I find even more admirable is when an organization commits from the C-suite down, gaining genuine buy-in and marching toward the same goal. This decision isn't left to a single department but inherent in the work ethos of every revenue-generating individual.

In short, it works because an optimized workforce is baked into their DNA.

Many companies who work with us at MBO Partners are stellar examples of doing this well, and many more are working hard to scale up to this journey. And it is a journey—one cannot simply flip a switch and impact any change to a large and often global enterprise. But other companies have unfortunately relegated management of their workforce programs to departments overly focused on full-time employees (such as HR, which in many cases does not have responsibility for driving revenue). Or they've burdened their labor acquisition leadership with restrictive procurement protocols, thinking they'll win by cost efficiencies alone—forgetting or minimizing the need for progress and innovation.

No one department can "win" the human capital game. Still, there is a commonality: the best programs are championed by the C-suite and operating leaders and disbursed throughout the company as a strategic imperative.

Leaders would do well to consider asking their most senior reports what they are doing to manage their human capital deployment best and appointing a global task force to examine and optimize their future workforce strategy.

The ideal blended team to take this on would mix functions known for their knowledge of necessary skills and talent recruitment (such as HR) with those responsible for driving revenue (operating leaders) and other necessary functions to articulate not just what one's ideal workforce mix should be, but what skills and functions should be prioritized for future growth. After all, it's one thing to declare a talent strategy and another to recruit for it in a climate where there are still more job openings than job seekers, particularly in high-skill areas.

The great Stephen Hawking once said that "the greatest enemy of knowledge is not ignorance, it is the illusion of knowledge."

Don't suffer from illusions. Dig in. Do the work. A clearly defined workforce mix drives results that will delight your clients, weather the ebbs and flows of the market, and drive profitability.[35]

* * *

Human capital scarcity is arguably one of the most significant issues a company faces. People are choosing not to be full-time employees. If you deny it, you'll lose the ability to source the people you need because so many people have moved to the world of independent professionals. Ignore the data to your peril; there's no time for losers.

To paraphrase that earlier quote from Queen's Brian May: You can no longer fight this. The fact is that talented people want to participate in the economy and help your enterprise, but they don't want to be your full-time employees. An enterprise cannot simply stand up front and dictate to the masses the terms under which they can be employed. Independents want to sing along, too, to be part of a two-way process. Independents want to participate, but without being owned. The labor force *is* shrinking, but innovative enterprises will dream and create new anthems—new ways to engage externals as the workforce they need.

The key is to remember a principle I'll refer to often, with due credit to bestselling author Peter Diamandis: Abundance *is* achievable through innovation and technological advancements, allowing us to overcome the constraints that have previously held us back.[36] And believing in abundance means believing in labor force abundance—and opening your eyes to see who *all* the people are.

In the war for talent, we can all be the champions, my friends.

6

~~I CAN'T GET NO~~ SATISFACTION

Force #6: The State of Independence in America

> There comes a time when you ought to start doing what you
> want. Take a job that you love. You will jump out of bed in the
> morning. I think you are out of your mind if you keep taking
> jobs that you don't like because you think it will look good on
> your resume. Isn't that a little like saving up sex for your old age?
> —Warren Buffett

I was born on January 9, 1964, the same week the Rolling Stones began their very first tour of England as a headline act. A year and a half later, as I was waking up in a crib in North Dakota, the Stones were waking up in a hotel room in Clearwater, Florida. Keith Richards, their 21-year-old guitarist, noticed that his cassette recorder was at the end of the tape. He kept the recorder by his bed in case he thought up new songs in the middle of the night. Richards hit the rewind button and listened to what was mostly himself snoring. But as he continued to listen, Richards heard what it was that woke him in the middle of the night and caused him to hit the record button in the first place. There, on the tape, was Richards laying down the guitar riff that became the opening to the Stones' most iconic song: "(I Can't Get No) Satisfaction."[1]

Richards took the riff to Mick Jagger, also 21, and they penned the lyrics together. One month later, on June 5, 1965, they released "Satisfaction" as a single, and within the week, it landed on the Top 100 charts. Another month later, the song hit #1. The Stones had tapped into the rock and roll desires of the baby boomers and gave them what they wanted: "Satisfaction." And in the sixty years since, they've played the song in concert over one thousand times.[2] If you go see the Stones in concert, you might wonder about the optics of octogenarians singing lyrics about lusty teen love. But you can take this to the bank: The Stones will sing "Satisfaction." Some things never change.

You can't say the same thing about the profile of the US labor force, which looked quite different in 1965 than it does today. Politicians, pundits, sociologists, theologians, and economists all like to weigh in on whether these changes have benefited or harmed society. I'm just presenting the data here as a factual reminder that so much *has* changed since 1965—the year that the first baby boomers turned nineteen and hit the full-time employee workforce.

- In 1965, only 49% of the adult population graduated from high school; only 9% had a college degree. Today, 91% graduate high school and 38% from college.[3]
- In 1965, 80% of working-age men and 40% of working-age women were employed.[4] Now, men's labor force participation is 68%, around 57% for women.
- The male/female ratio of the US workforce in 1965 was about 70/30; today, it is 55/45.
- In 1965, US companies employed 16 million workers in manufacturing.[5] Today, the US has about 13 million manufacturing jobs.
- Throughout the 1960s, the foreign-born population in the US remained under 10 million (less than 5% of the population); today, there are more than 40 million (around 13% of the population).

But do you know what *hasn't* changed? Sixty years ago, people wanted to be happy. They wanted to find satisfaction in their life, which also meant finding satisfaction in their work—or trying to. People are no different to-day in their *yearning* for job satisfaction. The main difference now from 1965 is that the social contract between employer and employee has broken down, and the barriers to entry for entrepreneurship have never been lower. So, show me one of your full-time employees with low job satisfaction, and I'll show you someone who may be preparing to leave your workforce—and may even be thinking of going independent.

THE SURVEY SAYS

What does every company want? Healthy, happy workers, right? But what will it take for "employee well-being" to move from being a corporate buzzword and instead become a reality in the lives of workers? How can a greater percentage of the workforce find satisfaction in their career? By now, it should not surprise you that I'll answer that question by pointing to independents, the segment of the workforce most satisfied with their work. Here's how I know that's true.

The company I lead publishes a widely read and respected annual report called "The State of Independence," grounded in original data collected by a third-party firm we commission for the research. MBO's founder, Gene Zaino, kick-started this annual study in 2012 to better understand his target customer base. The report helps us answer enterprises' question: *What do independents want?* Or, more precisely, *How can our business become the client of choice for skilled independents?*

With more than a dozen years of primary research now under our belt, we can see the compelling workforce trends that exist and even where there have been breaks in those trends. The data paints a rich picture of independent workers' motivations, needs, and desires. Year by year, we continue to probe the psyche and gauge the mood of America's rapidly growing independent workforce.[6] And here's what we find: independents are happier and healthier than they were as full-time employees.

Our original research published in 2023 showed that 87% of independents report they're happier working independently, and 78% say they are healthier since moving to independent work. That's up from 63% in 2015.

So, in those eight years, the number of respondents who reported "I'm happier and healthier as an independent" skyrocketed from about two-thirds to
almost 90%. I'll talk more about "satisfaction" later in this chapter, but first,
let's take a look at the overall numbers.

OVERALL GROWTH

An essential fact about the independent workforce in America is how it continues to grow. Only one year out of the past eleven showed a plateau in that
trendline. All the remaining years revealed growth. So it's no surprise that over
72 million Americans are doing some form of independent work today. Our
prediction about the trendline is that over the next five years, more than 60%
of the US workforce will have worked as an independent at some point in their
career—over half the US workforce. Independents cannot be ignored.

From 2020 to 2023, the total number of independents grew 89% (from
38.2M to 72.1M). And the number of *full-time* independents surged almost
100% during these four years, increasing from 13.6 million to 26 million
(for an average annual growth rate of 23% per year during this time period).
By contrast, between 2011 and 2019, the annual growth rate for full-time
independent workers averaged 2%. So clearly, there has been a surge.

The increase can be ascribed to several factors. Many people were
pushed out of full-time work in 2020 and 2021 due to COVID-19, to care
for children who weren't in school full-time or to care for parents who
couldn't seek full-time employment. But they still want to work, and there
is high demand for their skills. Others may turn to part-time work as a bul-
wark against rising costs due to inflation and insecurity stemming from the
volatile environment. These part-time independents don't work a regular
schedule but instead work irregularly and periodically.

One essential thing to keep in mind about the growth: even though
unemployment remains at record lows here in the United States, we still
have more people choosing to be independents. That is, they're not choosing
to be independent because they can't get a job. No, they're choosing a better
way of life. Independents live the life they want by taking control of their

destiny. They've flipped the "I can't get no satisfaction" script. They *do* get satisfaction—as our research shows.

Across the board, the old stereotypes and tropes about independent freelancers and workers are being upended. Independents are growing in number, becoming more centered in the economy and forming connections to one another and to companies large and small. They find work in different ways and have a fundamentally optimistic view about their prospects, health, and purpose.

As we have discussed, so many technical innovations have been developed to enable people to work independently. But another critical component driving this trend is that existing societal norms have changed over the past decade. People think and act differently about concepts like "remote work" and "external workforce." Ten years ago, if you were at a cocktail party and said you were an independent, the reaction would often be: "Well, what did you do before you got laid off?" This was the understanding: You worked independently because something went wrong, but you tried to escape that circumstance as quickly as possible.

In the future of work, however, a larger portion of the professional workforce will consist of independent professionals compared to full-time employees. In greater numbers, Americans are opting for the flexibility, autonomy, and work-life balance offered by independent work. And we know this growth will be sustained because of the generational surge of the external workforce. In 2021, the independent workforce grew 34%, with 68% of those independents coming from the younger generations (millennials and Gen Z).

It's safe to say now, after more than a dozen years of tracking the size and sentiments of the independent economy, we have finally reached a tipping point: Independent work has been mainstreamed. In a world where top talent is hard to find, many leading organizations strategically engage independent talent alongside or instead of full-time traditional labor.

OCCASIONALS AND PART-TIMERS

By far, the fastest-growing segment of independent work is the group we call Occasional Independents. These are part-time independents who work irregularly and periodically. We also refer to this cohort as side giggers or side hustlers. Most have other paid jobs or are busy with primary activities such as caregiving, homemaking, or attending school. Since we first started tracking Occasionals, their numbers have more than tripled, growing from 9.1 million in 2015 to 31.9 million in 2022. The fastest growth occurred over the past two years, with the number of Occasionals growing 51% in 2021 and 34% in 2022. But they grew an additional 15% in 2023—and that would still be the third fastest growth that they've had.

The biggest driver in the growth of Occasionals and part-time independents (independents who work more regularly than Occasionals—on average weekly but fewer than 15 hours per week) is the need for supplemental income. Amid rising inflation, many Americans have found that their income hasn't kept up with rising costs, especially for education, health care, and housing. For this group, part-time independent work has become crucial to making ends meet and to shore up shaky finances. Other reasons for becoming an Occasional Independent include starting a passion business, testing the prospect of going independent with part-time work, or developing new skills.

PROFILES IN COURAGE

The more the independent workforce grows and expands, the more closely it resembles the American workforce at large.

It used to be that the external workforce was weighted heavily with older workers. These people, now in the second half of their careers, already had credentials, and many became independent contractors to continue working for somebody they already knew. Once you had a career of twenty-five years, you could promote yourself or your products. The decades spent in your career as an employee became the shingle you hung out as an independent.

One thing's for sure: It's not 1980 anymore. Spending many years with one company or even working in one career is becoming rare. Now a much higher share of independent workers has a career of 10 years or fewer in a specific field. That's because half the independent workforce is younger than forty, and, as stated earlier, 68% of newcomers to independent work are either millennials or Gen Zers. The combined total of millennials and Gen Zers now outnumbers the combined ranks of baby boomers and Gen Xers in the external workforce. Let those numbers sink in as you consider the future of your workforce because the movement of the younger generations into the external workforce is surging—not plateauing or declining as some would have you believe.

Let's break down those generational numbers more, from oldest to youngest. In 2023:

- *Boomers* (the youngest of which is now 60) and *matures* (those over 77) accounted for only 19% of the independent workforce. And as we saw in the previous chapter, this group is retiring by the millions each year.
- *Gen X* (born c. 1965–1980) represented 29% of the external workforce. They are moving into middle age, and the oldest are in the latter stages of their careers—thus leaning more into independent work.
- *Millennials* (born 1981–1996) made up the largest cohort of the independent workforce at 33%.
- *Gen Z* (born 1997–2012) made up 19% of the independent workforce—a remarkable number given that half their generation is still finishing high school.

The pandemic and the accompanying recession of 2020 hit younger workers hard, so they turned to independent work to supplement their income or even to serve as their primary source of income. Millennials, many of whom entered the workforce during the Great Recession in 2007, knew better than to wait for the job market to recover. And for Gen Zers, dubbed the most entrepreneurial generational cohort of recent history, independence through independent work was a natural course when they weren't struggling to find desirable payroll jobs.

Many younger workers have also decided they don't want their lives defined by work. Instead, they're looking for the freedom, flexibility, and control to live and work in a way that fits their values and passions. And who doesn't desire those things?

MOTIVATIONS, NEEDS, AND DESIRES

"It's the economy, stupid"—that famous 1992 political maxim by Bill Clinton's campaign guru James Carville—taught us that current economic conditions determine how most people vote because that's the chief factor in people feeling happy and satisfied. Everybody knows this is true. But here's a paradigm shifter we've discovered: Independents have some immunity to turbulent economies. Even amidst the volatile economy of the past few years, independents' self-reported feelings on happiness, health, and perceived financial security are on par with or the highest they've been in the dozen years of data collected by MBO.

In 2023, 77% of respondents indicated that they are "very satisfied" with independent work, 87% said they were happier working on their own, 78% reported that independent work is better for their health. Also, 53% reported they earned more working on their own than they could at traditional jobs, and 66% said independence made them feel more secure than when they worked as a full-time employee (up from 32% in 2011).

To be sure, there are challenges embedded in working this way: the lack of job security, volatile income, and the need to set boundaries. The challenge most cited among independents is not enough predictable income (49%, down from 55% in 2012), followed by concerns about the next job/pipeline (33%). In the next chapter, we will look further into the erosion of the social contract and how its demise impacts the financial outlook of independents—especially the younger independents.

Even though satisfaction *and* confidence in their career prospects remain high year after year for independents, would independents go back to a W-2 job if they could? Mostly not. Sixty-three percent said that working independently was their choice completely, and 78% plan to continue working independently. Only 12% plan to seek a permanent full-time job. At a time when payroll jobs are plentiful, independent workers constantly weigh whether they should stay on the career path they're on. They know they could quickly jump back into a high-paying W-2 role. But they're not.

For example, by the end of 2022, 29 straight months of job growth had added 22.5 million payroll jobs, recouping all the jobs lost in the pandemic and then some. At 153 million, there had never been more payroll jobs in the United States. With an unemployment rate of just 3.5%, there were still over 10 million job openings in the nation. And yet, even with all that strength in the payroll jobs market, there have never been more people working independently than there are now—both in terms of overall numbers and also as a percentage of the total workforce.

In the past, the payroll and independent jobs markets were in tension—a strong payroll jobs market tended to drain people away from the independent workforce. But in the past few years, we have learned that a booming payroll jobs market can coexist with a rapid increase in the number of independent workers. This development shows the United States' power as a job-creating engine and highlights the forces and trends spurring the growth of independent work. And even beyond the macroeconomic climate, fundamental changes in work are increasing the demand for independent workers and helping to boost supply.

And again, the critical thing to remember here is that although unemployment has been at record lows in the United States, more people are choosing to be independent than ever before. They decide to be independent because they want a certain way of life: happier and healthier.

So here's the answer to the question "What does every company want?": Healthy, happy workers. And with 82% of the full-time independents reporting that they're happier working independently and 69% saying this is better for their health—now you know where to find a happier, healthier workforce.

LIFE GOALS AND THE WHY

All of this reminds us of the importance of knowing and working toward a bigger picture—the longer-term vision most of us probably describe as our "life goals" or the "why" we're doing what we do in our careers.

We know that people work not just to make a living and pay their bills but to realize their ambitions and achieve personal goals—however they define them. Our research asked full-time independents several questions about their success in meeting their life goals. The questions were the same as those used by our collaborative partner in research, Flywheel Associates, in their "State of Career and Work Success Survey." This allowed us to compare full-time independents with the overall US adult workforce regarding their views on whether they're meeting their life goals. Full-time independents self-ranked consistently higher on key personal elements. Some 65% of full-time independents said they were helping others, compared with 59% of US adults; 63% of full-time independents said they were spending enough time with family, compared with 55% of traditional workers.

Allow me to connect on this point in a personal way. I'm a very principles-based person in terms of the way I think about what to do and why to do things. I spent thirty plus years with a very prestigious firm and enjoyed the work immensely. Even so, I got to the point where I thought: *There is something more I can do. There's a better way for me to help people.*

While with my firm, I was also a builder of many different businesses. By way of analogy, I told myself it was time for me professionally to be a builder of a future that transcends the existing ways of working to improve the well-being of people *and* businesses. In my mind, the best way to do that was to make a move and help a company like MBO to maximize independents' future and well-being.

It sounds so simple, but it's really something that I have a passion for: helping these individuals—like you!—find success in their independent solopreneur life. To build their small business or enterprise. To improve their well-being.

Workers increasingly want the autonomy, control, and flexibility that independent work provides. If working independently wasn't satisfying, then we would not be seeing the phenomenal growth in the number of people making this move. Or at best, the numbers would be cyclical—determined more by the overall job market. But that's not the case. Independents become—and remain—independent because they find they are healthier, happier, and wealthier.

In sum: They get no satisfaction.

7

INTERLUDE:
TAKE THIS JOB AND SHOVE IT

The Changing of the Social Contract

> The real problem of humanity is the following: we have Paleo-
> lithic emotions, medieval institutions, and godlike technology,
> and it is terrifically dangerous, and it is now approaching a point
> of crisis overall.
>
> —E. O. Wilson, 2009[1]

Now that we've looked at all "Six Forces Shaping the Future of Work," here's the bottom line: The business models that survive and thrive will be built on a modern understanding of the workforce. Enterprises that view their workforce mostly in terms of having full-time, captive employees will be disrupted. To recap in shorthand, these are the forces—the "Everson's Evolutions"—that are shaping the future of work:

1. Change accelerates
2. Progress deflates

3. Everything fractionalizes
4. Knowledge flows
5. Talent wars will escalate
6. Labor will shift increasingly to independent work

And remember, the sixth force—*Labor will shift increasingly to independent work*—cannot be stopped or reversed because it's rooted in the first five macro trends, which themselves seem unstoppable.

In one of the final scenes of Mel Gibson's *The Patriot*, as the British general Cornwallis looks out over the Battle of Yorktown, he admits to a colleague that their British Army had lost the war to the Americans. Sighing deeply, he utters a statement of surrender, not simply because of that day's defeat or even the war itself. He sighed an admittance that the entire world order would be changing. If the ragtag American colonials could break away from Britain—warring and winning their independence—then *any* colony from *any* empire might do so. If the latest tools of education, technology, and mass communication in the hands of commoners could topple the mightiest army on earth, then Cornwallis understood the broader implication: "Everything will change. Everything *has* changed."

With that theme in view and before we move into the second part of this book with its emphasis on "the independent mind," I want to first "interlude" here in order to state clearly a belief I don't hear many talking about. After thinking about the future of work for the past few decades, I have come to believe:

The social contract is broken.

Or, to state it positively:

We must construct a new social contract.

Pertaining to labor, the social contract that dominated the American workforce for the past six or seven decades was mainly built on one big idea: workers promised their loyalty to a business in return for a *guaranteed pension* for life when they retired. But pension systems began eroding in the 1980s, fueled by corporate bankruptcies in the steel and airline industries. At the same time, more and more companies switched from defined benefits to defined contribution plans. No longer was loyalty essential. Blue- and white-collar workers alike could just port their existing benefits to a new company.[2]

The rise of the independent workforce, fueled by technological advancements and changing preferences in the labor market, has ushered in a new era of labor characterized by hypermobility, the gig economy, freelancing, temp work, contract work, solopreneurs, micropreneurs, and the self-employed. While this transformation has offered workers greater flexibility and autonomy, it has also brought forth a series of challenges that the traditional employment model did not anticipate—nor can it meet.

In the time period after World War II, people were able to live a better lifestyle: improved food, shelter, and keeping up with the Joneses. And they were able to do so with a single income, a breadwinner who worked a full-time job with a defined benefit plan. There was great security in this.

But by the 1970s and the onset of higher inflation, households began to realize they needed two incomes to support the lifestyle they wanted. So spouses started going to work. Then, by the late 1980s and early 1990s, the consumer credit markets were reengineered to make it possible to use your home as cash flow. Consumer credit began to balloon, and it has continued to skyrocket for over 20 years now.

As a result of all these economic trends, what we started to see in the 2000s (and it has really been ramping up for the last 10 to 15 years) is people doing side gigs to create incremental income because they've already maxed out the other options. Both spouses work. They've maxed out their credit and housing market options. But they need more income, so doing side jobs became the trendline for a greater portion of the workforce.

This chapter investigates the challenges the labor force faces in general—the symptoms of the busted-up social contract. Then we'll look at some particular challenges facing independent workers. We'll shed light on the gaps in labor protections and propose an updated social contract that addresses the unique needs of this burgeoning workforce.

NINE SYMPTOMS OF THE BROKEN SOCIAL CONTRACT

I'm neither an idealist nor a utopian. If history teaches us anything, it's that we are stumbling forward—and I believe both *stumbling* and *forward* describe the lessons of history. As Martin Luther King, Jr. famously said, "The arc of the moral universe is long, but it bends toward justice." And it also seems to be bending toward decentralization.

Today, whoever controls the distribution to the consumer is winning. Walmart, Target, and Costco went and moved out the small businesses throughout America. When Sam Walton's Walmart showed up in a town, you were in trouble if you were a local retailer. The large corporation's distribution systems made it impossible for the little independent entrepreneur to make it. But now, because of the high quality and low cost of doing business through digital platforms, the barriers to entry are lower than ever. The platforms make it possible for entrepreneurs to be back in the business because the distribution has been opened up.

Throughout history, the "powers that be" have often gotten themselves pulled into the future unwillingly, kicking and screaming because of the loss of power they knew would come. And, of course, the twentieth century saw tens of millions of people murdered by totalitarian leaders hell-bent on reshaping their nation into a heaven on earth. No system is perfect, but certainly, we can learn from history that some systems are awful—to put it mildly. As Winston Churchill said to the House of Commons in 1947: "Democracy is the worst form of government, except for all those others that have been tried."[3]

What difference does all this make? Why discuss this in a book about the future of work and the independent workforce? Well, I would argue that so many of the "labor pains" of the workforce we read about daily in the business headlines are symptoms of our need for a new social contract.

Though I could highlight several dozen, here are nine signs of the broken social contract that can probably be read about in the news any given week. The common sentiment running through all can be expressed by the title of Twisted Sister's classic rock hit "We're Not Gonna Take It." Or better, Johnny Paycheck's #1 hit on the country charts from 1977, "Take This

Job and Shove It." The signs are all around us: We *must* construct a new social contract.

Sign #1: No Golden Watch

As I said in the introduction, since at least World War II, when workers became employees of a company, they expected to remain with that enterprise for twenty or thirty years—until retirement. Loyalty was a two-way street based on the promise of defined benefits: "Stay with us for X number of years, and there will be a pension that will take care of you after you retire." That model is now unsustainable, and it probably was so even at its creation.

Here's an astounding fact: In 1980, nearly two-thirds of employees working for private companies in the United States had a defined benefit plan—otherwise known as a "retirement plan" or "pension." But today, less than 10% (and some estimate it to be only 3%) of American workers employed with private companies have a defined benefit plan. You read that right. That's all happened since the time I graduated high school, and that was the start of the break in the social contract bond with labor. There's no golden watch. No defined benefit plans.

We could debate whether those defined benefit plans were ever financially sustainable. My opinion: They were not, although with the shorter lifespans in 1945, one might argue that pension plans were sustainable. In 1945, a male in the United States could be expected to live 62.9 years; a female 68.4 years.[4] So, after giving thirty years to an employer, the retiree could hope to live ten more years in retirement and had some pension on which to do so. But now—and this is good news—life expectancy in the United States is approaching 80 years for males and 83 years for females.[5] That's great news for being able to stay alive and be with the people we love for longer, but how does the math work for private or public employers to provide 20–25 years of defined retirement benefits? It doesn't, and that's why I say the employer-employee bond has broken. The extra years are here but the money is not. The reality is that those pension plans that once existed as a promise to the worker are now mostly gone, and their disappearance broke the loyalty that an employee had to their employer.

Sign #2: Transitory Employment

If the employer-employee relationship isn't a 20- or 30-year relationship, how long *does* it last? Here's what we know: If you are under 45 years old in the United States, you will change companies on average every four years. If you're under 35, you will change companies every three years.[6] With stats like that, who continues to think the United States will have a permanent workforce for any company? The ideal of a permanent full-time workforce is dead.

Sign #3: Instability

Given the transitory nature of jobs, especially for the younger generations, it's no surprise that "Generation Z Yearns for Stability" (i.e., staying put in one job), according to surveys reported on by the media. In 2023, Handshake reported survey results showing that 85% of newly graduated Gen Z job seekers ranked "stability" as their top aspiration, rating it ahead of all other factors, including benefits (81%) and a high starting salary (80%).[7] They have older siblings or friends who bounce every few years from employer to employer, and deep down they aspire to something different.

But the reality is that "stability" does not equal "having a company job." I want to be careful here because our data shows that the fastest growing cohort of independent contractors is Gen Z. And we know from our State of Independence reports that independents feel more secure as independents than they did as employees. So when I report that Gen Z seeks stability, what I believe this means is that they are seeking purpose and economic stability—not simply the older ideal of having and keeping one employer.

Sign #4: Lack of Advancement

Related to job instability, the younger generations face high hurdles to career advancement within one company. How can you move up the ladder with one employer when you don't *stay* at one employer longer than three years? But it's a catch-22. Do employees leave for another company because they feel there's little opportunity to advance with their current employer? Or do they fail to advance because they're jumping ship too soon? The answer is probably "both." That said, I don't think I'd counsel a young worker to stay put at one company if they can advance simply by switching to another. Why gamble that your current employer will create a path for you to advance? But again, people want job stability too.

Sign #5: Not Knowing Each Other or the Company

People like to work with people they know. Still, with workers changing companies every three or four years, I'm hearing about "the knowing problem": coworkers don't know one another long enough to be bonded. Because of shallow relationships, they aren't in sync. The idea is that a lack of "knowing" creates a shortage of "flowing."

Related to this problem, there's a myth that independent contractors can't be known as deeply as full-time employees. But I'm saying that's a myth because, statistically speaking, employees in your workforce under the age of 45 will change jobs every three or four years. So, do you really have a knowingness with them—even if they are employees?

In contrast, I would argue that independents who work two, three, six, or eight months a year for a company will, after a few rotations or projects, be just as well-known to a company, if not better, than the full-time workforce. And again, if you're wondering about how and why these time arrangements are decided—just remember that independents serve their clients by solving problems or project execution. The mindset of the relationship doesn't involve punching a time card.

Sign #6: The Great Resignation and the Great Realization

In what was likely the most significant social experiment on work we will hopefully ever see, the COVID-19 pandemic showed us that people can work comfortably from pretty much anywhere. However, as noted earlier, the quits rate was the highest in the Bureau of Labor's tracking of this stat, as millions of people chose to leave their jobs every month.[8] The pandemic accelerated a long-simmering shift and changes many years in the making. We were dealing with a transforming workforce well before the pandemic revealed cracks in the foundations of many companies' traditional full-time employee-focused models. The so-called permanence of a full-time position filled by a single individual sitting at a desk in an office complex has become a relic of the past.

In response to these "quitting" trends, I have championed the "Great Realization," a movement that empowers individuals to have the freedom to do the work they love, the way they want, and for businesses to rethink how to break free of corporate rigidity and succeed in the future of work.[9]

Sign #7: Quiet Quitting

Quiet quitting describes how employees will show up physically to work but choose to disengage mentally or emotionally. They're not ready to quit and move into a new job, but they feel like they need to set boundaries. They've stopped "going the extra mile" and don't feel bad about it because of poor work conditions. They only want to do the bare minimum at work.

Matt Pearce, a reporter for the *Los Angeles Times*, traced the origins of the concept and argued, "Gen Z didn't coin 'quiet quitting'—Gen X did."[10] If in doubt, he argues, go back and watch the 1999 movie *Office Space* because the movie's central plot is the quiet quitting of the Gen X lead character, played by Ron Livingston. Jennifer Aniston's character finally completely quits her job as a server after her manager continues to hassle her because she only wore "the required minimum pieces of flair" on her uniform. And who can forget Milton, the "older guy" in the movie who was abused by management, forced to move to the basement, isolated, and even fired (without being told). Finally, when the boss took Milton's beloved red stapler, he responded with an ultimate "We're not gonna take it" move and burned the office down.

Depending on who is doing the analyzing, these workers are either lazy slackers or courageous workers who are putting down proper work-life boundaries. Arianna Huffington declared, "Quiet quitting isn't just about quitting on a job, it's a step toward quitting on life. Yes, we shouldn't be defined by our work. But at the same time, if work is at least eight hours of our day, are we saying these are hours we're willing to simply go through the motions, with the inevitable boredom that's bound to ensue? Work can give us meaning and purpose. It's part of a thriving life. We should absolutely reject 'hustle culture' and burnout (I believe this so strongly I founded a company with that as its mission). But rejecting burnout doesn't mean rejecting the possibility of finding joy in our work, loving our work."[11]

Sign #8: Quiet Firing

Some employees who feel no support from management and get little or no feedback, training, or a path for advancement, end up demoralized and move on to a new job. The term "quiet firing" describes the passive-aggressive maltreatment of an employee, to persuade them to quit their job—to get the employee to leave without having to terminate them with severance benefits or messy interactions. Do quiet managers intentionally do this, or are they just poor managers? Yes, no, does it matter the reason? Either way, such management strips employees of their agency to improve, learn, grow, and become more valuable to the company. And this behavior lowers morale across the team as the other employees wonder if they will be next.

Sign #9: The Four-Day Workweek

In an attempt to fix the problem of employee burnout or work-life misbalance, there has been a growing global movement toward establishing a four-day workweek. Sometimes the idea is that workers put in the same hours but only work four days a week—longer hours but fewer days. Or it could mean lessening the total number of hours worked, incentivizing employees to jettison the fluff and filler activities and just get the actual work done efficiently.

Either way, these are healthy movements toward a new social contract between employees and employers. That said, it should come as no surprise by now that when someone tells me they wish they could work a four-day workweek, I respond: "You can! Become an independent." And when enterprise leaders tell me candidly that their full-time employees aren't truly needed full-time each day or for an entire year, I respond by asking, "Then, why not use independents for this work?"

It's possible to cut through the debate about whether the four-day work-week actually works by using independents for focused projects and problems. How long they work each week is up to them and the expectations created by the arrangement. As an enterprise leader, does it really matter if people work five days a week for eight hours? Change your mind, and the rest will follow.

WE DON'T NEED NO REGULATION? IS THIS TRUE?

With so many symptoms of a failed broken social contract between labor and business, there's a temptation to bring in the power of the government to solve the problems. I've even heard people talk about getting the government involved in fixing the problem of people not connecting to one another in the workforce. The lack of connection may be one of the shortcomings of the existing social contract, but government regulation often brings with it an ominous feeling: Can't live with it. Can't live without it.

As the independent workforce grows (both low income/low skill and high income/high skill), I predict politicians will pursue protectionist and tax revenue policies. After all, two of the largest tax revenue sources are wage and income taxes. You've seen some of this with California's AB5 legislation, saying that everybody should be classified as an employee.[12] One school of thought is that corporations are picking on the little guy—the un-skilled worker—and taking advantage of them on these tech platforms. The other thought is that the government wants a consolidated tax collection system in place.

I would argue that the skilled independent workforce doesn't want or need governmental regulation to protect them from enterprises. From what I see, the independent mind has a bit of a libertarian bent, wanting to keep the government out of their business and live up to the full meaning of the word "independent." Without making this partisan, there's a famous

Ronald Reagan quote along these lines: "The nine most terrifying words in the English language are: I'm from the government, and I'm here to help."

You can't paint all workers with the same brush. For example, skilled independents who utilize MBO's platform are making $100K to $300K, and some earn over $1 million, a year. They don't need a government bureaucrat telling them whether they should be an independent business or whether they should be an employee. Further, I marvel at the hypocrisy of the government guaranteeing the right of workers to organize but not protecting their right to choose whether they contract as an employee or an independent.

But one of the challenges with working with a very diverse independent workforce is ensuring that you get them enrolled in a compliant way with federal and state tax laws and a whole host of other regulatory measures. So, the enterprise comes to MBO, and we enter into a master service agreement with them, providing them with three things.

First, we give them their own marketplace, riding on the MBO platform, where they house the talent they come to know—independents who may contract work with them and other companies at will. Second, we provide peace of mind from knowing that there has been compliant enrollment of these people on projects. And finally, you must be able to capture the time and manage and pay this diverse workforce. We do all of that for the enterprise, simplifying its access to and utilization of great independent talent. And for the talent, we give them access to more jobs than they otherwise could get. We match the two in between.

One of our independent professionals, whom I'll call "Glenn," worked as an executive at Nature Conservancy. Like me, he had 30 years of experience and tons of subject matter expertise in sustainability.

Glenn came to us because he was thinking of jumping from being an employee to being an independent. He wanted much more control and influence over who he worked for, when he worked, and how he worked. He wanted to work on projects he loved and no longer wanted to operate within a big company with all its bureaucracy. Now, he has multiple clients as an independent. He's as busy as he wants to be, but what's important is that he's busy with the stuff he chooses to do.

So, what does the relationship between Glenn and MBO look like? For starters, all the bureaucracy and administration that he didn't like in a big company—it's gone. Of course, when you have a little micropreneur or solopreneur company, you get other types of administration: tax filing, setting up legal entities, compliance issues, billings, etc. MBO took care of all that for him.

MBO started as a company called My Business Office to help people who wanted to be in business without having to deal with the bureaucracy. And now we're doing that at scale. At the same time, we're serving the needs of enterprises that need access to this top talent because more and more of the top talent are choosing to be independent.

So we've been pioneers in helping independents and enterprises partner, maintain compliance with regulations, and do great work together. The engine runs well. And yet, with several decades of involvement in this lane, we have thought about how things could be better—how the rise of the self-employed, independent workforce might help shape the new social contract.

THE CERTFIED SELF-EMPLOYED WORKER SOCIAL CONTRACT (AN MBO PARTNERS PROPOSAL)

The growth and innovation of the American workplace have outpaced the evolution of laws and rules, creating issues ranging from independent contractor compliance to guaranteed worker protections. MBO Partners has proposed a modern solution to address these issues and to remove the risks associated with hiring independent talent: the Certified Self-Employed Worker (CSE).[13]

As we have seen throughout this chapter, starting in the early twentieth century a "social contract" between employer and worker—ultimately overseen by government regulation—put the responsibility of supplying health and retirement benefits, maintaining minimum pay, and collecting and remitting payroll taxes squarely on the shoulders of companies. Employers, for their part, were willing to do so because it enabled them to negotiate labor contracts effectively and attract and retain employees.

But the old order is breaking down. Consumers and businesses can procure a growing range of services from non-employees over the internet, through apps, or from single-person microbusinesses who choose to be self-employed. With the rise of powerful platforms that broker and arrange such transactions and relationships, it has become increasingly difficult for all parties—workers, employers, regulators, and government—to distinguish between employees and independent workers. The ambiguity has led to the development of significant gray areas and gaps.

As is frequently the case, the rapid adoption of technology and innovation in business models has outpaced the evolution of rules and laws. Consequently, the rising popularity of independent work is being hampered by an overlapping and inconsistent patchwork quilt of federal, state, and local laws, regulations, and administrative worker classification enforcement positions. This conflict results in efficiency-destroying litigation and administrative delay surrounding the proper classification of workers.

Perhaps worse, these unresolved conflicts lead businesses to engage talent in suboptimal ways. They may outsource work overseas, pay independent workers through disguised methods like credit cards, or perhaps even bury them under other vendors. And pervasive misclassification can lead to the loss of tax revenues, negatively impacting governments and all taxpaying citizens. All this friction impedes innovation, adds costs to business, and lowers overall productivity. As the American independent workforce grows in size, strength, and importance, these circumstances will act as an economic sedative.

The growth of the American independent workforce has meaningful implications for individuals, companies, government, regulators, and society at large. Unfortunately, the current shape of the employment ecosystem often discourages the utilization of independents. Current laws and enforcement tilt heavily toward simply classifying independent workers as employees, as the system perceives that employee status is the "common preference," defaulting that all workers wish to have employer-provided benefits and entitlements, regardless of their worker classification. As a result, the many companies and organizations that want to retain independent workers often fear being penalized—subject to stiff penalties for not paying overtime, withholding taxes, and providing the overall protections and entitlements guaranteed to employees. Such penalties and associated compliance costs can reduce the economic advantage of working with independents. As a result, many organizations are hesitant to engage directly with American independent workers and instead send work offshore.

These questions have been brought to the forefront—and to the courts—partly due to the rapid rise of on-demand service platforms. While workers who utilize platforms like Uber and Handy comprise a small segment of the independent workforce, their appearances in courtrooms have generated an outsized amount of attention. Consequently, the legal system is defining the new terms of worker relationships in a haphazard fashion.

In response, many observers, experts, and stakeholders have proposed a range of solutions. For instance, former Clinton administration labor secretary Robert Reich has proposed the creation of a third labor category—the "dependent contractor"—which would seek to provide more certainty in classification and also require businesses to offer some benefits to contractors. The Brookings Institution's Hamilton Project has proposed that independent workers pool benefits from multiple employer contributions and be granted the right to organize.

At MBO, we think there is a better option. To provide certainty and clarity surrounding the norms and practices of employee-employer relationships in the twenty-first century, it is vital that we establish clear distinctions between formal employees and independent workers.

One appealing and sensible approach would be to create a formal federal certification for independent workers who meet specific criteria: the CSE designation. The goal of such a designation would be to remove roadblocks impeding the growth of the independent services market while embracing many of the elements of the safety net provided by the traditional employer-employee social contract.

By way of analogy, the proposed CSE designation for independents is like the professional certification requirements for being an "accredited investor"—requirements set by the US Securities and Exchange Commission. In order to invest in certain risky securities (with a higher risk, but a potential for higher gain), you have to meet the requirements established by the SEC: a net worth exceeding $1 million, an income over $200,000, and certain credentials issued by the Financial Industry Regulatory Authority. It's a process, to be sure, but it's all spelled out and clear.

Likewise, the CSE designation for independents would be a clear way of demonstrating that you have the level of sophistication needed to make your own choice. You know and have the ability to comply with the government regulations regarding the workforce.

Of course, one of the challenges of improving the situation through a simple regulatory solution or a new labor classification is that the independent workforce is not homogenous. Instead, we propose a more nuanced approach that can satisfy the needs of all independents. At one end of the spectrum, it would protect workers delivering routine services by addressing the power imbalance created by online platforms that commoditize work. Simultaneously, it would free from regulation those workers who wish to take control of their independent business and apply their talent and innovation to work the way they choose.

Protections are certainly needed for independents delivering routine services who may earn low to moderate incomes by depending on "commodity service platforms" (CSP) such as Uber, Lyft, Handy, Upwork, and Taskrabbit. These contractors may be caught in a "race to the bottom" when they offer commodity services; the protections are particularly necessary when the CSP that delivers the work also sets the pay and markets these workers as an integral component of their business model. Technology can be applied to easily track their hours regardless of how the services are delivered and paid for. These workers certainly seem more like employees than independent businesses, and the protections offered by our current system of laws and regulations are valuable to those who want them.

However, for other independent workers who want to pursue earning income and perhaps a full-time career as a responsible, self-employed independent contractor, it's clear the focus of worker regulations—geared toward employees—is no longer appropriate. Today's growing independent workforce economy requires worker regulations to provide for liberation from the "one size fits all" restraints and economic friction caused by the safety-net protections for those who only want to be employed and do not want to take on the risks and opportunities of self-employment.

A common misconception in the current approach to reducing misclassification is that all independent contractors wish to be employees. Many independent professionals truly wish to run their own businesses and to utilize their specialization and skill set to differentiate themselves from other workers, build a diversified and multiple client income stream, focus on working when and where they want, and deliver valuable services to buyers that see their value. We should encourage those who wish to be self-directed, who create their own jobs and businesses.

Regulations in the Tax Cuts and Jobs Act further incentivize workers to strike out on their own thanks to provisions that allow a 20% reduction in taxable income. A balance must be struck whereby these independents are not taken advantage of by their clients yet can also pursue their work and engage with clients in an effective, misclassification-free manner while funding their own safety net and taxes.

Any such proposal should meet several essential criteria. It should be implemented quickly and be preemptive by all states. A federal solution leaving workers subject to the threat of reclassification in other state or local jurisdictions would not be effective. It should ensure that government-mandated worker protections—traditional employee benefits—are preserved for those who need them without creating obstacles for those who wish to be accountable for their own personal security and protections, including benefits, self-employment-related taxes, FICA, Medicaid, and for some structures even state unemployment insurance. It should support the continued funding of the appropriate level (the amount and frequency) of taxes and prohibit companies from abusing the new system to avoid their employer responsibilities. It should enable people who wish to embrace the opportunity to be a self-employed business to thrive without burdening their clients with the real risks created by ambiguous worker reclassification rules that put these aspiring independents at a disadvantage competing with offshore workers and more inefficient service providers.

Accordingly, at MBO we propose the creation of a federally recognized safe-harbor worker classification—the CSE. A worker who seeks and obtains CSE status would be "certified" as an independent contractor. Clients could engage the CSE worker without having to worry about litigation, administrative enforcement action, or other entanglements. With the CSE, America can get back to the business of business and out of the business of inefficient self-examination.

CSE certification creates a mechanism for willing independent professionals to run their business through a government-approved process and commercially available systems to provide the tools and access to build their own safety nets and properly fund their taxes with third-party verification. The CSE solution is a people-implemented privilege that liberates workers to become independent on their own terms.

The mission of the CSE solution is simple, direct, and critical: It creates worker-driven steps that empower independents to create partnerships with customers and clients, thus removing the paternal dependences of traditional employment in which a business provides benefits that limit the independents' mobility. As is the case with obtaining other credentialing and certifications, the process for achieving CSE status would be thorough but fair and enabling. We propose a certification system as follows:

- When applying for certification, applicants would represent that they understand they are waiving the protections of employment laws. A test or legally binding form would verify that applicants understand what this means.
- Applicants would agree to comply with applicable tax funding rules whether they are (1) pass-through entities budgeting and setting aside funds from their income so that they are able to pay quarterly taxes or (2) paying themselves as a W-2, withholding taxes each time they receive payment.
- Applicants would represent that they bear the risk of loss and opportunity for profit and understand what is needed to cover their own business expenses, benefits, and self-employment taxes.
- Applicants would represent that they hold themselves out to the

public as offering services and that they have or anticipate having multiple sources of income and thus do not have economic dependency from any one company that could appear as an employer.

- Applicants would certify that they are free from more than de minimis direction/control from clients concerning the details of their work.

- Applicants should be able to represent and show proof of how they are developing their own skills independent from those provided by any one client.

- Certification would be valid for a set period and would be subject to renewal.

- Applicants would agree to verify their tax payments via an approved service provider, such as a certified accountant or financial management platform.

- Certification would bar the classification of the worker as an "employee" under any federal, state, or local law and would preempt contrary laws.

- Workers who do not go through the certification process would be subject to existing laws and regulations that favor employee status.

- The recipient of the service (or the platform that delivers the worker to perform the service) must adhere to local and federal employer-employee responsibilities.

- First-time applicants could apply based on their anticipated business model. Renewal applicants would need to represent that their business has been compliant with CSE terms over the previous certification term.

* * *

I hope this discussion has been helpful in thinking through the social contract. I truly believe we are at a pivot point in human history regarding society's relationship with the workforce. And I believe the independent workforce will play a central role in the future of work and the building out of the new social contract.

The challenges are significant, but they are not insurmountable. With the rapid technological changes coming at us each decade—and even more will now come faster with AI—some fear we cannot find solutions fast enough. But I'm betting that we can figure this out. When I think about this, a point by Seth Godin resonates with me: "Perhaps our job is to create the conditions for things to get better, not to predict that they won't."[14]

EVERSON'S ACTION POINT: FOR CURRENT EMPLOYEES

Note: Beginning with this chapter and continuing through part 2 of the book, I'll close each chapter with some action points—mostly for enterprise leaders, but also for independents. However, this chapter's action point is for the reader who is currently an employee but is thinking about the independent life.

I understand Arianna Huffington's point about "quiet quitting" and agree with much of it. But I find even more compelling Adam Grant's tweet on the subject: "'Quiet quitting' isn't laziness. Doing the bare minimum is a common response to bullshit jobs, abusive bosses, and low pay. When they don't feel cared about, people eventually stop caring. If you want them to go the extra mile, start with meaningful work, respect, and fair pay."[15]

To Grant's tweet, I would add the following question *to employees* who find themselves stuck in toxic work environments: *Have you considered just going independent?* Huffington is right when she says, "Work can give us meaning and purpose." And I would argue that independent work can provide meaning and purpose, but without the toxicity or the need to quit. Don't wait for society to rewrite the social contract: Rewrite it for yourself and gain your freedom!

PART 2

THE INDEPENDENT MIND
OF A FREE BIRD

8

I LOVE STORY [MILES'S VERSION]

Own Your Own Narrative

> The most powerful person in the world is the storyteller. The
> storyteller sets the vision, values, and agenda of an entire gener-
> ation that is to come.
> —Steve Jobs, 1994 (one year before Pixar released *Toy Story*)[1]

In August 2019, Taylor Swift went on *CBS News Sunday Morning* to an-
nounce her intention to rerecord her first six albums and release them as
"(Taylor's Version)" recordings. This move was Swift's response to a bitter
dispute with her former record label, Big Machine Records, which owned
the rights to the "masters" of the six albums but not the "publishing rights"
(the lyrics, arrangements, composition, etc.). Big Machine tried to get Swift
under a new, decade-long contract, promising her the rights to the original
recordings *if* she produced another six.

To complicate matters, Swift had bad blood with the owner of Big Machine, Scooter Braun: "All I could think about was the incessant, manip-
ulative bullying I've received at his hands for years." If she stayed with Big

Machine, she believed, "Essentially, my musical legacy is about to lie in the hands of someone who tried to dismantle it."[2]

The record label thought she was bluffing. To rerecord the albums would be an unprecedented power move that would devalue the original recordings—if the musician had broad support and people bought the new rather than the old. There was a risk involved (there always is in such things) because popular support for any type of highly paid entertainer—musician, actor, athlete—can erode quickly if it is perceived that money is their motivation.

But for Swift, the principle of the matter transcended the dollar calculation. She wanted the freedom to own her creation—the artist's right to determine the destiny of her musical legacy. "The reason I'm rerecording my music next year is because I do want my music to live on," Swift told *Forbes* in 2019. "I want it to be in movies. I *do* want it to be in commercials. But I only want that if I own it."

She wasn't bluffing. Swift swiftly did just what she said she would do. The first song she rerecorded and released was "Love Story (Taylor's Version)." Politicians, other musicians, and her fan base showed their support with purchases of the new music and by creating viral hashtags on social media: #IStandWithTaylor. The rerecordings were extraordinarily successful, and her entire catalog is now valued at over $400M.[3] The popularity of Swift's Eras tour vaulted her into billionaire status—as a 33-year-old.

* * *

You have undoubtedly heard the basic gist of the Taylor Swift story I recounted above, especially if you're a fan. Swifties don't need me, a man in his early sixties, to tell them about the epic battle their heroine won. But if you do want to read more about it, Wikipedia has a lengthy entry dedicated to this one event, this singular battle fought by the young singer. Printed out, the "Taylor Swift masters dispute" article totals 39 pages of reading material. By contrast, Wikipedia's article about "The Battle of Gettysburg" runs only 37 pages.[4]

But opening this chapter with the Swift saga gives me a chance to talk about "story"—which also serves to explain why I use so many anecdotes from pop culture, music, and the history of technology. I've mixed in quite a few tales about famous musicians and entrepreneurs like Steve Jobs, Steve Wozniak, and Bill Gates throughout the book because these stories are in the common domain. There are a half dozen bestselling books or movies about Jobs alone, and he was profiled repeatedly by major magazines over the course of several decades. There's a lot I don't have to explain about these famous founders of the world's most valuable companies. We know these narratives because these entrepreneurs became larger than life.

Besides all that, the company I lead as CEO, MBO Partners, has as its mission "to make it easier for enterprise organizations and top independent professionals to work together." That makes us part of a larger, global story—a movement and revolutionary moment of people walking away from full-time employment and into the external workforce. For many, that journey begins with small steps as they venture into the gig economy doing side hustles of various types.

The word *gig* is how jazz musicians of the 1920s referred to performances. These artists were genuine independent contractors, freelancers of pioneering music that swept across the nation and the world—American originals. They didn't have jobs as jazz musicians. They hustled and marketed and created and built their "company of one" (themselves) or perhaps a company of a few, if they played in a band. They took on the burden of providing their income not through 9 to 5 labor (or in those days, more like a 50-hour workweek in manufacturing). They played when and where they wanted to or could—and if they didn't get a gig, they might not get a meal, as the clubs often comped their food and drinks after the show.

So, I've got a good historical reason to talk about musicians and music in the context of the gig economy, side hustling, and the future of work being independent. It's natural.

* * *

Because I love stories, I love history. Seeing where we've come from and how things developed (or didn't) fascinates me, but not simply for their entertainment value. History—and the *story*telling part of talking about the past—helps us "superforecast," to use the term coined and popularized by Philip Tetlock. His research, including the Good Judgment Project, has shown that individuals can improve their forecasting accuracy through deliberate practice, feedback, and a growth mindset. The process "involves gathering evidence from various sources, thinking probabilistically, working in teams, keeping score, and being willing to admit error and change course."[5]

Though I've never participated in Tetlock's project, with three decades of experience as a businessman, entrepreneur, and corporate leader, I've honed my own abilities to analyze the past, live wide-eyed in the present, and forecast the future. Specifically, I'm continually learning about economic and technology trends that impact the future of work, including the major thrust of this book: the future of work is independent.

But business concepts tend to be too abstract, and abstract ideas can tend to induce sleep, like Thanksgiving turkey. I know there's a place for academic material and scholarly white papers, but I wanted my book to aim for the lower rungs of the ladder of abstraction. To explain the concepts with concrete examples and historical anecdotes. To tell stories.

"In the beginning, there was the story," Seth Godin once wrote. "Stories make it easier to understand the world. Stories are the only way we know to spread an idea."[6] I consider Godin one of the great storytellers of our age because every concept Godin writes about comes with a story that analogizes the concept—all in less than a page. The "story" might just be him describing something he saw while walking down the road. Like the parables of Jesus or the fables of Aesop, Godin tells a story about something we understand in order to help us understand something we don't.

Also, it can be fun to *hear* stories and to *tell* stories. And fun stuff stimulates the release of endorphins—the chemical messengers in our body that make us feel happiness and well-being. Who doesn't want to do the things that make us feel better? I'm Miles Everson and I endorse endorphins.

So let me ask you—and this question is for everyone reading this book: entrepreneur or business leader or anyone in between—what are the stories you tell about your career or business? "Storytelling is by far the most underrated skill when it comes to business," wrote the famous entrepreneur Gary Vaynerchuk in his bestselling book *Crush It!* (which is, as you might expect, stuffed full of Gary V stories).

So again, what's *your* story? What's the autobiography of your small business? If you're a corporate executive or the leader of a nonprofit—how the heck did you get there? Are you just entering the job market or within a decade of retirement? Have you worked for the same company for most of your career, or have you had a different employer every three to five years? Or are you an entrepreneur? Have you started your own business? Have you done gig work? Are you an employee fighting to retain your remote work location and schedule, or are you a freelancing, nomadic independent?

What genre has your career story been so far? Horror? Comedy? Tragedy? Sci-fi? Thriller? Inspirational? No matter what your story is and how you are currently engaged in the workforce, I want you to know I've got you in mind as I write these pages. I hope that this book—and particularly this part 2—will help you to stop telling the wrong kind of stories about yourself and your career. I hope you'll read these pages as a way of growing or expanding "the independent mind" within you. It's time to write the next chapter of your story, or a brand new story altogether.

✦ ✦ ✦

Taylor Swift wasn't bluffing. Her masters had been sold to a private equity group and that ticked her off. "None of these investors have ever bothered to contact me or my team directly, to perform their due diligence on their investment; on their investment in me," she recounted in 2019 while giving an acceptance speech for Woman of the Decade by *Billboard*. "To ask how I might feel about the new owner of my art, the music I wrote, the videos I created, photos of me, my handwriting, my album designs."[7]

Swift knew the story she wanted to write about her career and it didn't involve losing her personal agency, authenticity, or voice. In a very real sense, Swift wanted to be an "independent" so she could build her music and legacy the way she wanted. Without manipulation by other parties. With the freedom to learn and grow and be true to her values—come what may, in terms of the market's support of her. Swift believed what I'm hoping you'll believe about your own career: I want to break free.

EVERSON'S ACTION POINT: FOR EVERYONE

Taking agency begins with knowing your story: past, present, and future: Where have you come from, where are you now, and where do you hope to be? But far too many people and businesses (through their leadership) invest no time or energy in such reflections. Of course, you can't change the past and you can't predict or perfectly plan the future. But here in the present, my action point for everyone—independents and enterprises alike—is this: write your story.

Literally, not figuratively. Not for publication or marketing or public relations. Just do it for yourself. Take out a sheet or two of paper (seriously, I do recommend doing this exercise old-school with paper and pen). Limit it to just a couple of sheets and spend no more than an hour on it. You can do more later, but if you think of this as a big undertaking, you may never take your first step.

9

I WANT TO BREAK FREE

Freedom | Courage | Decentralized Authority

> I can't convince you to want freedom. But if you do want free-
> dom, it can't come to you in the form of a centralized system,
> whether that's communism, backdoored cryptography, or cen-
> trally controlled AI.
>
> —Marc Andreesen[1]

What begins in the mind eventually flows out through your hands and feet. The way we think determines the way we act.

Therefore, having an independent mind about life in general seems to be a prerequisite for jumping into an entrepreneurial life. And I find that the opposite is also true. Show me someone who *lacks* an independent mind and I'll show you someone who doesn't have the temperament or drive for being an entrepreneur. Even if they have sufficient capital, a good head for numbers, sales skills, and a strong product or services, it also takes an independent mind to be a successful business builder.

I'm not alone in thinking that a person's *thinking* determines whether or not they will create or find success. Even when we're talking about full-time employees of a company, the brightest enterprise leaders know to look for independent-minded people to join their team. For example, in his bestselling book *Principles*, Ray Dalio wrote:

> We look for people who think independently, argue open-mindedly and assertively, and above all else value the intense pursuit of truth and excellence, and through it, the rapid improvement of themselves and the organization. Most important, they must be able to put their egos aside and assess themselves candidly.[2]

Peter Diamandis, a medical doctor, futurist, and an entrepreneur I greatly admire, tweeted this statement I couldn't agree with more fully: "What made Steve Jobs or Elon Musk succeed? Was it their technology, or was it their mindset? Personally, I think mindset is an entrepreneur's most critical asset. Yet few of us ever take the time to craft it—to purposefully select and sharpen the mindset(s) we desire."[3]

Or consider Peter Thiel, a venture capitalist guru who closed out his 2014 *New York Times* #1 bestseller *Zero to One* with these words:

> Our task today is to find singular ways to create the new things that will make the future not just different, but better—to go from 0 to 1. The essential first step is to think for yourself. Only by seeing our world anew, as fresh and strange as it was to the ancients who saw it first, can we both re-create it and preserve it for the future.[4]

As Solomon wrote 3,000 years ago: "As a man thinks in his heart, so is he" (Proverbs 23:7).

Don't get me wrong. I'm not describing a "power of positive thinking" attitude, although I will discuss the importance of grit and resilience in this chapter. And I'm not saying that entrepreneurs will think themselves into being entrepreneurs through daily affirmations, like a modified Stuart Smalley sketch from *Saturday Night Live*: "I'm good enough, I'm smart enough, and doggone it, people like my small business."

What I *do* mean is that entrepreneurs—and independents in

particular—own a mental toolbox of mindsets that are helpful for success as an independent. And to be honest, these mindsets are helpful to enterprises, too, and the "intrapreneurs" who work within enterprises. Many people in full-time employment just haven't developed them yet. Worse, some full-time employees with an independent mind get shut down or stifled by the company's bureaucracy. Of course, some employees work for companies that value innovation. Such companies give employees the freedom to work like "intrapreneurs"—to have an entrepreneur's mindset *within* the company. That's fantastic, and I applaud those open-minded companies and independent-minded employees. I wish there were more of them, because businesses that act with an entrepreneur's mindset will be better off than those that have lost their entrepreneur's spark.

Freedom: That's the second characteristic of "The Independent Mind of a Free Bird." When you get to know the business builders like I do, you realize that independent-minded people are the rule in that crowd, not the exception. It's their independent mind that *led* them to join the independent workforce. And it's their love of freedom that keeps them an independent even when things get rough.

FREEDOM

I was in the spring semester of my sophomore year of college when Queen released "I Want to Break Free," one of my personal favorites from the band and the inspiration for this chapter's title. The song's video got them in hot water with American viewers because the band dressed in drag as a spoof of a popular British soap opera. The video's message was about how these bored "housewives" wanted to cut loose and "break free" of other people's expectations, norms, and assumptions.

"We had done some really serious, epic videos in the past, and we just thought we'd have some fun," Roger Taylor later explained. "We wanted people to know that we didn't take ourselves too seriously, that we could still laugh at ourselves. I think we proved that."

Rolling Stone explained the varied reception the video received internationally:

Brit fans got the joke, but fans in America viewed the cross-dressing as a coming-out for Mercury, who wore a wig and fake breasts in the video and onstage (the video was banned by MTV, and rocks were hurled at Mercury during a concert in Brazil). Conversely, *in most of the rest of Europe, the song was viewed as an anthem of resistance against political oppression.*[5]

Remember, this was April 1984. The Soviet Union wouldn't collapse for almost eight more years. Though the song didn't crack the Top 40 in the United States, it landed in the Top 5 throughout most of Europe. South Africans catapulted the song to #1 precisely because they understood "I Want to Break Free" as an anthem of freedom during those days in which apartheid still subjected nonwhites. Apartheid ended there in 1991, and in April 1994, exactly ten years after the release of the song, citizens of all races were allowed to vote in elections. Ideas have consequences.

The independent mind values freedom above all else, fueling the engine of entrepreneurship. How does this play out in their careers? I believe the desire for freedom manifests itself as:

- entrepreneurial courage;
- a distrust of centralized authorities;
- contrarian thinking;
- a desire for authenticity (the theme of the next chapter).

Independents frequently tell me they love and value freedom the most— over and above any other aspect of working independently. When surveyed, 75% of independents report a desire to be their own boss, compared with only 44% of traditional jobholders who say the same. A 31% difference! That's telling, and what it says is this: Independents are wired differently. They take ownership and innovate, and doing so is an integral part of who they are in their work. They want the freedom to be this way.

People who choose to be independent and go on their own have mental gears that operate differently than those who want to be employees their entire lives. I'm not saying one is good or bad. I'm just saying that, as a company, you want to engage both mindsets in your business. That's where you'll find the diverse workforce your business needs.

Entrepreneurs choose to be independent because they want a different way of life—a life of freedom. They believe individual freedom is critical to finding fulfillment in life and work. And when you engage them as independent workers, they bring that mindset to the project you've engaged them to do. Wanting to be their own boss is an asset, not a liability.

So here's my question for enterprises: Doesn't your business need people like this?

COURAGE AND CONTRARIAN THINKING

In chapter 7, I talked about Mel Gibson's 2000 movie, *The Patriot*, which many people described as "*Braveheart* set in the American Revolution." Ah, *Braveheart*. Who can forget the blood, guts, and blue face paint of Gibson's 1995 blockbuster? In the most meme-worthy scene of the film, the Scottish hero William Wallace rode back and forth on a beautiful horse to address the predominantly peasant army of Scotland before they were to fight an insurmountable English army.

The Scottish elites, however, wanted to barter with their overlords and leave the *field* of battle without actually battling! They had wealth and lands—so why risk death? Sure, they'd rather be free, but not at the cost of sacrifice. The spirit of the landed elites infected the commoners with fear.

But Wallace had other plans, and so he shouted out to his fellow commoners:

> I see a whole army of my countrymen here in defiance of tyranny. You have come to fight as free men, and free men you are. What would you do with that freedom? Will you fight?[6]

A soldier, probably just a feudal farmer by trade, stood on the front line, pointed at the English across the field, and said, "Fight? Against that? No, we will run, and we will live."

The cowardice of realism had already infected them—and fear enslaves. But Wallace appealed to the men by appealing to a higher cause. He knew that "Every man dies. Not every man really lives." So, Wallace shouted back to the army these words of moral courage:

Aye, fight, and you may die. Run, and you'll live, at least a while. And dying in your beds many years from now, would you be willing to trade all the days from this day to that for one chance, just one chance to come back here and tell our enemies that they may take our lives, but they'll never take our freedom![7]

Inspired and led by Wallace, the Scottish won that battle and more that followed. Wallace ended up—even in real life—being executed by the king of England. But the people of Scotland did go forth and win their freedom.

Say what you will about the historical accuracy of the film, but its central theme—finding the courage to live free—will continue to inspire anyone who watches the movie.

Someone may complain that the analogy breaks down. That there's no comparing freelance work with the courage it takes to join an army, pick up a sword, and battle against an army led by a king who would enslave you.

On the other hand, did you know the word *freelance* was literally coined to describe independent soldiers (fighting with swords and *lances*) who a foreign king would hire as mercenaries? They'd show up with their lances and fight for pay, as opposed to fighting for their own land or freedom. Sir Walter Scott's novel *Ivanhoe* marks the first occurrence of the term in print: "I offered Richard the service of my Free Lances ... thanks to the bustling times, a man of action will always find employment."

Indeed, a man or woman of action *will* always find independent work—although BYOL (bring your own lance) is no longer required.[8] At any rate, we're not talking about life and death here in this book, just the opportunity to work *like* a medieval freelancer: independent, on one's own terms, and without any permanent commitment to an employer.

That's why I say that joining the external workforce *is* a bold declaration because independents face the financial pressure and bear it alone. Plus, cultural stereotypes have, at least in the past, sought to shame people from striking out on their own.

In the 2010 movie *The Social Network*, we are introduced to Sean Parker (played by Justin Timberlake) in a scene from 2004, just before he learned about Facebook and Mark Zuckerberg. Though it's an invented scene between Parker and a college student he had just spent the night with, the snappy dialogue (Aaron Sorkin wrote the screenplay) reflected the zeitgeist prevalent even twenty years ago:

> AMY   So what do you do?
> SEAN PARKER   I'm an entrepreneur.
> AMY   You're unemployed.
> SEAN PARKER   I wouldn't say that.
> AMY   What would you say?
> SEAN PARKER   That I'm an entrepreneur.

Thankfully, the view of "Amy" is more the stuff of movies than real life.[9] Most independents don't become indie-entrepreneurs in response to being unable to get a job (though there's nothing wrong with making entrepreneurial lemonade from the lemons of unemployment). Today, saying "I'm an entrepreneur" or "I'm self-employed" doesn't carry the same stigma or evoke the same eye-rolling it once did.

But even with a broader acceptance of independent work, going out on your own still requires a great deal of courage. It takes money to make the world go round, and earning money means finding work; independents are no exception to that rule.

As stated earlier, when surveyed for MBO's "State of Independence in America" report in 2023, independents cited "not enough predictable income" the most (40%). The good news is we've seen that number trend downward from 55% in 2012. In addition, we have seen platforms bring liquidity into other markets and disrupt traditional business models. We are now seeing talent platforms, like MBO Partners, on the rise. In 2012, only 4% of independents used a platform to find work. But by 2023, we have seen a tenfold-plus increase to over 40% of independents using talent platforms to find work.

DISTRUST OF CENTRALIZED AUTHORITIES

In 1984, Steve Jobs launched the Macintosh personal computer with a legendary television commercial. One of the most famous advertisements of all time, the commercial paid homage to George Orwell's novel *1984* with its dystopian future ruled by a televised "Big Brother." The commercial's message was that the Macintosh would revolutionize computing, contra the "Big Brother" of IBM, and bring individualized freedom rather than centralized control. The message was compelling, and the Mac became one of the bestselling and most iconic computers of its time.

As early as 1981, when Jobs talked to national news media about how personal computers contrasted with mainframes, he described the PC's surpassing value in terms of decentralization. He compared an Apple computer to an automobile and the mainframes as a passenger train: "The Volkswagen isn't as fast or as comfortable as the passenger train. But the VW owners can go where they want, when they want, and with whom they want. The VW owners have personal control of the machine."[10]

That's the *Braveheart* language of freedom, applied to the dawn of the personal computer. Personal computers would later catch up to mainframes in speed and power, but Jobs made the point that even with a PC's inferior power and speed, the individual consumer still wins overall with the PC because of the freedom of decentralized computing.

Likewise, independents value freedom because it comes with this added, built-in bonus: decentralized authority. Independents (and I suspect most people) don't trust centralized authorities the same way society did 50 or 100 years ago. We certainly don't want to be controlled and manipulated by central authorities. Like Dr. Seuss wrote in *Oh, The Places You'll Go!*: "You have brains in your head. You have feet in your shoes. You can steer yourself any direction you choose."[11]

And it cuts both ways: independents and enterprises alike want freedom from control and manipulation. More transparency. More value and accountability and fewer org-chart power trips. You end up with fewer unwanted products and unused services that exist only because they're forcefully bundled with that one product or service you want.

I agree with Linux creator Linus Torvalds when he said, "The way to survive and flourish is to make the best damn product you can. And if you can't survive and flourish on that, then you shouldn't . . . Success is about quality and giving folks what they want. It's not about trying to control people."[12] And yes, Torvalds had the 1990s-era Microsoft policy of enforced bundling in mind when he wrote these words.

This same spirit hearkens back all the way to the birth of the United States. In the lead-up to the American Revolution, the printing presses ran day and night, producing pamphlets on the theme of freedom and decentralized power.

> Thomas Paine threw gasoline-soaked ink on the fiery spirit of American independence by publishing his pamphlet *Common Sense* six months before the Declaration of Independence in 1776. Upon independence from King George III, Paine promised, "The birthday of a new world is at hand." This new world would be born free from a king.[13]

It's worth remembering that these authors, printers, and most of the colonists were either farmers or small, independent businessmen in "cottage industries"—skilled craftsman producing goods or services from their own home or property. The industrialized factory system with its hierarchical management and division of labor—all that came much later in American life. But at its start, Americans were independent entrepreneurs with a distaste and distrust of centralized authorities.

Can I mention Tucker Carlson, Fox News, Elon Musk, and Twitter without anyone thinking I'm trying to sneak politics in here? I'm not, but when Fox News fired their most popular host in 2023, Carlson wiped the "full-time employee" dust off his feet and headed back out into the world as an independent worker. Here's what Megyn Kelly—also a former Fox host who is now independent—said at the time about Carlson's potential next move: "He will no longer answer to a corporate master. He will be free to say whatever he wants to say, within the bounds of defamation law, of course, and he'll be totally unleashed."

For people on either side of the political aisle, it was hard to imagine that Carlson had been on a leash during his time at Fox. And yet, we found out later that he was. Fox is a publicly traded company with a board and executives who set the company's direction. They were in the process of shifting Fox, if ever so slightly, and Carlson answered to them—until he didn't.

Genevieve Roch-Decter, the founder and CEO of GRIT, a "financial media company which is democratizing access to institutional-quality market insights for the masses," said, "Elon Musk should hire Tucker Carlson and start a video service to compete with YouTube."[14]

She wasn't alone in thinking this, but Musk replied with a different vision: "Or we don't hire anyone, but simply enable content creators to prosper on this platform without applying censorship that goes beyond the law."[15]

Hear that? "We don't hire anyone" is the spirit of an enterprise that believes in the power of free independents. And when Musk writes, "without applying censorship"—that's the language of decentralized authority.

* * *

Freedom, courage, and a desire for decentralized authority: those three mindsets walk in the door when an independent arrives. Smart enterprises will make the shift toward this way of thinking.

EVERSON'S ACTION POINT: FOR ENTERPRISES

Prioritize providing ample space for direct reports to accomplish their work. Train managers to oversee hybrid teams comprising both remote workers and contractors effectively. Discourage micromanagement and promote trust management instead. Encourage managers to delegate decision-making to their teams and employees whenever possible. Shift focus from counting hours to common sense behaviors, continuous learning, achieving goals, and meeting deadlines. When attrition occurs, consider reconfiguring teams to leverage independents strategically, prioritizing enhanced efficiency, creativity, and output over cost savings.[16]

10

GO YOUR OWN WAY

Authenticity

> Any belonging that asks us to betray ourselves is not true belonging.
>
> —Brené Brown

> All I can do is be me—whoever that is.
>
> —Bob Dylan

B y the time Stevie Nicks broke up with Lindsey Buckingham in 1976, they had known each other for over a decade. Going all the way back to high school, they had been friends, then lovers, then a singing duo called Buckingham Nicks. In 1973, they produced an album together, but poor sales led to their music label dropping them.

"I loved him before he was a millionaire," Nicks said. "We were two kids out of Menlo-Atherton High School. I loved him for all the right reasons. We did have a great relationship at first. I loved taking care of him and the house."[1]

In 1975, they joined a band and helped it become a rock music legend: Fleetwood Mac. The first album the band produced with Buckingham and Nicks on board went all the way to #1 in the United States and led to an epic tour full of sold-out concert venues. Nicks contributed "Rhiannon" and "Landslide" to the album, songs that still receive airplay five decades later.

But the sudden success, fame, and influx of money brought stressors, as Warner Brothers expected the band to deliver a follow-up album with even more commercial appeal. Behind the scenes, two of the couples in the band—Buckingham and Nicks and Christine and John McVie—were breaking up. The strain of the music life had taken its toll on them, to be sure, but for Nicks, there was more.

"From the very beginning, Lindsey was very controlling and very possessive," Nicks told *Rolling Stone* forty years later. "And after hearing all of the stories from my mother and how independent she was and how independent she made me, I was never good with possessive people or controlling people."[2]

Buckingham said he was "completely devastated when she took off" and that "there was a lot of pent-up frustration and anger towards Stevie in me for many years."

Fueled by the angst of Nicks breaking up with him, Buckingham picked up his guitar and wrote "Go Your Own Way," the band's first release off their next album, *Rumours*.

"The song became this symbol of independence for each of us and where we were heading as individuals," Buckingham said. "It also crystallized the band's collective desire for a new creative direction on the album we were about to record."

Nicks was livid about some of the song's lyrics. "I very much resented him telling the world that 'packing up, shacking up' with different men was all I wanted to do. He knew it wasn't true," she later told *Rolling Stone*. "It was just an angry thing that he said. Every time those words would come onstage, I wanted to go over and kill him. He knew it, so he really pushed my buttons through that. It was like, 'I'll make you suffer for leaving me.' And I did."

Nicks wrote "Dreams" as her own musical response to the busted relationship. That song went #1 in the United States, fueling even more album sales.[3] "'Dreams' and 'Go Your Own Way' are what I call the 'twin songs,'" Nicks said. "They're the same song written by two people about the same relationship."[4]

"Go Your Own Way" peaked at #10 on the US charts, and the album sold 10 million copies in the first month. In 1977, Fleetwood received the Grammy Award for Album of the Year. As of 2023, *Rumours* has sold 30 to 40 million copies, making it one of the top 10 bestselling albums ever.

Ken Caillat, the engineer for the album (but probably better known now as "Colbie's dad"), gave his explanation for the success of the album: "By vanquishing, ignoring, and burning through the personal tragedies and turmoil, sacrificing the connections that each band member lost, the members of Fleetwood Mac created one of the greatest rock and roll albums in history."[5]

In other words, the album conveyed *authenticity* because the band refused to hide their raw emotions or produce music unrelated to their actual life.

"The *Rumours* album went way through the ceiling, you know, and at some point, became a phenomenon in which the sales and the, the success of it really became disproportionate to what the music itself was," Buckingham later reflected. "I always perceived it as having something to do with the fact that it was kind of a musical soap opera, and I think all of that came through. I think the emotion of that, the truthfulness of that came through on the grooves."[6]

* * *

The message of "Go Your Own Way" eventually transcended the original context of lost love and heartbreak, becoming an anthem of freedom, independence, and personal agency. As such, I think the song—and the story behind its creation—serves as a powerful metaphor for this crucial aspect of the independent mind: authenticity. Just as Buckingham wrote about

Nicks breaking away from a relationship and forging her own path, independent workers are breaking away from traditional employment models and forging their own careers. Independent workers are carving out their own paths, creating their own businesses, and defining success on their own terms. They're not afraid to take risks, and they're not afraid to fail. They're charting their own course and doing it their own way.

People possess "agency" when they have the ability to fulfill their unique potential, to have the power and resources to control their own destiny. When you've got life's steering wheel firmly in your hands, that's agency.

Traditionally, members of the workforce have had limited agency regarding their careers. Management held the winning hand, determining significant aspects of a worker's career path, income, and even the number of vacation days they could take in a year. But the scales seem to have now tipped, as evidenced by the growing population of independent professionals.

Independents *take* agency like the free agents they are. If you are an employee working for a company, you are beholden to the manager you report to. They determine your destiny. But when you are an independent—especially in the "war for talent" job climate we discussed in chapter 6—you get to choose who you work for. Further, independents view *themselves* as the company. Ultimately, everything begins and ends with them, even if they outsource back-office responsibilities and hire executive assistants. They take ownership and responsibility for growing their "company of one." They preserve and expand their identity rather than identifying as an employee of a single company.

In years past, if you walked in and handed someone your resume showing that you had ten years of professional work but had been in five companies, the immediate reaction would be: "This person cannot keep a job. They change jobs every two years." But now, if your resume says you've been in the same place for a decade, the response would likely be: "This person must not be effective because they could not get another job." The narrative has completely flipped. Today, it's a sign of strength and professional prowess if you have experience with multiple companies. What once was a weakness is now a strength.

Across the generations, people are seeking better work-life balance and the ability to pursue their passions. Health and wellness are taking center stage as top priorities. When MBO commissioned a survey for our "Life Goals Report" in 2023, we found that independents lead traditional employees in nearly every measure of work-life satisfaction.

What might this mean for company leadership? How can enterprises build agency into their talent programs? Will this allow them to be more competitive for high-value employees and independents? Answering those types of questions will be our mission in this chapter.

AUTHENTICITY AND JOBS

I send articles to an email list every day along different themes, depending on what interests the person who signed up. The newsletter I publish on Fridays receives the most traffic of all. Titled "Mindfulness by Miles," I try to answer a question I get asked often: "How do independent-minded people *think* in order to become successful?" They want to know some secret sauce mindset that leads to successful entrepreneurship. Look, I'm not Tony Robbins, but here's one core answer I genuinely believe: independent-minded people define *themselves* and refuse to let other people define who they are.

In 2005, Steve Jobs gave the commencement address at Stanford University, a speech now ranked as one of the greatest of all time and viewed more than any other—50 million and counting. With a tone of urgent authenticity and an efficient use of time, Jobs spoke for only fourteen minutes—2,225 words.[7] The following 66 words from the speech are the most often quoted:

> Your time is limited, so don't waste it living someone else's life. Don't be trapped by dogma—which is living with the results of other people's thinking. Don't let the noise of others' opinions drown out your own inner voice. And most important, have the courage to follow your heart and intuition. They somehow already know what you truly want to become. Everything else is secondary.[8]

People question whether it's sound advice to "follow your heart" because if you want to succeed in life, then it's *skills* you need—and, preferably, skills supported by market demand. Author Cal Newport argues that the "follow your passion" vocational advice can lead young people astray if detached from skill development and market realities.

Likewise, Arthur C. Brooks, the author and social scientist, says that the *first* step in seeking happiness is to answer this question: *Who am I?* "Only after we answer that can we understand our needs and desires," Brooks writes. Because "only that understanding can allow us to get on with the serious business of what we are supposed to do with our life."[9]

But even with all that nuance, I still *love* the Steve Jobs quote, and here's why. Jobs told us we must do our own thinking and that life is short, so we'd better get on with it. He's saying to "go your own way" by building your life on the thinking of your own mind and heart, not that of "other people's thinking" or the "noise of other's opinions." This mindset was core to Jobs's identity as an entrepreneur, and it's probably the main difference between Jobs and Wozniak.

In the 2014 Ashton Kutcher-as-Steve Jobs movie, there's a scene set in 1974, when 19-year-old Jobs worked for Atari and his colleagues greatly disliked him. In the film, Jobs commiserates with his friend Wozniak, saying, "I just can't work for other people. I need my independence." Wozniak understood what Jobs was saying, though he himself didn't mind working for other people. At the time of Apple's incorporation, Woz had to be coaxed, pleaded with, and basically ordered to quit his "day job" at Hewlett-Packard. Woz wrote that he felt he "didn't need my own company," that he "would never become someone authoritative," and that he "would stay at HP for my full-time job and design computers for fun."[10] Woz loved and planned on making a career at HP, to engineer whatever a boss told him to. Woz wasn't inclined to "go his own way" as an *entrepreneur*—and that's okay because he *was* gifted to be one of the greatest engineers of all time. *That* was his own way.

Jobs was wired differently. Very early on at Apple, Jobs clashed with Michael Scott, the outsider brought in to serve as the company's first CEO from 1977 to 1981. Wozniak served as the engineering genius, and Jobs the visionary and marketing wunderkind. But Scott came to Apple a decade older than Jobs when Mike Markkula hired him to organize the company and create systems and structure.

Jobs found himself in a conundrum: unprepared to be the CEO, yet unable to simply shut off his own thinking and obey orders, "and not just because he had an adolescent problem with authority," Jobs's biographers Brent Schlender and Rick Tetzeli wrote. "He had seen now that his *contrarian thinking* was essential for the kinds of breakthrough products he wanted to engineer, and he had also seen that his irascible methods could prod a group of people to deliver that vision."[11]

In 1981, the solution became apparent: Markkula fired Scott. But four years later, with Jobs once again chafing under a new CEO—this time John Sculley—the shoe was on the other foot. The board took a vote, sided with Sculley, and Jobs was out of a job at the company he had begun a decade earlier.

Was Jobs right or wrong? Yes, both. He wasn't a saint, as the biographies have shown, and he caused hurt in many of his personal relationships. But deeply ingrained into Jobs's psyche as an entrepreneur was this desire to be free and authentic. As a result, Jobs experienced a decade of wilderness years, exiled outside the company he had begun. And Apple floundered without its founder.

During this time, however, Jobs led the movie company Pixar into greatness and founded another computer company (NeXT). When Apple called for him to return in 1997, Jobs came back but changed—better than he had been before, yet with the same commitment to authenticity. That same year, he launched Apple's "Think Different" marketing strategy, with a commercial featuring images of Einstein, Gandhi, Muhammad Ali, Bob Dylan, and Picasso—and a now-legendary script narrated by actor Richard Dreyfuss:

> Here's to the crazy ones. The misfits. The rebels. The troublemakers. The round pegs in the square holes. The ones who *see things differently*. They're

not fond of rules. And they have no respect for the status quo. You can quote them, disagree with them, glorify or vilify them. About the only thing you can't do is ignore them. Because they change things. They push the human race forward. And while some may see them as the crazy ones, we see genius. Because the people who are crazy enough *to think* they can change the world are the ones who do.[12]

Grounded in this philosophy—this mindset of thinking independently and being authentic to yourself—Jobs led Apple to its most extraordinary breakthroughs from 1997 until his death in 2011.

* * *

Having spent a lifetime surrounded by entrepreneurs—and being one myself, with a string of side hustles I built even while I was a leader in corporate America—I can state this fact with certainty: Entrepreneurs think differently. They think *independently* and with a desire for *authenticity*. I'm not downplaying the role of ambition or a desire for status, recognition, and money—those factors all have their place. But independents feel most of all a desire to be authentic in their working lives—to have the *freedom* to be *authentic*.

A 2022 survey of employees (not independents) by PwC sought to discover what the "most important factors were when considering a change in work environment." Seventy-one percent said "pay"—that's no surprise, of course. But coming in second and third place were responses about fulfillment and authenticity:

- 71% responded: "I am fairly rewarded financially for my work"
- 69% responded: "I find my job fulfilling"
- 66% responded: "I can truly be myself"

And even further down the list, we see responses that can be characterized as "going my own way":

- 60% responded: "I can be creative/innovative in my job"
- 50% responded: "I can choose when I work"
- 47% responded: "I can choose where I work"[13]

Again, take note that this reflects the responses of people employed full-time in a company—not independents. But here's the point: if two-thirds of *your* company's employees desire to be fulfilled at work, to be creative and innovative, and to "truly be myself," then how long will they remain as your employees if those felt needs are not met? And with more people jumping into the independent workforce—and reporting that they have better pay, health, and satisfaction than they did as an employee—your employees may take that jump too.

People want to live authentically in their vocation and will make the necessary moves in order to gain it.

NORMALIZING FREQUENT JOB CHANGES

That leads me to ask you this question: How do you see yourself five years from now? Do you envision still having the same job, or do you see yourself pursuing a different career path?

Some people seem to think they're locked into stagnant careers. They wouldn't use that word, of course, but their "stuck" actions speak louder than any words they may use to describe their career. They seem to believe that once they've chosen a particular career path, then that's it for them for the rest of their lives. But that idea couldn't be further from the truth! Denying yourself opportunities for growth just to stay comfortable can be a more significant risk than a reward.

That's why I'm joining in with the chorus of others to argue that we are long overdue for a new way of thinking about employee tenure. Jack Kelly's opinion piece in *Forbes*, "It's Time to Normalize Frequent Job Changes," nailed this theme. "There would be no job shaming for switching jobs, as it would be normalized," Kelly wrote. "Companies will continually hire people who have a fresh new perspective from working at several different firms. It's as if you're bringing in management consultants, who've been at several businesses, learned what works and what doesn't, and offers this valuable information to the company and its management."[14]

That's so true, except I'd like to take it even further. Instead of switching jobs every five to seven years, people should go independent. Let's normalize independent workers instead of simply normalizing the idea of short-term employees. Being independent means having "job change" baked into the cake.

According to statistics from the US Department of Labor, people nowadays change careers on average five to seven times throughout their lives. These changes are not always drastic, life-changing moves. They could be in the form of:

- Pursuing a degree or course in a different field
- Finding a job in a loosely related profession
- Moving to a different specialty after a few years
- Starting a business
- Dabbling in nonprofit or contractual work

Having the courage to change careers is a good thing. At the same time, however, this can also make it hard to determine whether you're *truly* on the right path.

If you're starting to feel bored or discontented with your work, then ask yourself who or what is to blame—the job, field, industry, or you? Every job has its frustrations and challenges, and that's why you shouldn't easily give up. That's why finding the right career is a powerful way to build purpose and enjoyment into your life! Having a vocation you enjoy doing will help you accomplish goals, earn a living, and develop your skill sets.

Here are three signs that independents know they are on the right career path. First, independents feel a sense of purpose in their work. Do you? According to a study by Glassdoor, 50% of millennial and Gen Z workers are willing to accept a lower salary for a job more aligned with their core values.[15] What does this tell you?

When employees feel their work has a social impact, they demonstrate greater levels of loyalty and dedication not only to their jobs but also to the companies they work for. So, as a highly engaged employee, you have to know what you're working for and how you'll win, as these will inspire you to do your best.

Being in the right industry or career path will give you a sense of purpose, and your efforts will not feel like a burden because you feel connected to your organization's success.

Second, independents spend more of their work hours using their strengths instead of their weaknesses. Because they choose their clients and projects, they can align their work with the skills they have an abundance of and avoid projects that will only serve to highlight skill sets that aren't in their toolbox.

What about you? Everyone has their own strengths and weaknesses, so the key to job success is to identify your strengths and find a role that lets you bring your best skills to work for most of your workday. If you ever find yourself questioning the career decisions you've made, take a pause and re-evaluate your strengths. Identify the talents and skill sets you were born with and those you can improve eventually. If you spend your time doing what you're naturally good at, you'll be more productive and happier. On the other hand, if you force yourself into a role that isn't the right fit for you, it's only a matter of time before you stop growing and find yourself overwhelmingly frustrated. The right job or career won't make you dwell too much on your weaknesses and spend time trying to become someone you're not.

Third, independents achieve a balance between work and life. Before, having a healthy work-life and personal life balance used to only mean the ability to "turn off" work at 5 PM (or whatever time your eighth or ninth work hour is) and "turn on" life afterward. However, lifestyle changes and technological advancements have redefined what this balance means to different people over the last decade. For example, having more flexibility in the when and the where of work allows working parents to drop off and pick up their children from school. Thankfully, the pandemic pushed "work from home" into the mainstream, so now even employees benefit—if their workplace allows it.

Do these describe your work as an employee? If not, I think you're a candidate for becoming an independent.[16]

TO THE BEAT OF HIS OWN DRUM

To use a cliché, living an authentic life in your work is like marching to the beat of your own drum. Or, if it's the case that you actually *are* a professional drummer, it's no cliché at all.

The "Fleetwood" of Fleetwood Mac is British drummer Mick Fleetwood, who cofounded the band in 1967. As a child, he wasn't a great student and dropped out of school altogether at fifteen, with his parents' support, and moved to London to pursue drumming as a career.

Fleetwood describes his drum style as "capitalizing on (his) own ineptness"—a reference to the fact that he has dyslexia. When Jeff Porcaro, the drummer for Boz Scaggs, watched Fleetwood play "Go Your Own Way" in concert, he was mesmerized by the unique approach he took to the song.

"I've watched, I've tried to understand it. Nothing you do up there makes sense, but it sounds beautiful," Porcaro said to Fleetwood. "What's your method? What are you doing in that last fill of 'Go Your Own Way'? I can't figure it out! I've been watching every night. What do you do in the last measure on that last beat? Is the snare ahead or behind?"

Fleetwood told him about his dyslexia and how it "prevented him from understanding the minutia of his drumming." In other words, Fleetwood couldn't explain what he was doing in his work; it just flowed as an authentic expression of who he was—strengths and weaknesses.

"It was only after we continued to talk that Jeff realized I wasn't kidding around," Fleetwood later said. "We eventually had a tremendous laugh about it."[17]

After fifty years of playing drums professionally and with his unique approach to percussion, it's safe to say that nothing would stop Fleetwood from marching to the beat of his own drum—literally.

Fleetwood's dyslexia led to his different drum technique—he

"capitalized on his own ineptness." I'm sure there's something in your life you'd "fix" immediately if you could. Something you feel is broken or missing or just not right—and that is the reason why you do X differently than others. Okay, so you don't want a heart surgeon that, objectively speaking, has poor motor skills or shows up to work drunk. Limitations can be good and helpful, to say the least. But in areas where your "limitation" just means you'll do things different and that's all—then by all means, don't be afraid to be different!

NO REGRETS?

There's a saying that perception is reality. I think nothing could be more false when it comes to one's own well-being. When you go around projecting that you're something you're not, that's a painful experience. You constantly regret your decisions or indecisions, and these memories bring unpleasantness with every passing.

Having conducted a dozen-plus years of research into the world of independents at MBO, we know how they're wired and feel. I'll say it again because it bears repeating: Independents are happier, healthier, and more financially secure than when they were full-time employees. And I attribute that largely to an independent's ability to express his or her own authenticity.

When I interviewed Daniel Pink in 2023 about his excellent book *The Power of Regret*, he confirmed my thoughts here:

> I'll be your hallelujah chorus on that analysis. Absolutely. One of the things that you see in the language of people's regrets—and my research on this goes back to when I wrote *Free Agent Nation*—is the concern that people have for authenticity. The sense that people are squelching who they are. I traveled around America twenty years ago, interviewing people who had made this decision to go independent. They'd say things like, "I wanted to leave that job at that big operation, that big organization, because every time I went into work, I had to put on a game face. I had

to put on a mask. I had to be somebody who I really wasn't. They literally use the language of authenticity: "I regret not being my authentic self." Or, "I regret living someone else's life." Legions of people—dozens and dozens and dozens around the world, saying, "I regret caring too much about what other people think and not enough about who I really was."[18]

Note: To see the entire video of my interview with Daniel Pink, go to TheIndependentMind.com

Then, Pink reminded me of his own story of jumping into the independent workforce, leaving behind a job as a speechwriter for Vice President Al Gore!

I went out on my own because I wanted to be bolder. I wanted to do my own thing. I wanted to be self-determined. I wanted to be authentic. I didn't want to be controlled. I wanted to do my own stuff. You know, there are too many people who look up after thirty or forty years of a kind of a lackluster career where they weren't authentic, where they weren't self-determined. They say, "Crap, I totally blew it." I don't want to be that person.

How many people can say they became a freelancer after working for the White House? Yet, no matter how good that job might have been, Pink wanted freedom, autonomy, and authenticity for himself. As he wrote in 2001, "In the new flight to quality, more and more of us are pursuing work that will celebrate, rather than suffocate, our authenticity."[19]

Two decades later, those ideas are even more true and are being lived out in the lives of the independent workforce. As work becomes more about doing what you love and doing it the way you want, it becomes much more fulfilling. Everyone can directly see how they are impacting what is important to their personal passions and purpose. That's how independents think.

Contrast this with employees who must adapt to a company's purpose. Their game of work becomes competing with other employees for the next promotion or raise, all while checking their individuality at the corporate door.

EVERSON'S ACTION POINT: FOR EVERYONE

The action point here is mental. Start thinking differently about "the obstacle" that is your "limitation" (remember Fleetwood's dyslexia-influenced drumming). Don't just think about it as something to be endured. Or worse, don't just put on a happy face as if it doesn't suck. But instead, think on the journal entry of the Roman emperor and Stoic philosopher Marcus Aurelius (rebirthed for us now by Ryan Holiday): "The mind adapts and converts to its own purposes the obstacle to our acting. The impediment to action advances action. What stands in the way becomes the way."[20]

11

GONNA FLY NOW

Grit

It's not whether you get knocked down, it's whether you get up.
—Vince Lombardi

In 1975, a relatively unknown actor with less than $200 in the bank wrote a screenplay for a movie he desperately wanted to play the lead in. When a studio offered him $300,000 for the script if he agreed to *not* be in the film, he turned them down. They relented and committed to a lowball budget with the actor, Sylvester Stallone, who created *Rocky* for less than $1.5 million.

The movie, released in late November 1976, became the year's #1 box office draw. The Academy Awards nominated *Rocky* in 10 categories, and the film won three, including the coveted prize for Best Picture. Stallone became a household name, and the character Rocky Balboa became a national icon—an embodied metaphor of grit, underdog determination, resilience, tenacity, a refusal to quit even after failure, and the barreling through of barriers. In other words, everything this chapter is about.

What's fascinating is how, both in Stallone's creation of the film and in

Balboa's storyline itself, we find all the defining characteristics of an under-dog survivor. Stallone created his big break on a tiny budget and long odds. And the titular character Rocky was just a local impoverished nobody with big muscles but scant credentials who "went the distance" in the boxing arena against Apollo Creed, the world's heavyweight champion.

Years later, Stallone reflected on how the making of *Rocky* paralleled his own life at the time:

> I was a complete unknown—even unknown to myself. And I had this idea. A lot of people were feeling kind of the way I was—going nowhere fast. And I didn't know whether I had it or not. So I wrote this story about an underdog—a person who wasn't very appreciated. And I was given a break by United Artists. Now, you had to put up or shut up. So I couldn't believe my good fortune. And every day, we'd go to the studio and work on the script a little bit. Of course, I had a bit of an odd personality, I guess. Maybe I was born to play this part, I don't know. But it just seemed to fit into all the things I sort of believed in.[1]

And that's exactly why moviegoers loved the film: They either saw themselves in the character of Rocky or aspired to become like him. Rocky Balboa was an everyman, and every man wanted to be a Rocky. With no boxing industry insider connections, what mattered most was Balboa's mindset—what he carried within him on the inside.

In a poignant scene between Rocky and his girlfriend, Adrian, he ex-presses his belief that he can't possibly beat the champ in the ring. Adrian doesn't pull a Pollyanna or tell him to "just believe in yourself." A boxing ring isn't the place for bullshit (and, I might add, neither is the world of business). Adrian just asks Rocky what he is going to do. Considering the overwhelming talent and training of Apollo Creed, what was Rocky's game plan, his mindset? Rocky said:

> It really don't matter if I lose this fight. It really don't matter if this guy opens my head, either. 'Cause all I wanna do is go the distance. No one's ever gone the distance with Creed, and if I can go that distance, you see,

and that bell rings and I'm still standing, I'm gonna know for the first time in my life, see, that I weren't just another bum from the neighborhood.[2]

Rocky was motivated by a desire to show others—or better, to show himself—that "I weren't just another bum from the neighborhood." And it wouldn't even take him "winning" (i.e., defeating the world's champ) to prove he wasn't a "bum" because the public's expectations were so low for Rocky that all he needed to do was to "go the distance." To stay in the ring and on his feet for fifteen rounds.

Likewise, entrepreneur-independents know the expectation is low for starting a business because most businesses *do* fail. They know they can always return to full-time employment and nobody will shame them if that's what they must do to make their living. But independents don't want to return to full-time employee status. They want to stay on their feet and go the distance as an independent. They want to play the lead role in the movie they wrote—not living out someone else's script and dream.

In the case of the real-life Stallone—and just about every artist, actor, and musician—these people work as independents, literally. I'm not shoehorning their stories for use as illustrative fodder. As I mentioned earlier, jazz musicians coined the term *gig* in the 1920s to describe their live musical performances—shows they did not perform as employees but as independent workers. One performance at a time. One satisfied audience at a time.

These people are solo entrepreneurs, business builders who develop and market themselves and their creative talent. Behind every successful business builder are several who have failed, and even those who have been successful have often failed multiple times in their quest. But they don't quit when rejected a time or two—or 20. For example, book authors (aka "independents who write books") take rejection like Rocky took punches to the ribs—with a "is that all you got?" sneer:

- J.K. Rowling: The author of the Harry Potter series submitted her manuscript to 12 publishing houses, all of which rejected it.
- William Golding: His novel *Lord of the Flies* was rejected 20 times before it was published.

- Marcel Proust: Proust faced so many rejections that he decided to pay for the publication of his work himself.
- Jack Canfield and Mark Victor Hansen: Their book *Chicken Soup for the Soul* received 134 rejections before it was published.
- Dr. Seuss: The beloved children's author, Theodore Geisel, faced multiple rejections before finding success.

Or how about inventors—independent entrepreneurs who created products and launched businesses that sold those products?

- Sir James Dyson: The inventor of the bagless vacuum cleaner faced 5,126 failed prototypes before finally creating a successful product.
- Walt Disney: Disney was fired from a newspaper job for "lacking imagination" and faced multiple rejections before finding success with Mickey Mouse and Disneyland.
- Henry Ford: Ford's first two automobile companies failed before he founded the Ford Motor Company and revolutionized the automobile industry.
- Robert Goddard: The media and scientific community ridiculed Goddard's early rocket experiments. However, he persisted and is now considered the father of modern rocketry.
- Alexander Graham Bell: Bell's telephone invention was initially rejected by Western Union, but he continued to improve and market the device until it became a commercial success.

Independents develop a high resilience to failure. They build mental and physical agility, knowing that if necessity is the *mother* of invention, then rejection must be its *father*.

THE "FREE YOUR MIND STARTER PACK"

In a recent study of high-performing leaders within the British Royal Navy, researchers discovered this about motivation: "Findings suggest differences in motivation are more important than differences in general intelligence, or personality traits, in predicting assessed performance, potential within, and actual rate of advancement to, senior leadership positions."[3]

When it comes to motivation, independents become Free Birds because they want their work to be about more than hassle avoidance and the fear of being fired. So what *does* motivate an independent-minded person when they're having their own "I can't defeat Apollo Creed" moment of Balboa blues? Here are four items in the "Free Your Mind Starter Pack."

First, independents refuse to buckle under or whine about their "lot in life." Are there obstacles and impediments that nobody would willingly have scripted into their life? Yes, of course, but independents get on with it. Without glamorizing suffering, they see the challenges and hardship as part of the excitement of entrepreneurship. They believe, as Ryan Holiday wrote into the title of his bestselling book, *The Obstacle Is the Way: The Timeless Art of Turning Trials into Triumph.*[4]

In one of the most poignant scenes in the film version of J.R.R. Tolkien's *The Lord of the Rings*, the hobbit Frodo laments to his friend, the wizard Gandalf, about the burden of being the ring-bearer.

FRODO   I wish the Ring had never come to me. I wish none of this had happened.

GANDALF   So do all who live to see such times, but that is not for them to decide. All we have to decide is what to do with the time that is given to us.[5]

No matter what their religious or philosophical background, Gandalf's thinking illustrates the mind of an independent. I've found that independents operate with a sense of calling and mission—I know that's true of me—that carries them along whenever they walk through their own "realm of Mordor."

Which leads me to the second point: I don't believe that most business builders wake up thinking primarily about money. Money *is* a metric, a data point for determining whether things are working, but it's not the ultimate concern. Like Frodo, independents embrace the pain because they believe the journey has a greater purpose. That's just as true in the mind of an entrepreneur who cleans septic tanks ("I'm helping people maintain a sanitary dwelling") as it is for Elon Musk ("I'm helping people become Mars dwellers").

Third, independents know entrepreneurship doesn't come with a guarantee of success. When you buy an unassembled bicycle for your kid, you know it will have all the pieces and instructions needed to build the bike. You know that if you do what you're told, you'll have a functioning bike—and hopefully, a happy child. But if pieces are missing or the instructions are gibberish, you'll return the hot mess to the store for a refund.

Entrepreneurs know that building a business isn't like that. There's hardly *any* set of instructions—at least not in the particulars of their business. There's no guarantee that they've got all the parts needed to complete the job to the point of success and happiness. There's no map. There's no refund policy. There's a chance of failure and disappointment. And yet, independents love what they're doing. "The fact that you don't know if it's gonna work is exactly what makes it worth doing," wrote entrepreneur Alex Hormozi. "It's why entrepreneurship isn't for the faint of heart. Embrace uncertainty."[6]

Fourth, entrepreneurs know that "iron sharpens iron," and they gravitate toward other independent-minded people for friendship and personal development. They look for a growth mindset as they choose books to read and social media accounts to follow. When your business hires an independent for a project, they'll quickly get a sense of whether your company's culture is free or restrictive—and this evaluation may determine whether they'll take on another project with you.

And when independents contract to work with other independents—or even when they hire employees for critical positions—they look for these same qualities of mind. Independents don't want soulless, clock-punching zombies any more than you do. "Mediocre people don't like high achievers, and high achievers don't like mediocre people," former Alabama football coach Nick Saban loved to say (quoting Jim Collins). "Get the right guys on the bus, get them in the right seats, and get the wrong guys off the bus."[7]

FINDING SUCCESS

My first advice to any individual looking to set out as an entrepreneur is that they should know who they are—what kind of builder they are. Not all business builders are wired the same way. An efficient and economic way to find out who you are is to take the Gallup Builder Profile 10 (called the BP 10 assessment). Next, focus on something you are passionate about and are committed to. I use both passion and commitment intentionally because, often, you hear that you should work only on what you have a passion for. We discussed this in the previous chapter with Steve Jobs's 2005 commencement address. I've often observed people who have a passion for something but are unwilling to put the work in, so that's why commitment is equally important.

To be successful, you're going to have to work every day. Yes, you *do* need to have a sense of reality in terms of understanding what it will take to be successful, but you don't need all the answers on day one. Occasionally, you'll find the lucky person who seems to win at everything the first time around. But that person is an exception, and for the rest of us, we've got to be prepared to put in the work. Business builders start wherever they are!

Here's more secret sauce for builder success: talk to some of your *potential* customers and ask them what they think about your *potential* product or service. Get feedback even before you launch. The more people you draw into advising you on whether you should make the change, the more people will have an implicit ownership in your decision. So you should always ask yourself: *When I do my own thing, who will be my first half dozen customers?* The best way to secure those first half dozen customers is to have them be a part of your decision-making. They will feel a sense of commitment and ownership of the decision they helped you make.

And I must put an exclamation point on two philosophical points that drive my business builder mindset. It's really very simple—just two words: Start. Finish.

So many people will plan and plan, but they won't actually act. So, I say: Just start! Send the email. Register the entity. Make the phone call. Write the article. Just do something.

And then, don't try to do so many things simultaneously that you can't finish any of them. As I get up every day, one of the first things on my mind is the answer to this question: *What will I finish today?* Not just *What am I going to think about?* or *What am I going to start?* But when you put the "start" and the "finish" together, that can really cause somebody to go out and build a real business as a successful entrepreneur.

THE BARRIERS HAVE NEVER BEEN LOWER

Tony Robbins addresses the fear independents have when starting a business and says what we have been saying throughout this book: Entrepreneurship begins in the mind. Independent startups start with right thinking.

> Launching a business is a process fraught with hurdles ... It's easy to see how, in searching for answers to the question of what are barriers to entry, many business owners understandably come to believe that they must achieve perfection (i.e., complete funding, a fully-staffed team and perfect economic conditions) in order to compete. Although ideal conditions make entering an industry easier, it is not conditions or circumstances that ultimately create market entry barriers. It's your mindset, and the biggest barriers to entry stem from your own fears.[8]

Now, to enterprises I would say this: If you want to utilize independents, work on getting rid of barriers that keep them from working with your company. They have enough fears to face down and fires to put out to also deal with your company's HR and procurement friction.

What? After you've read an entire chapter where I've likened independents to brave hobbits and heavyweight boxing champions, it might seem odd for me to say the following, but I'm just being truthful. Independents aren't going to put up with your bureaucratic hassles.

"*What?!*" I can hear you shouting at me: "I thought they were resilience freaks?"

Yes, all that is true, but this is also true (and now I'm speaking to independents too): the barriers to entry for entrepreneurship have never been lower.

Think about what it takes to start a business in the digital age compared to even the mostly analog 1980s (a decade many of us still remember well). Marketing, communications, HR, insurance, legal compliance, networking, inventory, etc.—everything needed on the back end of a business can now be obtained quickly and cheaply.

Also, before the internet, my ability to reach the people who would buy from me had geographical and physical limitations, not to mention so much spent up front in sunk costs. But today I can reach millions of people within minutes digitally.

Let me say it again: Barriers to entry to independent work are the lowest they've ever been. The pandemic accelerated remote work by a decade at least, and with the acceptance of remote work comes a liquidity to the opportunities that an individual can seek. And the liquidity goes in both directions, giving companies a larger population of people they can seek out for their workforce.

So, in a world where so many barriers to entry have been lowered, and an independent can find clients and projects on their iPhone while sitting next to their kids on a fishing boat, what's keeping you from becoming an independent? Fear? Lack of determination?

Or to business leaders, do you really think they're going to put up with your archaic onboarding systems? Why are they filling out ten forms like your employees do? They don't need a parking badge or a handbook showing them where the fire exits are. Why does your payroll department send them their money "in four to six weeks" as if they are your coffee supplier for the company break room?

I know it sounds like I'm speaking out of both sides of my mouth, but I'm a realist. Yes, independents can eat nails for breakfast. But they'll also remember which company fed them nails and which gave them croissants.

To independents, I say: you *have* to be like Rocky if you want to succeed.

To enterprises, I say: Rocky's body can remember every punch that landed on him. Make sure your business isn't on the giving end of that equation.

YO, ADRIAN, I DID IT!

Stallone wasn't alone in being a hard-working, unknown independent who really needed *Rocky* to succeed and launch his career. Movies need music, and music takes musicians and composers! Enter Bill Conti.

Close your eyes and think of that classic music from the first Rocky film. No, not "Eye of the Tiger" by Survivor—that song didn't come until 1982 when Rocky took on Mr. T in the third installment of the film franchise. No, I'm talking about Conti's theme song from the original film. Titled "Gonna Fly Now," the song starts with those escalating trumpet blasts:

"Bum bumpa bum, bum bum bum, bum bumpa bum, bum bum bum..."

The song's opening measures are so iconic and well-known now that playing just a few seconds of them serves as a metaphor for the idea of grit and determination in the face of overwhelming odds. You don't even have to be an athlete for the song to do its magic on you in this regard.

This has to be one of the greatest motivational songs in the history of film. Watch the movie again and scroll over to the "training montage" (now an essential trope of any movie in the shadow of *Rocky*). As Balboa runs through the streets of Philadelphia, it's Conti's "Gonna Fly Now" blaring away—all the way to the top steps of the Philadelphia Museum of Art. Hands raised high, Rocky jumps up and down in triumph—though the big fight is still ahead of him. That's what great music like this can do to inspire us all.

But before *Rocky*, almost no one knew Bill Conti. That's why he took the job scoring the film's music for only $25,000—and he had to pay the musicians himself out of that. But after the success of *Rocky*, Conti never lacked for steady work in film. He went on to win an Academy Award for his score for the movie *The Right Stuff*, along with the nomination he received for "Gonna Fly Now."

My high school marching band, with me on trombone, played this song my freshman year. Fans of the movie became purchasers of the music, pushing "Gonna Fly Now" to #1 on the *Billboard* Hot 100 chart. On the day that happened, I bet Bill Conti jumped up and down and said:

"Yo, Adrian, I did it!"

EVERSON'S ACTION POINT: FOR ENTERPRISES

The question is: How can you, as an enterprise, be more effective at appealing to a broader number of people who can contribute to your company's growth?

First, every executive I talk to says they want the best talent, but if your company doesn't allow for *independents* to be "on the bus," then it's just a lot of empty talk. Instead, free your mind to utilize free minds. Doing so will change your company's culture (iron *will* sharpen iron), it will make you a magnet for independents, and it will back up your claim that you want the best talent.

Second, you'll want to eliminate point-of-entry friction and increase liquidity so individuals and your company can work together efficiently. It's not a long-term permanent relationship, so the onboarding has to stop feeling like you're building the Hoover Dam. People now can choose who they work for and how long they work for much more easily than before. So if you want to compete and win in the twenty-first century, you've got to take all the friction out of their being eligible to work for your organization.

12

FOREVER YOUNG

Lengthened Life, Health Span, and Work Span

Some age. Others mature.

—Sean Connery[1]

Though he never climbed the famous mountain, Ernest Hemingway camped near its base while on safari in 1933 and used the setting for his bleak, semi-autobiographical short story "The Snows of Kilimanjaro." With hyenas and vultures circling ominously, the main character, Harry, lay dying of gangrene while waiting for a rescue plane that never came. Reflecting on his life while drinking copious amounts of liquor, Harry concluded that his life and talent as a writer had been wasted because of perpetual procrastination and a love of luxury. Hemingway ends the story with the hyena howling. Like I said, it's bleak.

Thankfully, my own Tanzanian experience bore absolutely no resemblance to Harry's. Instead of a death wrapped in loneliness and regret, in 2014 I celebrated my fiftieth birthday by camping on safari with my family and climbing Kilimanjaro for eight days with my son, Luke, and another father-son team. Instead of being drunk on sorrowful scotch, I drank in the view of a sunrise more intimate than any I had ever seen before.

This was an eight-day trip—six days up and two days down. Kilimanjaro rises 19,340 feet above sea level, making it Africa's tallest mountain and the world's largest freestanding mountain. About 30,000 people climb Kilimanjaro annually, with about 60% of them reaching the top. The mountain is not dangerous, with only about ten deaths a year, a remarkably small number compared to other mountains. But it takes a significant amount of training to be able to make the climb. You have to build stamina into your legs and mind if you're going to make it to the top.

The months of preparation and then the execution of the climb taught me many lessons about grit, determination, and resilience—everything we discussed in the prior chapter. Independents climb their own Kilimanjaro every week, showing resilience by overcoming stress and living outside their comfort zone. Also, the idea is that you focus on the next goal (i.e., the next summit), but once you've hit that one, you can start to look further and ascend another, higher summit. We knew the goal was to hit Kilimanjaro at the top at the summit, but there were many summits between sea level and the top of the mountain. And each one of those summits created an opportunity for us to surrender to the mountain or push on and reach the goal. Likewise, independents think about setbacks and challenges like that—seeing them as impossible obstacles if not broken down into subparts. They achieve the subpart and then push on after that.

I know, I know—the "climb a mountain" metaphor is the ultimate motivational-meme-cliché. If you close your eyes, I'm sure you can see the framed, poster-size photo of a mountain. In super big letters at the top is the word: **RESILIENCE**. Down at the bottom, in a smaller font size, the poster declares something profoundly obvious, like:

"If you want to reach the summit, don't ever quit."

—Anonymous

It's anonymous because it's asinine. It's pure saccharine drivel when it comes to building a resilience mindset.

Or perhaps the poster would picture me, Miles Everson, in training for the climb. I could supply the photos. For almost a year before the climb, I carried a 40-pound backpack around the neighborhood for my exercise. And for extra practice, we climbed five different mountains in New York State—nowhere near 19,000 feet, of course, but if you put on a 40-pound pack and climb a mountain for a day, you'll feel the burn. Ironically, I'm in better shape now than I was at 50, and it would probably be easier for me today than it was a decade ago. I don't know that I would ever call it "easy," but it wouldn't be as difficult. So the quote underneath the large word **PREPARATION** would be accompanied by a quotation like this:

> **"It's not the will to win that matters. It's the will to prepare to win that matters."**
>
> **–Paul "Bear" Bryant**

I find value in that kind of quote. A highly successful college football coach's claim that the preparation mattered most—that has meaning to it because of the man's accomplishments.

Or I've got one even better. The poster pictures me standing alongside the 20 sherpas (local mountain guides) we hired to help us navigate and carry gear. As the four of us outsiders carried our own water and rain gear, the sherpas lugged all our food, tents, and equipment. Let me put it this way: We had assistance. So, the large word on this motivational poster would be **TEAMWORK**—and the quote would say:

> **"It takes a team to reach the top. And when I say 'team,' I mean twenty or more strong-backed people who make sure we don't die. Remember, there's no 'I' in sherpa."**
>
> **–Miles Everson**

I'm being cheeky here, but that's because I'm actually not telling my Kilimanjaro story to talk about grit and resilience and preparation and teamwork. I could. That's all true—and those qualities certainly embody the mind of the independent. But there's a more profound point I want to make throughout this chapter: I believe that the increased lifespans—and improved quality of life in our later years—directly impacts the mind of the independent. "Forever Young" is more than the title of this chapter, it's a major focus of my own life and leadership.

So, the large word on the poster would be: **LIFESPAN**.

As I said, I climbed Mt. Kilimanjaro for my fiftieth birthday. In 1900, the average life expectancy in the United States—for males and females combined—was less than 50 years, and on average, men died even younger than that.[2] Let me state the obvious: you can't climb Kilimanjaro at 50 if you don't live to 50. You can't start or build a company at 70 if you're in the grave at 60. Life expectancy now hovers around 80 years, an increase of 21 years in the past 100 years (the 1925 average was 58).

So, the text at the bottom of the **LIFESPAN** poster should convey this quote from Peter Diamandis, MD:

> We are edging closer toward a dramatically extended healthspan—where 100 is the new 60. What will you create, where will you explore, and how will you spend your time if you are able to add an additional 40 healthy years to your life?[3]

Or maybe use this Diamandis dandy:

> Entrepreneurship is beautiful because there is no pre-set time frame for success. You can build a massively successful company at age 19 or age 70.[4]

In Hemingway's story, we have no idea how old the broken-down Harry was supposed to be. But in 1933—the year Hemingway camped at the feet of Kilimanjaro—the average lifespan for an American male was 61. When Hemingway died in 1961, he was 61 years old. He was exceptional as a novelist but altogether average in lifespan. Like most men of his time, Hemingway had a career spanning about four decades, and he packed an incredible amount of output into those forty years. But to state the obvious, his productivity could have been even greater had Hemingway lived longer.

With an extra decade or two, might he have given us another *Old Man and the Sea*?

In 1935, when Social Security began and established 65 as the year a person could collect benefits, average life expectancy was 60 for men and 64 for women. That shorter life expectancy, combined with the ability to collect benefits, institutionalized the idea of retiring at age 65—or sooner, if you could manage it.[5] But with the increase in lifespans, the "retire at 65" mindset has also been changing for a generation now: 41% of the US workforce expects they will work *past* 65, up from 12% 30 years ago.[6]

This trend in thinking differently about "retirement" directly impacts the future of work for both employees and independents. Our increasing lifespans will increase our work span—and that's a good thing, except where the work is physically taxing or requires the strength of one's youth (more than the wisdom and experience of one's age). And independents are leading the way here, taking advantage of the expanded work span years to stay productive, earn income, and find more fulfillment than people often imagine they will have in a twenty-year "retirement" period before declining health begins.

THREE BOXES

Richard Bolles wrote a now-classic book in 1981 called *The Three Boxes of Life*, which accurately predicted and directed how, in the postindustrial world, we would rethink and reshape the landmarks of our lives.

> The arc of our lives—defined in the industrial era—includes "three boxes": A glut of learning, then a glut of work, then a glut of leisure (in what I call "the period formerly known as retirement"). Millions of Americans have followed those Old Rules of Work, which included learning a trade or getting a degree; doing that work for most of their careers; buying a house, having a family, and educating their kids so they'd have a better life. But following those rules no longer results in widespread economic benefit.[7]

Three gluts, and then we die? And the third glut is . . . endless golf and the beach? Gee, great. Can't wait. And the worst part is that, with increasing lifespans being what they are, the "glut of leisure" box is constantly getting longer.

Similarly, columnist David Brooks wrote in *The Atlantic* about the changing mindset about "retirement," comparing it to how the concept of "teenager" developed in the 1940s as society and lifespans changed. "Gradually people began to accept that there is a distinct phase of life between childhood and adulthood," Brooks wrote.[8]

The point being, these are malleable concepts. The notions about what we are supposed to do at a certain age, they're rooted in societal expectations—and those expectations are rooted in reality about lifespans and longevity. If the average lifespan is 30 or 40, then people getting married at 15 makes sense. But if, on average, we live to 100, then we'd make "lifelong" decisions differently.

Brooks completes the analogy by showing how "retirement" is a malleable concept too—and how it's our longer lifespans that have transformed our thinking about work spans:

In the 21st century, another new phase is developing, between the career phase and senescence. People are living longer lives. If you are 60 right now, you have a roughly 50 percent chance of reaching 90. In other words, if you retire in your early or mid-60s, you can expect to have another 20 years before your mind and body begin their steepest decline.

We don't yet have a good name for this life stage. Sara Lawrence-Lightfoot, a notable scholar in this area, calls it the "Third Chapter." Some call it "Adulthood II" or, the name I prefer, the "Encore Years." For many, it's a delightful and rewarding phase, but the transition into it can be rocky.[9]

Now, let's bring this discussion to bear on the theme of this book. Independents are contrarian thinkers regarding retirement as consisting of two or three decades of leisure time. That mindset is so prevalent in our culture that it can feel like a mandate. If you color outside those lines by continuing to work, people begin to make assumptions or ask, "What went wrong? Did you not plan for retirement?"

But independents think independently, right? Even as young independents (Gen Z and millennials) are starting their careers, they're thinking about longevity and lifespan: How would I think about my career if I knew I would live to 100 and have strength of body and mind until 90?

Interest in the topic of health span and longevity has grown exponentially in the twenty-first century, and it has become a primary focus of my own life. Accordingly, I've begun to see just how important it is to have an independent mind if you are to pursue improved health. You have to think for yourself. Thinking independently impacts not just how you work, but also how you manage your money and your health.

Independents see the lifespan stats and know they *don't* want to retire at 65. But—and this is crucial to understand—just because independents want to continue working longer than age 65 doesn't mean they want to be in a stressful job full of unnecessary friction, toxic office politics, and no flexibility in where and when they work. If working past 65 means all of that, then yes—a life of leisure might be preferable. In other words, independents *want* to find purposeful and engaging work well into their 70s and even 80s—and they believe they can—*if* they work independently.

"The human hunger for meaning and fulfillment is strong," Brooks concluded. "And yet America today is too awash in workism and too short on purpose. We shouldn't have to wait until we're sixty-five to learn how to transform our lives."[10] I agree with Brooks and would add that the younger generations don't plan on waiting to find fulfillment, nor do they plan on retiring from purposeful work simply because their birth certificate says they've been on the planet for three score and five years.

And let's be honest about the economic realities, because for many people, longer work spans might be more about finances than self-actualization—and there's nothing wrong with that. Workers no longer retire at age 65 with a gold watch and pension. Due to economic cycles and financial setbacks that happen no matter how well one has planned, many people find themselves unable to retire from full-time employment at 65. But they do want flexibility in how they work, so they can spend quality time with friends and family. That's why many baby boomers are taking up second careers as independents, allowing them to control when, where, and how much they work. This trend will most certainly continue, with workers pursuing passion projects well into their 80s and beyond.

WHAT ABOUT BOB (DYLAN)?

Even if you live to 100, life still goes by quickly—too quickly. And as the old saying goes, "No one on his deathbed ever said, 'I wish I had spent more time on my business.'"[11] Actually, that quote *isn't* so old—it only emerged from the mind of labor negotiator Arnold Zack in the mid-1980s. Zack was active in his work at the highest levels even into his 80s, having been appointed by President Obama to a board that negotiated labor disputes with the railroads, the USPS, the Internal Revenue Service, and state governments. And here's the irony: Zack, now in his 90s, continues to be quoted in major newspapers about current issues, and he still serves as a senior research associate—at Harvard!

That said, I do understand and accept the point of Zack's famous quote: life is more than business and work.

♦ ♦ ♦

There's snow at the top of Mt. Kilimanjaro, and it's freezing cold, especially at night. Everything in your body tells you to stay put once you're bundled up in your sleeping bag and tent. But if you want to reach the summit before sunrise, you have to break camp around midnight and climb the final leg in the darkness. If you ever get the chance to ascend one of the tallest mountains in the world, you definitely want to be there at sunrise, because the sunrise at those elevations is unlike anything you've seen before. You can see forever, and the view takes your breath away.

You can't stay long, of course—only about thirty minutes—because you've got to get back down to base camp. You're so low on oxygen by that time in the journey that your legs and feet are moving slowly, a little less than one foot per step. After preparing a year to reach the summit, my son, Luke, and I sat there, took pictures, and soaked in the experience alongside the two other non-sherpas in our group. They were also a father-son duo and friends of ours from back home. Luke and the other boy were from the same Boy Scout troop and became Eagle Scouts together, just as I had become an Eagle Scout years earlier in North Dakota.

* * *

After being born in Duluth, Minnesota, in 1941, the great Bob Dylan grew up in Hibbing—another relatively small, cold outpost of the northern Midwest United States, a few hours closer to Canada from where I went to college. Aspiring to be a musician, Dylan left for New York City in 1961 and released his debut album in 1962.

On January 9, 1964—the same year Dylan launched his fourth album—I entered the world as my parents' third-born child. With my entrance, my dad had a son.

In 1965, Dylan went "electric" at the Newport Folk Festival, a turning point for the songwriter/musician, who was already being labeled the "spokesman for a generation." Then, on January 6, 1966, Dylan became a father to *his* firstborn child, a son named Jesse. Dylan owned the 1960s, becoming one of the most impactful forces on the music scene and culture.

In January 1974, Dylan released "Forever Young" from his fourteenth album, a lullaby-styled prayer of blessing on his son, Jesse. The song almost didn't make it onto the album after a friend teased Dylan: "C'mon, Bob. What! Are you getting mushy in your old age?" But Dylan relented and added the song, embracing that being a father does allow for some sentimentality.[12]

Old Testament verses inspired Dylan's lyrics; the "Priestly Blessing" found in Numbers 6:24-27 (NKJV):

> *The Lord bless you and keep you;*
> *The Lord make His face shine upon you,*
> *And be gracious to you;*

The Lord lift up His countenance upon you,
And give you peace.[13]

These verses and his Jewish background also influenced actor Leonard "Mr. Spock" Nimoy, as he invented his famous Vulcan greeting and introduced it to the world in 1967 during the second season of *Star Trek*. Nimoy saw the hand gesture and heard a form of the "live long and prosper" phrase as a boy in his Jewish synagogue.[14]

I was seven when that episode of *Star Trek* first aired—too young to take notice. And I was 10 when Dylan's "Forever" song was released, close to the same age as his son for whom he wrote the song. Dylan is now in his 80s—just like the first entrepreneurs I knew: my mom and dad. Dylan is in his sixth decade of his career—yes, as an independent professional musician—and I'm now in my 60s. There's no connection between those two facts except this: Time passes quickly. Did I mention I'm a grandfather?

But guess what? I've got no plans to retire at 65. Why would I? Oh, I'll chart a course for my work that involves doing different types of work than what I did in earlier decades of my career. But I have no desire for a "glut of leisure" during a decades-long period of retirement idleness. Call it what you want: the "Third Chapter" or the "Encore Years." Whatever. I've got as much fire and drive as I've ever had in my life.

Longevity is the work-span mindset of the independents I know and work with through MBO and other spaces. Young independents and those who are my age and older, in either direction of the age spectrum, their independent mind says, "Me retire? No way."

CAN WE ALL AGREE IT'S A GOOD THING?

This trend line is also good for the American and global economies because individuals will engage financially at a higher level for more years. Production and consumption are part of the way you get continued growth, so healthy workers working longer will be higher producers and consumers. Experience is like interest—it compounds. So why not be healthy to take advantage of the compounding effects of your experience? If you're not producing income, you get a lot more conservative with your expenses.

What happens to people's spending patterns within five years of their retirement? With retirement looming, spending patterns go down dramatically. While working, people think, "I still have an income, so we can go out for dinner on Fridays and take a vacation." Compare that to the retiree who enters into a frugal mindset: "I've got to button down."

I predict that 100-year-olds will eventually be in the workforce— with joy and of their own desire. And if my prediction is off, I can almost guarantee that 90-year-olds will work in greater numbers with each passing decade. Rapid mental and physical health advancements are converging and will make this possible. Of course, I'm not talking about 90-year-old construction workers or grand piano movers. I wouldn't want to hire an 80-something to mow my grass. But maybe the 80-year-old owns the business and oversees the work being done by the young whippersnappers?

And I'm not saying that people in their 80s and 90s will want to work 40 hours a week and 2,000 hours per year. But just think of all the areas of our knowledge economy where the wisdom and experience gained in a long life can be an invaluable asset to an enterprise—especially within a project-focused work environment.

* * *

It's fantastic that the workforce—and independents especially—are transitioning away from the mindset of an extended retirement. But the question remains: Have businesses adjusted *their* mindset about older workers? And when the work can be done by independents—*older* than 65—are enterprises thinking strategically about how to utilize such talent? Or do they respond to people based on outdated notions of what it means to be older than 65? "People work longer into their lives, yet we've found it rare to see organizations put programs in place to fully integrate older workers into their talent system," said James Root of Bain & Company, who commissioned research on this subject.

> Before age sixty, [the Bain report states] the average worker in developed markets is primarily motivated by good compensation. Averages are often misleading, but not in this case. In nearly all developed markets, good compensation is the top priority across archetypes [i.e., personalities and motivations]. Around sixty, there's a tipping point. Interesting work becomes the No. 1 job attribute, and both autonomy and flexibility significantly increase in importance.

As we'll see in future chapters, schedule and work location flexibility is a significant motivation for all independents—not just those older than 65. And who doesn't want their work to be "interesting"?

007

Some people respond to all the advances in health by asking a cynical question, "Are you trying to live forever?" No, that's not the point—except maybe for the people who believe that artificial intelligence and the coming singularity will make it possible for humans to "upload their consciousness" into quantum computers. But that's not what I'm talking about when I refer to "Forever Young."

I opened this chapter with climbing Kilimanjaro and Hemingway's lifespan, so let me wrap up our lifespan talk by referring to two well-known novelists from roughly the same period as Hemingway: Jack London (1876–1916), famous for *The Call of the Wild*, and Ian Fleming (1908–1964), famous for Bond. James Bond.

In 2021, actor Daniel Craig ended his run playing James Bond in five films with (spoiler alert) his death at the end of the appropriately named *No Time to Die*. A few of his colleagues gathered in the office of M (played by Ralph Fiennes) for a toast in 007's honor. M read the following lines, spoken by London to his friends and published in 1916 a few weeks after his death:

> The proper function of man is to live, not to exist. I shall not waste my
> days in trying to prolong them. I shall use my time.[15]

Fleming actually did write the Jack London quote in his 1964 novel *You Only Live Twice*—except that Bond was only presumed to be dead in the novel. And Fleming himself died that year, so the last pages of his final novel published while he was alive contained an obituary for 007, with the Jack London quote carrying the dramatic load.

Anyhow, London's words are a fantastic way to close *this* chapter, because I can both agree and disagree with London's quote.

First, London sounds too cavalier with the "waste my days in trying to prolong them" lines—and in his own life, he died at the age of 40, possibly from a fatal dose of morphine. But to his credit, the average lifespan for a man born in 1876 was in the low 40s. With that perspective, he may have considered his life to have already been long and fruitful. We have different ideas today, of course, but he may have viewed his life as being nearly over at 40.

Second, London asserts that "The proper function of man is to live" and "I shall use my time"—and to these sentiments, I agree. Don't spend your life trying to stay alive just to stay alive. Instead, stay "Forever Young" so you can make a difference through your life and relationships—and that includes your work.

Independent-minded people know that, on average, they will live longer and stay healthier than at any time in recorded human history. And as a result, they're rethinking the idea of having a "glut of leisure" to be found in the "third box" of life. They want the kind of meaning and fulfillment that work can bring, and they don't want that to end at age 65.

That said, you don't get the work if you can't keep up. So, independents know there's one vital piece they must have if they're going to work for extra decades. You must have a growth mindset. You must see yourself as a lifelong learner—and that brings us to chapter 13.

EVERSON'S ACTION POINT FOR ENTERPRISES

For enterprises, this chapter's action point is pretty straightforward. Either you have "programs in place to fully integrate older workers" (as Bain wrote) or . . . you don't. And if you don't have a program, then you probably don't have the people either. This probably isn't about anything nefarious in your HR: we're not talking about age discrimination. But it's going to take a change in mindset: that's always the first step.

First, I recommend that for your enterprise's bucket list of "projects" or "problems" (the kind that take a year or two to accomplish), don't hire another employee. Instead, find an independent who has a CV showing a track record of doing several dozen such projects in their career. Chances are they're older because it would take a few decades to accomplish "several dozen" of these.

Second, when valuable existing employees start talking about retirement and "cutting back," proposition them with the idea of working independently for your business once they retire. Who knows, maybe their desire to retire was rooted in a desire to have more flexibility in where and when they worked, and they'd love the chance to continue on, but independently. Maybe they didn't know that was an option because nobody at your enterprise had done it before. There's always a first.

13

LEARNING TO FLY

Growth Mindset | Lifelong Learning

Live as if you were to die tomorrow. Learn as if you were to live forever.

—Attributed to Mahatma Gandhi

On March 29, 1982, the Georgetown University basketball team and its star center, Patrick Ewing, led the University of North Carolina by one point with 32 seconds remaining in the NCAA national championship game. UNC inbounded the ball at half-court and passed it back and forth around the perimeter for 12 seconds before the sixth pass went to its freshman guard—Michael Jordan. In one fluid motion, Jordan leapt high and sank a game-winning jump shot that launched him into a career that's turned him into one of the most recognized faces on the planet.

Whereas Jordan was not even in the photograph when his coach and teammates were featured on the cover of *Sports Illustrated* the previous November, he has now graced the cover of the magazine 50 times—more than any other athlete. During his freshman year of college, Jordan still wrote home to ask for spending money; now he's worth $3 billion and has landed on the Forbes 400 list of wealthiest people.[1] Beyond being gifted with a certain-sized body and natural athleticism, what set Jordan apart from his peers? What made him become the "GOAT" (greatest of all time)?

At one point in his career, Jordan was asked to name his best skill—the thing that set him apart. Scoring? Defense? Playmaking? Slam dunks? No. Jordan said, "I was coachable. I was a sponge and aggressive to learn." His UNC coach, the legendary Dean Smith, reflected that Jordan was "inconsistent as a freshman" but that "he was one of the most competitive [players] we've ever had in our drills. He wanted to get better, and then he had the ability to get better."[2]

In *The Last Dance*, the 2020 documentary about Jordan, Roy Williams, an assistant coach during Jordan's time at UNC (and who later became the head coach), recounts how he told the freshman that he would need to work harder at the collegiate level than anything he had known during his successful high school career. Would the young man listen? Would he be teachable, or would the early successes make him think he had already arrived?

Jordan told Williams he had always worked harder than anyone else in high school. Williams responded, "Excuse me. I thought you just told me you wanted to be the best player to ever play here." Jordan understood the point: Forget the track record and prior accomplishments. Learn and keep learning. Put the work ethic into practice and admit just how much growth you've got left to do. "I'm going to show you. Nobody will ever work as hard as I work," Jordan told Williams.[3]

"You can't learn what you think you already know," Ryan Holiday wrote. "If you want to get smarter, stop thinking you're smart. If you want to learn, focus on all the things you don't know. Humility, admission of ignorance—these are the starting points. This is the attitude that gets you further in life."[4]

* * *

Major League Baseball kicked off its 1982 season one week after Jordan's UNC won the championship. The St. Louis Cardinals of the National League were predicted to compete for the Eastern Division, with strong starting pitching, tight defense led by Ozzie Smith, and a speedy offense. Their bullpen featured Bruce Sutter, a bearded and bushy-haired pitcher who had never started a game in the major leagues, which was a rarity in those pioneering days of bullpen duty specialists. Sutter saved 36 games for the 1982 Cardinals, then saved two more in the World Series that year—including the final pitch of their game-seven victory over the Milwaukee Brewers.

Sutter racked up 300 saves and an armful of individual awards during his career, earning him entrance into baseball's Hall of Fame in 2006. But the amazing thing is that his career almost ended before it even got started. While pitching in the minor leagues in 1972 at age 19, Sutter was forced to undergo arm surgery—and he had to pay for it himself. After rehab, Sutter was dismayed to realize his pitches weren't as effective; his fastball wasn't so fast. This was a career-threatening crisis.

That's when his minor league pitching coach, Fred Martin, taught him the split-fingered fastball, a new variation on the old forkball pitch of yesteryear. The pitch looks like a fastball to the batter, but the splitter clocks in around 85 mph—seven to ten miles slower than most fastballs. Plus, the ball's spin causes the bottom to drop out as it crosses the plate. "Even though hitters knew it was coming, they still weren't able to hit it," remarked Hall of Famer Jim Katt, a teammate of Sutter's in 1982. Because of Sutter's success with the split-fingered fastball, other pitchers learned and used it with success, and it became known as "the pitch of the 1980s." At the Hall of Fame, Sutter's plaque begins with these words: "A dominant closer who revolutionized the split-fingered fastball, which confounded batters."

To recap: Sutter injured his arm in 1972, learned the splitter in 1973, made it to the big leagues in 1976, and played until he retired in 1989. But *if* Martin hadn't been Sutter's pitching coach, or *if* Sutter had quit after his injury or refused to learn a newfangled pitch—he wouldn't have even made it to the major leagues. Think about that: 16 post-surgery years of a Hall of Fame career in the highly competitive field of professional baseball made possible because a 19-year-old turned his surgery setback into an opportunity to learn and grow into something new. Like the Michael Jordan story,

Sutter combined his growth mindset with the lucky break of having an aggressive mentor—and the rest is history.

* * *

A growth mindset is the belief that one's talents and abilities can be developed through hard work, lifelong learning strategies, and timely input from others. When individuals and organizations embrace a growth mindset, they tend to be more innovative, risk-taking, and committed to learning and growing. This can be particularly important for independent workers because entrepreneurs need to be adaptable and willing to learn new skills in order to succeed in a constantly changing job market.

Independents show a lifelong commitment to learning—a mindset of continual growth, exploration, and improvement. They look for the constructive critic who challenges and coaches them into improvement. And independents know that the best critic might even be the one looking at them in the mirror each morning: themselves.

"I think it's very important to have a feedback loop," Elon Musk said, "where you're constantly thinking about what you've done and how you could be doing it better. I think that's the single best piece of advice: constantly think about how you could be doing things better and questioning yourself."[5]

To "become great and stay great," Ryan Holiday wrote, people "must be always learning. We must all become our own teachers, tutors, and critics."[6]

Learning how to learn—that's the idea. The most valuable mindset an individual can have is an enhanced learning capability—and it's both the capability and the interest in learning.[7] If you are good at learning and practice a discipline of learning, you will be able to adapt to changing skills, careers, and jobs.

Whether you learn through formal education like college or through less formal learning mechanisms—that's a personal choice. But, the most successful and satisfied individuals will pursue a path of becoming constant and continual learners. It used to be that people would pick a job based on their education, whether that was high school or college, and then they would go and work in that job for decades. That's no longer the case because it doesn't have to be. If you know how to learn, you can continue to pick up new skills and capabilities that help you work well into subsequent decades beyond what has historically been the experience. This advice applies to any knowledge work and any job that requires technical skill development. So, learn how to learn because that's the lifelong trajectory of the independent mind.

MACHINE OF THE YEAR

When *Time* magazine famously made the computer its "Machine of the Year" for 1982 (and allegedly displaced Steve Jobs from being "Man of the Year"—so he thought), the article mentioned the concerns many had that computers would displace jobs. "Theoretically, all unemployed workers can be retrained," *Time* explained, "but retraining programs are not high on the nation's agenda. Many new jobs, moreover, will require an aptitude in using computers, and the retraining needed to use them will have to be repeated as the technology keeps improving."[8] Gone would be the days of learning a set of skills and then toiling at a repetitive task until retirement. (When you put it that way, why was eliminating *that* type of work a bad thing?)

A computer industry founder speculated that companies "who put in computers usually increase their staffs as well," but that "one industry may kill another industry. That's tough on some people." *Time* correctly concluded that "new technology eventually creates as many jobs as it destroys, and often more." The catch, however, was that the workforce would need to learn how to use the computers—and then learn more. Lather. Rinse. Repeat.

Even executives had reason to worry, as a bank vice president explained: "Managers who do not have the ability to use a terminal within three to five years may become organizationally dysfunctional." Look, nobody wants to become "organizationally dysfunctional"—that's business speak for workers becoming stale amidst change, suddenly lacking the knowledge or skills to do their job. "Lifelong retraining is expected to become the norm for many people," said a US government report quoted in the *Time* article.[9]

That was true in 1982 and is even more true four decades later. Replace the phrase "training to use computers" with "training to use AI" and you get an idea of the importance of having a growth mindset and a commitment to lifelong learning.

What's interesting, though, is that the "training" and continuous education that's actually needed at the *advent* of a new technology isn't always what people think it will be. Two decades after the publication of the "Machine of the Year" article, the *Wall Street Journal* reflected on the *Time* article: "Looking back, it was globalization, not automation, that became the bogeyman of job losses and the need for retraining—your average office worker never did learn to program a PC."[10] The early stereotype of "computer geeks" who built their own computers (hardware geniuses like Wozniak) or wrote their own programs (software gurus like Gates) wound up *not* being the norm for most of us who simply use computers without knowing precisely how they work.

Likewise, when the iPhone launched, and Apple introduced the App Store, there was a rush to become a professional app creator—learning how to code into existence the actual apps. In hindsight, we can see that it's the widespread entrepreneurial *use* of apps—not their creation—that has enriched the most people. People barely old enough to vote are making bank using TikTok to create and "influence"—and I guarantee that most of them do not know how to code. And, of course, it was the *use* of apps that fueled "the Uber of *X*" gig economy.

Recently, we've seen a tidal wave of interest in monetizing the use of AI, with each breathless article promising that if you don't learn how to use artificial intelligence, you will be obsolete and out of business. Okay, so that's true and *not* true, depending on what is meant by "using AI." Will your small business have to learn how AI works "under the hood" and employ coders and engineers dedicated to building AI products for your business? No, of course not—that would be the equivalent of your company building its own computers from scratch or writing its own version of Microsoft Excel. That said, you *will* need to utilize some AI-fueled "software as a service" geared for your industry. At the very least, your customer service inputs can begin to be automated, saving labor costs and increasing customer satisfaction. Five years ago, you probably didn't even think about AI, but five years from now, your use of AI may be the key to your enterprise's survival. The point is that incorporating AI *will* take a mind willing to learn new things—a mindset for growth.

If none of your *employees* know how AI works, don't worry because I know independents who eat, sleep, and breathe AI and are ready to take you on as a client. As new as AI may be, these independents are lifelong learners; they've already upskilled to discover what's under the AI hood and how to tune your company's engine accordingly. For example, my friend Salim Ismail, founder of OpenExO, helps businesses get "AI Ready"—a concept that would not have been comprehended by most people even a decade ago. Or at the very least, getting "AI Ready" wasn't on the radar for most businesses at that point in time.

In 2024, MBO Partners released the findings of a study that showed a wave of "AI-upskilling among independent workers: 37% of independent workers currently incorporate generative AI into their daily tasks and 74% are already familiar with AI and are planning to enhance their skills in this area."[11]

And that illustrates the broader theme of this chapter: Free Bird independents practice lifelong learning and believe in a growth mindset. But would you believe that the "growth mindset" idea, as we currently talk about it, has only recently been developed?

THE DWECKS OF SOCIETY

In a world where publishers consider a book successful if it sells 5,000 or 10,000 copies, Carol Dweck's book *Mindset: Changing the Way You Think to Fulfill Your Potential* has sold over a million copies since first being published in 2006. Even if you didn't know it, she has influenced you through endless articles or books by other authors who built their own material on a foundation of Dweck's teaching. She pioneered the idea of "two mindsets," conveying that "it's not just our abilities and talent that bring us success, but whether we approach our goals with a fixed or growth mindset."[12]

Dweck asks a question, "Is success about learning—or proving you're smart?" Setting up the question that way, you can tell you're supposed to answer that it's "about learning," but the point is to reflect on whether you act on that idea. Actions and thinking go hand in hand. "You have a choice. Mindsets are just beliefs," writes Dweck. "They're powerful beliefs, but they're just something in your mind, and you can change your mind. As you read, think about where you'd like to go and which mindset will take you there."[13]

Dweck advocates for people to change their beliefs, to change their minds, and to build the habit of having a growth mindset. The independents I know have this growth mindset, and if you're thinking of becoming an independent—you should too. Open your mind to the idea of having a mind that can grow. And it will.

Lifelong learning is *continuous* and *compounding*. The more things change, the more you *cannot* stay the same. The more your skills can be automated by AI or outsourced to someone across the globe, the more your own wages will deflate—or worse, your job will be eliminated. If the value of your skills is being deflated, then you need to upskill, retrain, learn, grow, and adapt. In that sense, this chapter applies the trends from part 1 (those "Everson's Evolutions," with their emphasis on the escalated rate of change, the fractionalization of everything, knowledge flows, and the deflationary nature of progress). Let me explain.

If what you're doing in your business or job is constant with what you did yesterday, then by definition, you are falling behind because of technological and societal changes. Thinking you can stay where you're at in business without working hard to increase your knowledge and skills is like thinking you can park your butt on top of an inflatable tube in the middle of a fast-moving river and not be swept downstream.

"There's no shortage of competition in the computer industry," Bill Gates declared in 1993—even before the internet exploded onto the scene. "You'll never have anybody in a very dominant position for very long because they have to prove themselves constantly. You can't just sit on a market position; the fact that you have a seventy to eighty percent share means nothing in the next round."[14] That's the language of continual growth.

Business innovation thrives within a growth mindset, as Keaton Swett, a young tech entrepreneur and colleague of mine at MBO, said, "Whether as an individual, team, or organization, we need to guard against becoming set in our ways. There are always new and exciting ideas to consider, so long as we aren't the ones unwittingly turning off the innovation faucet."[15]

The fixed mind can't keep up—it can't adapt to the rapid changes coming our way every month. "The mind is alive when it is flexible and adaptable. It can be updated, take new form, endure change," wrote James Clear, author of the massive bestseller *Atomic Habits*. "The mind is dead when it is fixed and immovable. It cannot absorb new ideas or thoughts. It is stiff and brittle. When we lose our ability to adapt, to move with the environment, to tolerate new beliefs and reshape our old ones, our mind is at risk of becoming outdated. The fixed mind becomes a relic."[16]

To be clear, lifelong learning isn't about chasing after every shiny new object and trending piece of information—not at all. Lifelong learners learn new things—new to *them*—but that doesn't mean the knowledge itself is brand new. A lifelong learner dips deeply into existing pools of knowledge and discovers fresh wisdom from the past, applying it to the present-day situations. They "must all know what came before, what is going on now, and what comes next," wrote Ryan Holiday—the bestselling author who lives this out, seeing how he's single-handedly reintroduced ancient Stoicism to modern readers.[17]

A growth mindset prevents us from hemorrhaging confidence when we fail and make mistakes. As long as we learn something from the process and grow, then we have no reason to fear making some right turns or even U-turns in our business. "Anybody who doesn't change their mind a lot is dramatically underestimating the complexity of the world that we live in," explained Jeff Bezos.[18] Or as Dweck teaches us, failure isn't about failing, but "is about not growing. Not reaching for the things you value. It means you're not fulfilling your potential."[19]

This is the path of wisdom. And from my experience, a growth mindset characterizes the mind of an independent.

NICHE, BESPOKE, LONG-TAIL SKILLS

The story of Bruce Sutter learning the split-fingered fastball that saved his young career (and saved 300 games in the majors) also illustrates a characteristic of independents: they become specialists. Independents focus on a few areas of skills they love and get extremely good at executing—just like Sutter became a split-fingered fastball specialist. The independent mind thinks in terms of specialization.

Look, you can either go a mile wide and an inch deep with your professional skills or go an inch wide and a mile deep. Except for behemoth corporations, companies can't afford to hire *employees* who are a mile deep and an inch wide in every area, but they do need access to this expertise for bursts of work seasons when they must complete projects requiring a variety of niche expertise. And that's where independents play a vital role. They bring that narrower bandwidth to the marketplace. They work with clients who need their "inch-wide, mile-deep" niche expertise.

This is "long tail" thinking, selling low volumes of hard-to-find or made-to-order, customized ("bespoke" is the trendy term) products and services. This approach can be particularly effective for independent workers who can offer these bespoke services to clients looking for specialized skills or services that are not commonly offered by others. By focusing on niche markets and offering tailor-made services, independent workers can stand out in a crowded market and build a reputation as a specialist in their field.

Once upon a time, businesses could depend on "scalable efficiency" as the engine of their growth. Once upon a time, individuals trusted institutions and centralized authorities and bought whatever they were selling. Not so anymore. "Scalable efficiency works best in stable environments that are not evolving rapidly," wrote John Hagel and John Seely Brown. "It also assumes that the constituencies served by these institutions will settle for standardized products and services that meet the lowest common denominator of need. Today, we live in a world that is increasingly shaped by exponentially improving digital technologies that are accelerating change, increasing uncertainty, and driving performance pressure on a global scale.

Consumers are less and less willing to settle for the standardized offerings that drove the success of large institutions in the past."[20]

Enterprises now realize that their workforce must possess niche and bespoke skills to provide niche and bespoke offerings—the opposite of a "cookie-cutter" mindset. And where will enterprises find talent with these bespoke skills? You guessed it: independents.

Independents only want to do what they're good at. They don't want to be an employee who spends precious time doing administrative items or programs that some manager thinks they should be doing. And they certainly don't want to be "kept busy" with work simply to justify a pre-set 40-hour work week. Independents want to do what they love and have a passion for. They think, *Can I just do* that? And when independents possess the marketable skills in "that" area, the answer is "yes." So you get people who are really good at what they do and love to do it instead of generalists.

I can hear the objections. "Miles, a duck with only one leg will swim in circles. You must diversify your skills."[21] Okay, sure, that's true—in fact, I'm arguing for "lifelong learning" that prompts you to do just that: continue to learn new skills. See? That said, you don't expect your accountant to also be the guy you call to clean out your septic tank and bake the wedding cake for your daughter's wedding. You can't be a gifted, talented professional who commands high wages if you're the "jack of all trades but the master of none."

An earnest amateur attempts to be in every market, but experienced independents know to focus their efforts into a specific lane. Independents complete projects and solve specific, focused problems that enterprises are willing to pay good money to get fixed. To borrow a Warren Buffett quote spoken in a different context: "You can't produce a baby in one month by getting nine women pregnant." That is to say: independents focus.

MERGERS, EMERGERS, AND SURGERS

In my thirty years with PwC, I was involved at all levels in helping organizations through hundreds of transformational changes, including mergers and acquisitions, so you could say I have a toolbox of niche skills related to adapting. So here's something I've noticed repeatedly: Whenever you do an acquisition of a company, you run the risk of losing very talented people. They're not interested in being part of the new entity, so they move on. I've seen this happen in nearly every acquisition I've been involved with. So that seems like a loss—a negative outcome of the merger or acquisition.

But a positive spin on that talent-loss problem is that the M&A opens opportunities for less seasoned people to emerge as new leaders. It's surprising how quickly a person will emerge as a leader to fill a void in the acquired company. More often than not, a young, high-performing talent who was previously unidentified suddenly emerges as a leader and fills the void.

These opportunities often come quickly, so a word to employees: Be ready to surge up. Advancement goes to the bold, and often, it's not a one-step-at-a-time happening. The person advances ahead of the pack, and—this is key—the "formal credentials" of earned degrees did not create the surge. The surge happened because the person upgraded and upskilled their brain through learning—and learning how to learn.

And the learning I'm talking about is actually a three-step process: learning, applying, and building. Lots of people talk about continuous learning, but learning without application is meaningless. And this is especially true when it comes to commercializing what you've learned.

We've become the "search generation," I think, where everyone goes online to search for things, to watch podcasts and discover information. But if they don't apply and build, have they really learned anything? Fact gathering is not the same thing as learning any more than having knowledge is equal to having wisdom. For example, think of someone who searches every day for facts about health but never applies what they learn in order to improve their health.

I think that's an important message, and it goes with the themes from a book I've profited from and have used with my executives—*Limitless* by Jim Kwik. It's about how continuous learning helps you rise above others in the workplace. I've seen it repeatedly: While others were keeping their heads down, collecting a paycheck and hoping to get that 5% a year raise, the surger was thinking, "What do I need to learn and how do I need to improve to maximize my potential?" The M&A opened the door for the upskilled surger, illustrating a maxim of Branch Rickey, the general manager of the Brooklyn Dodgers who signed Jackie Robinson: "Time is of the essence and luck is the residue of design."[22]

SKILL SET IS THE NEW DEGREE

Skill set is the new degree. That's why, within higher education, we're seeing a move toward focusing more on specific skills and capabilities rather than generalist degrees. *Dirty Jobs* creator Mike Rowe critiqued industrial modes of production (including education) when he said, "Mass production is a great thing—the Model T, right? But people aren't cars. So how did we turn our public education system into this thing that reeks of all the factory protocols I've ever seen?"[23] I believe this mindset, this yet nascent turn away from industrialized education, will drive the growth of the independent economy, as we see a movement toward businesses needing people with deeper skills—not degrees. But that also means independents must invest in themselves to hone and market these deeper skills.

Here's a trick question: Are independents smart or intellectual? "There's a difference between intellectual and smart," writes Seth Godin. "A plumber is smart, they know how to do a skilled and effective job on the task at hand. Intellectualism isn't about practical results, it's a passion for exploring what others have said, though this approach is sometimes misused to make others feel uninformed or to stall. If you want to know what the scholars have written, ask an intellectual. And if you've got a problem worth solving, it might pay to ask a smart person . . . Access to smart is easier than ever before. But we need to seek it out."[24]

In that sense, independents are smart, not scholars. Oh, they may have a scholarly background and may be considered intellectual. But the value they bring to your enterprise flows from their "smarts"—as Godin uses the term. After all, do you need someone to write a white paper on your problem or fix your problem?

In chapter 2 we talked about Ivan Illich and the "Tools of Conviviality."

Illich said convivial tools should be free, creative, and can be used by anyone with minimal special training. He critiqued the industrial mode of production, including the educational systems and the tools and technologies that support it. Illich argued that we need to create tools that promote individual autonomy and creativity rather than tools that create dependency and restrict freedom. As we saw, this philosophy directly influenced Wozniak and Jobs—and by extension, conviviality undergirds on-demand learning tools like Udemy. Low-cost or no-cost lectures by world-class leaders in any field you're interested in? That's conviviality.

The technology powering on-demand education may be relatively new, but the concept of "learning to learn" isn't. Albert Einstein once debated Thomas Edison over the inventor's belief that a college education was of little worth. Einstein, a college professor himself, nevertheless gave this nuanced reply: "It is not so very important for a person to learn facts. For that he does not really need a college. He can learn them from books. The value of an education in a liberal arts college is not the learning of many facts but the training of the mind to think something that cannot be learned from textbooks."[25]

* * *

Employees who launch out as independents have a genuine love of learning—that's a fact I can prove by both experience *and* logic. When independents worked as employees for your company as an engineer, did they have to understand marketing? Communications? Social media? Did they know their way around HR issues? Accounting? Sales? Corporate leadership? No, you hired them to be an engineer—other people in the company took care of the rest. But when they traded in a W-2 for a 1099 and life as an independent engineer, they knew they'd have to learn a panoply of new skills and knowledge—all of that "how to build and grow a small business" stuff.

Where do independents go to get all that extra learning—the upgraded knowledge packs of "Entrepreneurship 101"? Some may choose to go back to school for an MBA, and I won't knock that approach. Okay, maybe I'll knock it a bit because I don't think an MBA necessarily equips anyone to be an entrepreneur. For the same investment of time, energy, and tuition, a solopreneur can choose instead to learn through MOOCs (Massive Open Online Courses), seminars, books, certification programs, and getting "badges" that prove competence in a skill. And now, AI provides an instant tutor, available 24-7 and relatively free, to teach anyone about anything. Best of all, AI doesn't lose patience with you for asking a dozen follow-up questions until you fully understand the material.

In sum, convivial tools for learning lead to bespoke skills, and bespoke skills lead to more employees becoming independent. The social contract is changing, and people no longer want a life of "three gluts" (learning, working, retirement). People want the gluts to be blended—so no gluts at all. Instead, they want a holistic life with learning, work, and restorative ease blended throughout all the years.

So I'll say it once more: Lifelong learning marks the mindset of an independent. And as lifespans expand and lifelong learning becomes the norm, the independent workforce will organically grow—that's the surest bet one can make.

PETERSON, PRICE, PARETO (A WORD TO ENTERPRISES)

"How does all of this impact my business?" asks the leader of an enterprise or institution. "Miles, put the cookies on the bottom shelf!"

Fair enough. To get there, let's talk quickly about Peterson, Price, and Pareto. First, Dr. Jordan Peterson, the psychology professor and bestselling author of *12 Rules for Life*, said this in a lecture: "As your company grows, incompetence grows exponentially, and competence grows linearly."[26] I believe this is true—do you? The learning that your enterprise needs *tomorrow* just to stay where you're at *today*: this keeps you awake at night. This quote echoes much of what I said earlier in the chapter about how you cannot stay in one place without falling behind.

Second, Peterson referred to Price's law (named after Derek J. de Solla Price) that states "the square root of the number of people in a domain do 50% of the work." In other words, "if you have ten employees, three of them do half the work. If you have 100 employees, ten of them do half the work. If you have ten thousand employees, 100 of them do half the work."

That's awful but true—especially in knowledge work societies like ours. If you're carrying bricks for a living and you don't have ambition, it will show up visibly in your work. Either the pile of bricks got moved (and so, you get paid) or it didn't (and you don't). But in a knowledge economy, we need workers who think, iterate, lead, respond, and create value by bringing their emotional and mental selves into their work. No mindless cogs. No piecework. No programmed robots or automatons.

Similarly, the Pareto principle (better known as the 80/20 rule) says that 80% of consequences come from 20% of causes—or that 80% of the work comes from 20% of the people. Perhaps it's better to say that 80% of the finished work—or the work that really counts—comes from 20% of the people, because it's not as though the rest of the workforce is sitting on their backside. They're doing *something*—maybe even what they've been told to do. But they're not creating the kind of value that will keep the lights on or move your enterprise to be the leader in its category.

The hardest part of hearing these three principles is that you can't easily identify who among your workforce will help you do the opposite—to grow your competence linearly. Or which workforce members are definitely the "20%" people (Pareto)? Who is doing 50% of the value-creating work (Price)? People don't wear badges that say, "I'm part of the 80% who only does 20% of the value creating around here." Even worse, the high-performance people who do 50% of the work or create 50% of the sales—they know their value. Retaining them will be difficult.

If only you had a pool of talented professionals who love and live to create substantial value. When integrated into your workforce, this pool of people could be the catalyst for your company to grow its competence linearly. But where can you find such people for your workforce?

By now, you know my answer: independents.

Independents are lifelong learners who possess a growth mindset. But they also apply themselves to deep learning within their niche, so they're getting better and better within their lane—and that's all you need them for individually: to excel in the project-focused work you need done well.

So utilize independents and find that you're getting a "twenty percenter," a person who "creates fifty percent of the output" and fuels the level of your enterprise's competence.

WHEN TO STOP

"But when will the learning stop?" you ask. It won't. Though there are plenty of hacks to make the process more efficient, there's no hack that eliminates the learning altogether. That's because a learning hack *about* learning is itself . . . a form of learning! See how that works?

So, if you want to leap into the independent workforce but fear the learning curve, just remember that you don't have to know everything on Day 1. In fact, you won't. Entrepreneurs—like you want to become—get started where they're at, but they also commit to an ongoing and perpetual learning process. That's it. That's the path: you do *not* know everything, and that's okay because the learning is part of the life of the entrepreneur.

+ + +

In his 1984 rookie year in the NBA, Michael Jordan immediately became a scoring sensation and a human highlight reel. But after six seasons, his Chicago Bulls teams still had not won a championship. Meanwhile, Jordan kept learning and growing and working—including his understanding and acceptance that he could not possibly win a championship single-handedly. The other teams would double- and triple-team him whenever a game was on the line. Jordan needed to grow. In Bulls coach Phil Jackson, Jordan found a mentor who taught him how to improve his mental game and lead a team to victory by distributing the success.[27]

Finally, on June 12, 1991 (2,547 days after being drafted by the Bulls), Jordan and a group of mostly non–All Star teammates broke out. They won the NBA championship, beating Magic Johnson's Lakers. Jordan's eyes gushed tears, to the amazement of his teammates. "Sometimes we'd question whether he was human, whether he had feelings," former Bulls center

Will Perdue said. "He was just a guy that was focused on one thing and one thing only. The only emotion we'd seen out of him was anger or frustration. We were literally stunned to see those emotions."[28] Jordan's growth mindset led him not only to the 1991 championship but to six championships altogether in the 1990s. What a decade!

On June 17, 1991, Tom Petty and the Heartbreakers released "Learning to Fly"—a song that hit #1 on *Billboard*'s rock chart. When the Chicago Bulls produced a documentary of their team's season later that year, they titled it "Learning to Fly" and used Petty's song in the closing credits of the video. Players being interviewed even sang these lines of the song.

Thankfully, contrary to what the word "independent" seems to imply, you don't have to "start out all alone" (as Petty sang). Like Jordan, successful entrepreneurs discover they do better when they "get by with a little help from my friends." And to *that* theme, we now turn our attention.

EVERSON ACTION POINT: FOR ENTERPRISES

Set up mechanisms for developing the skills of your workforce—employees and independents alike. Not only will your business benefit immediately from having these upskills in your workforce, you'll also find it easier to attract and retain talent. Study after study proves this to be true.[29]

In their 2010 book, *The Power of Pull*, John Hagel, John Seely Brown, and Lang Davison persuasively argued that forward-thinking institutions will provide pathways and platforms for talent development. They warned that those who don't will "find its most talented people fleeing their cubicles and corner offices for other 'homes' (or perhaps even literally setting up business from home) . . . Any corporate 'vision' that fails to put talent development of individuals at the heart of its strategy will surely fail."[30]

14

WITH A LITTLE HELP FROM MY FRIENDS

Community | Connection | Communication

Friends are medicine. Close relationships reduce our stress, improve our health, and extend our life.

—Daniel Pink[1]

A month after Michael Jordan led the Bulls to their third consecutive championship in 1993, his father, James, was murdered. That tragedy, combined with Jordan's feeling of boredom and burnout, led him to retire from basketball, missing almost all of the next two seasons in favor of trying his hand at baseball with the Chicago White Sox.

As Jordan exited the Bulls, the team signed free agent point guard Steve Kerr, one of several players who had big Air Jordan shoes to fill in the absence of the superstar. The Bulls made the 1994 playoffs without Jordan, but they could not advance to the finals.

Then, in March 1995, Jordan made a two-word announcement: "I'm back." He played the final 17 regular season games and six playoff games, but the Orlando Magic eliminated the Bulls in the first round. Jordan didn't intend to lose the next time around.

Several months later, during a preseason practice game, Coach Phil Jackson tasked Kerr with guarding Jordan. "We're on opposite sides of the scrimmage, and he's talking all kinds of trash, and I'm pissed because we're getting our ass kicked," Kerr recalled.[2]

"Phil sensed my aggression, but he was trying to tone me down, and he starts calling these ticky-tack fouls," Jordan said. "Now I'm getting mad because for you to be protecting this guy, that's not going to help us when we play New York. That's not going to help us when we play these teams that are very physical. The next time he did it, I just haul off on Kerr. When I fouled Steve Kerr, I said, 'Now, *that's* a f-----g foul.'"

Kerr jumped up and shoved Jordan in the chest, who responded by giving Kerr a black eye with a punch to the face. Jackson tossed Jordan from practice. Not a great start for the return of the king.

But here's the surprise ending to the story. Jordan expressed remorse for his actions and apologized to Kerr. The two began to bond as friends, finding they unfortunately shared a similar tragic history of losing their fathers to murder; Kerr's father had been assassinated by terrorists in 1984 as the president of the American University of Beirut.

"I would say it definitely helped our relationship, and that probably sounds really weird," Kerr said years later, reflecting on the fight. "I wouldn't recommend that to anybody at home. It has to be understood in the context of intense competition."[3]

The Bulls went all the way that season, kick-starting the team's second "threepeat" championship run of the 1990s. Jordan trusted Kerr so much that he surprised everyone by passing the ball to him with the game on the line in the 1997 finals—Jordan being double-teamed. Kerr made the shot, and they won the championship.

Kerr won five NBA titles as a player—three with Jordan's Bulls and two with the San Antonio Spurs. Now, as a coach, he's led the Golden State Warriors to the NBA Finals six times, winning the championship in four of them.

Kerr credits Jordan as the factor that "changed the entire course" of his life and career. "I was able to play on these championship teams, made a name for myself, was able to get into TV, broadcasting, management, coaching and the reason people hired me for these jobs later on is because I played next to Michael Jordan. I owe him everything."[4] And to think it started with a black eye. That's the power of connection—it binds a team together even in the presence of oversized ego, ambition, and intensity.

"Some people think it's all about winning. In fact, quite the opposite," Kerr said years later as he coached the Golden State Warriors to become a dynasty. "A strong culture is when things *aren't* going great, but we still work hard, have joy and fun being together as a group."[5]

This chapter focuses on how the three Cs (community, connection, and communication) will impact retaining independent talent at your enterprise. Of course, much of what I write here applies to *everyone* in your workforce—independents don't have a monopoly on the human need for friendship and clear communication. But I'll point out specific challenges and opportunities for independents in relationship to your enterprise.

TEAMING UP

From the research collected by MBO, about one-fourth of full-time independents said they had teamed up with other independent workers or microbusinesses in their work.[6] The independent workforce is not simply a group of isolated, atomized contractors sitting in front of screens by themselves. Work increasingly gets done in teams, not only inside organizations and between companies, vendors, contractors, freelancers, and other business partners but also among independents themselves. Not surprisingly, independents thrive when it comes to working in teams.

Traditional jobholders also report that teaming with independent workers is increasing. In 2022, 22% of traditional jobholders reported they had teamed with an independent worker or microbusiness at work over the past year. That's up from just 12% in 2020.

The main advantage here is to be able to get more done in a cost-effective manner. Independents are starting to mimic bigger service firms—striving to accomplish more and earn more by deploying teams of workers instead of working alone. Independent workers who are good at what they do—but who are not necessarily skilled at generating business or who don't like to sell—are learning that teaming up allows them to focus on what they like best: doing the work.

Clients are learning that hiring teams is more productive, and that it makes good business sense to purchase a finite and cohesive result rather than individual components of a project that they must manage. In the growth of teaming, we see more independents behaving like owners of larger work outcomes, not just as deliverers of spot projects.

SHOULD I STAY OR SHOULD I GO?

Around 25 years ago, I learned something from the late Don Clifton, who was the chairman of the Gallup organization and one of the smartest men I've known, regarding human capital and psychology. Clifton said something to me that has stayed with me since. Business leaders would often ask him, "Why are my employees leaving?" and think the answer is some combination of pay and benefits.

But Clifton said they're asking the wrong question. They should ask, "Why do people *stay*?" Clifton said the reason people stay at companies or in the environment they're in is because they don't want to let their family and friends down. That is, if people have friends in their community, they will not leave the community.

That piece of wisdom can help you lead your business regardless of your use of independents—and I hope that it does. When your employees feel connected to relationships at work, they're more satisfied and stay with you longer.

Now, let's apply this principle to independent professionals. External work can be lonely, especially if someone spends the first years of their career in emotionally satisfying workplaces with fellow employees who become more than just colleagues. No matter what perks come with working externally, a drawback for many is the sense of being cut off from the human connection that's organically experienced in a workplace. Independents may miss the camaraderie and collaboration that comes with working in an office environment, and this can lead to decreased motivation and productivity.

Further, independents may struggle to build a network of professional contacts, thus limiting their opportunities for work and professional growth. After all, career advancement comes from who you know, not just what you know. Independents counter these difficulties by the intentional development of networks, community, and friendships—both digitally and in person.

Of course, loneliness and lack of networking opportunities can also hit full-time remote work employees. So even if you're not utilizing independents, your enterprise cannot stick its head in the sand regarding these challenges. And remember what I said earlier in the discussion about the broken social contract: you don't want government regulators to think it's their job to improve connection-making within the workforce! People want a sense of community and connection with other humans so they can improve their own well-being or status, but you can't regulate that.

Businesses that want to engage and retain independent workers must make their organization feel like it's a place where they're welcomed and there are opportunities for human connection. Reverse engineer Don Clifton's question "Why do people stay?" for your company. If I were to provide specific tips, those tips probably would work for some companies and fail miserably for others because every business has its own unique DNA.

If all this sounds too "touchy-feely" and unrelated to the bottom line—think again! Some business leaders seem to believe: *Independents get paid well. What more do they want? If they wanted friends, they should become employees.*

If that's your thinking, I hope I can persuade you to take a different perspective. A friendship mindset comes easier when connected to an abundance mindset. The pie *can* grow—the pie *is* growing. So as you utilize independents, network them into your employee relationship ecosystem (whatever that looks like for your enterprise) and find ways to practice the Golden Rule: "Do to others as you want others to do to you."

I hope you'll do this without thinking *What's in it for me?* That said, independents *will* help your enterprise thrive economically (see chapter 16,

"Has Life Been Good to Me?"). So why not put more humanity into your workplace by dropping the false view that independents aren't part of your team? They are! Remember Clifton's wisdom—"Why do people stay?"—and give independents the intangible benefit of finding friends and networks within your enterprise.

FINDING WORK

The ability to find work and progress in that work tends to be dependent on word of mouth—what others who are familiar with you say and think about you. In MBO's original research from our State of Independence in America report, we note that, for independents, finding work has always been about leveraging the power of peers, communities, and connections. But the shape of those communities and the places where that communication takes place have evolved swiftly. What's changed is the form word of mouth takes, the forums in which it takes place, and the folks who provide the relevant information.

In a nutshell, there has been a huge shift away from former employers influencing the ability to work in favor of digital platforms. That makes sense, given the way that we communicate. But there's something deeper at work. For individuals around the world, the community in which they operate is less centered on where they might have worked and the people they encountered in the office. Today, with so much "finding work" business, commerce, and communication taking place online, new communities are instead forming around these powerful platforms and networks.

In 2015, 81% of independents surveyed said they found work through word of mouth. By 2022, only 51% said word of mouth was important. Independents are relying more on one another. Twenty-four percent said other independents are a source of work. But the real boom has come from online marketplaces and social media. The pandemic and the shift to remote work led to a big jump in independents using both online talent and commerce marketplaces. Online talent marketplaces have increasingly become a key sales channel for independent workers who sell services to businesses. In

2012, only 3% of independents used an online talent platform to find work during the course of a year. By 2022, 41% did so—that's an amazing stat.

Using social media to find work or customers has also substantially increased. In 2022, 36% of independents found work on social media, up from 17% in 2015. This doubling speaks to the rise of social selling and the growth of the creator economy, both of which rely on social media to find customers. Three-quarters of independents also said social media is very important (34%) or somewhat important (41%) for building a reputation. More broadly, given the fact that people relate to, refer to, celebrate, and acknowledge one another on TikTok, Instagram, Twitter, and LinkedIn, social media *is* word of mouth now—and this trend will only continue to escalate with each passing year.

REX

Empirical research of "forty previous studies and a meta-analysis of 65,826 entrepreneurs observed through that research" has led business scholars to conclude that emotional intelligence (EQ) benefits entrepreneurs even more than IQ. "Within the domain of entrepreneurship, emotional intelligence was the stronger predictor of success."[7] That's because "EQ is linked to social skills such as accurately perceiving other's needs, making good first impressions, and influencing others in interpersonal interactions. These skills are important for developing business networks, which can aid in signaling legitimacy and in acquiring resources."[8]

In layman's terms, EQ helps you build relationships, and those relationships help you build your business. Independents are on the front line of living out this principle because there's nowhere to hide as solopreneurs. Independents can't just be good within their skill set but a lemon when it comes to building relationships and connecting with others.

You know who was awful at building relationships? *Tyrannosaurus rex.* Well, actually, that's a matter of hot debate among paleontologists. They're not sure whether this alpha predator (whose name means "king of the tyrant lizards") lived alone or as part of a pack. Were T-Rexes social creatures or solitary? Did they need the help of others to eat, or did they just eat all others? Or both?

T-Rex is a metaphor for independents and also full-time employees who work remotely. Are they sociable or solitary? Loners, team players, or a combination of both?

I heard from an IT worker named Rex (yes, that's his name) whose story illustrates the concepts of this chapter even though he's *not* an independent—though based on his remote work setup, he just as easily could be. So if you're a business leader reading this chapter, much of what I'm saying here can also be applied to your remote work employees.

In his early forties, Rex shifted his career by going into IT. He learned to code and completed a one-year internship with a local company, but then failed to receive a permanent job offer from the company. They preferred to churn through low-paid "interns" as part of its workforce strategy. He was discouraged but not defeated.

A few days later, as his mom scrolled through Facebook, she saw a post created by Josh, a friend of the family and a high school friend of her son, whom she had kept up with over the previous 20 years. Josh now lived three states away from Rex and was leading the IT department for a natural-gas distribution company. He wrote on Facebook how he was looking for an IT worker for a remote position. This hire would join his existing IT team, which was distributed throughout the world.

Rex connected with Josh and turned in his resume. Though their personal connection weighed in much heavier than formal credentialing, Rex possessed the skills and ambition needed for the work. He got the job and now works out of his own home, earning many times more than he would have through the local company that wasn't hiring.

Rex works from home and sets his own hours—keeping in mind the need to connect with colleagues who live on the other side of the globe. He takes a few trips a year to connect with the larger team and to perform IT work related to physical hardware components. To be clear, Rex earns his living as a W-2 employee, *not* as an independent. But at some point, we're just talking semantics, right?

Ever since COVID-19 and the rapid escalation of remote work

acceptance, the stories we're hearing have narratives that blur the old hard-and-fixed lines between employees and independents. Now, when you listen to someone talk about their work, you often have to stop and ask them if they're an independent or an employee, because there's nothing inherent in their story about their work that gives away their status.

Returning to the themes of this chapter, Rex wouldn't have even known of this job without social media. He wouldn't have applied if the job had required relocating to Colorado, and he may not have gotten it apart from the friendship factor with Josh, which added in a layer of organic trust and respect. Further, he wouldn't be as successful in the work without the teamwork of global colleagues, as they talk frequently throughout the day on phone and video calls—as well as email and texting.

So, in thinking about Rex at work—is he social or solitary? Yes, both. He's in tight communication and collegiality with a team of professionals, *and* he works from the quietness of his own home—plugging away at the actual work instead of being caught in commuting traffic or office politics. Rex is the king of his daily schedule—hear him roar.

I AM *NOT* A ROCK. I AM *NOT* AN ISLAND.

As a businessman, I've had it ingrained into me that being a leader requires having a brave face, even in difficult times. But I have learned throughout the years that honesty is another vital part of being successful. This means I must embrace vulnerability because it's a huge part of honesty—of telling the truth. As Marcus Aurelius once said: "Don't be ashamed to need help. Like a soldier storming a wall, you have a mission to accomplish. And if you've been wounded and you need a comrade to pull you up? So what?"

Brené Brown, author of the bestselling book *Daring Greatly*, has significantly impacted my thinking here. "Vulnerability is not winning or losing," Brown writes. "It's having the courage to show up and be seen when we have no control over the outcome. Vulnerability is not weakness; it's our greatest measure of courage."[9]

What? Vulnerability is a measure of courage? That idea runs contrary to prevailing notions of courage and strength. But Brown is right.

No one likes feeling vulnerable. Many of us associate the feeling with being weak or helpless. Feeling exposed or uncertain places an extreme amount of emotional pressure on oneself, causing us to make rash decisions that may get us out of the spotlight or camouflage our vulnerabilities—decisions that don't help us in the long run.

Again, please hear me carefully. I'm not saying independents are unique in this regard. Full-time employees also need connection and can find inner strength through embracing vulnerability. People are people. But I am saying that independents must prioritize this more intentionally and proactively, lest they take on a Simon & Garfunkel vibe. The independent mind knows it needs "help from my friends," refusing to equate independence with being a rock or an island.

This is one reason why networking is so important—you're going to need help and support that goes beyond the merely financial. Independents know that staying connected can help accomplish long-term goals. For example, lots of people knew that I was going to climb Kilimanjaro. During the yearlong training season, I told friends about my plans to scale the famous mountain. If I had failed to summit, I would have had to come back and tell people that I didn't make it to the top. Sharing your goals with people motivates you to complete them. But again—this takes a willingness to be vulnerable and open, because both strengths and weaknesses are revealed within such relationships.

Practically speaking, here's how I cultivate my network. Because I get energy out of relationships, every day I reach out to five people directly that I wouldn't have to for the business of the day. It sounds simple and small, but five a day and 35 a week really adds up over the years. That's how you build a massively extensive network of people who can count on you and that you can count on. It's a huge discipline, though, to say, "Okay, did I get to the five today?" And I'm not talking about contacting somebody because you're negotiating a deal. I'm talking about reaching out when you have no reason to do so for that day, except for the personal connection. Remember: Aim for the relation, not just transaction. That's the key.

WHAT WE CAN'T HAVE IS FAILURE TO COMMUNICATE

Google "misheard song lyrics" and you'll get a kick out of all the misunderstood lines from popular tunes. Music lovers today just look up lyrics online, but if in "the old days" you didn't buy a physical copy of the music and get the liner notes, you were often left guessing. People heard Mick Jagger singing, "I'll never leave your pizza burning," instead of "I'll never be your beast of burden." When Bon Jovi is "Livin' on a Prayer" and belts out, "It doesn't make a difference if we make it or not," many people thought he said, "It doesn't make a difference if we're *naked* or not." And nobody likely knows most of Pearl Jam's lyrics, given how Eddie Vedder's distinct voice combines with his incomprehensible and ever-changing lyrics to confuse even the most die-hard fans.[10]

It's all fun and games with misunderstood lyrics, but in the real world of business, communication snafus create inefficiencies and havoc. And if this is true when dealing with internal communications between employers and employees, how much more so when communicating with independents.

"Communication is the number one factor that drives satisfaction among independents," writes Gene Zaino, my friend and the founder of MBO Partners. "Defined project goals and objectives, timely feedback, and a clear project scope are must-haves for each high-value project they choose to attach their reputation to."[11]

So, for readers who are leaders, here are five ways your enterprise might be fumbling how it communicates with independents.[12]

First, a *lack of clarity*. Since freelancers and independent contractors work remotely, they often don't have daily face-to-face interactions with their clients the way employees would have with their managers. This can lead to miscommunications and misunderstandings, particularly if there is no clear communication plan. Of course, the problem of "unclear tasks" is often present even with employees—especially with employees who now do their work remotely. Because this is a problem for everyone, it makes sense to work hard to fix it for everyone—including independents.

Second, people have *different communication styles*. These differences can be magnified when working with an independent, external workforce. For example, some freelancers prefer to communicate primarily via email, while others prefer phone calls or video chats. Establishing communication preferences and expectations early in the working relationship is important.

I suppose it's at this point in the discussion that I'm supposed to go into great detail talking about various technologies and strategies: Zoom, Slack, synchronous vs. asynchronous, etc. But I'm going to skip that because since the pandemic hit, a dozen books and hundreds of articles have laid all that out. Plus, the tech changes each year, and the "everybody is doing it" strategy goes stale fast. So don't lay down draconian policies or think that some SaaS will work for everyone and for all time because it won't—just like your workforce has a variety of opinions on cubicles, open office layouts, and remote work.

What I *do* recommend is for you to communicate early and often with your independents about communication. Talk to independents about the *how*, the *when*, and the *how much* they desire to talk to you and your team. And tell them clearly your own desires too.

What's interesting, though, is that full-time employees may have individualized preferences as well—but since they are employees, management might pull the "I'm the boss" card and force communication in a way that management alone prefers. Perhaps the surge of growth in the external workforce will cause business leaders to consider and value different communication styles throughout their entire workforce. After all, if you value independents enough to be flexible in your communication style, then why not show the same flexibility for your full-time employees?

Third, *limited access to information.* This hearkens back to the "knowledge stocks vs. knowledge flows" discussion earlier. Independent workers may not have access to the same information and resources as in-house employees. This can make it difficult for them to stay updated on company news and changes, leading to misunderstandings and miscommunications.

Enterprises should embrace full transparency by making information as accessible as possible. While this might challenge the status quo of maintaining opacity in many areas, it's essential to explain how the strategies drive change, their impact on workflows, and expected outcomes. You must ensure clarity of expectations and easily understandable reasons behind them. Train your managers in effective "knowledge flow" communication practices, encouraging them to find new and efficient ways of doing business while incentivizing innovation.

Speaking of good communication and knowledge flow, if you go to the headquarters of a large enterprise today, the person on the one side of the building who's using independent talent most likely doesn't share the fact that they have that tremendous independent talent with the person on the other side. They literally can sit down the hall from one another but not know or share this invaluable intel about available talent.

Fourth, *cultural and language barriers*. When utilizing independent workers from different cultures or who speak other languages, there may be additional challenges in communication. For example, idiomatic expressions or slang may not translate well, or there may be communication norms and etiquette differences. This factor will continue to grow in importance as enterprises utilize more and more independents from the global workforce.

I've always been able to find how to make that connection. I certainly had lessons over the years regarding how you create that connectivity and what you learn from it. I learned there are some countries where when you sign a contract, you're done negotiating. In other countries, however, once you've signed a contract, that's when the negotiation begins. And if you don't understand that, you'll be at a disadvantage, frankly, in the whole negotiation.

The firm that I used to work at had a book with facts on hundreds of countries—a "How to do business in _____" guide—so we'd understand cultural norms and what to expect. By the way, it doesn't mean that one norm is good and one norm is bad. What it does mean is that they're different. Understanding and celebrating the differences in how business gets conducted, how people think, and what's normal for them is really important. Taking the time to learn and appreciate where other people may be coming from is an essential skill for building a business or leading teams.

Fifth, a *lack of feedback*. Independent workers may not receive regular feedback from their clients or employers, making it difficult to know whether they are meeting expectations. Every situation and company is different, but establishing a feedback system that allows for open and honest communication is important.

FREE AS A BIRD

The Beatles released "With a Little Help from My Friends" in June 1967 as part of their *Sgt. Pepper's Lonely Hearts Club Band* album. Then, in April 1970—just over 1,000 days later—Paul McCartney announced the band's breakup after 10 years together.

Rock historians and fans have written endlessly to analyze why the Beatles split, but the withering of the friendships certainly played a part. What had held them together became weaker than the forces that pulled them apart. Perhaps they would have gotten back together as many rock groups do after a lengthy separation. But with the murder of John Lennon in 1980, Beatles fans had their hopes crushed.

And yet, in 1994, the three surviving members received from Lennon's widow, Yoko Ono, some homemade demo audio tracks of unfinished songs by the late singer. With a certain sense of fear and trepidation, Paul, George Harrison, and Ringo Starr returned to the studio together and worked with the audio from their late band member . . . and friend. And that's how it came to be that in 1995—25 years after their breakup—the Beatles released two new songs with contributions from all four original members.[13] The first song, "Free as a Bird," launched on December 5, 1995.

On that same day, the Chicago Bulls owned the best record in the NBA, shooting out of the gates of the new season with a 13-2 record. It had just been months since Jordan gave Kerr the black eye, but that was all behind them now.

"Free as a Bird" hit the Top 10 charts in America and went on to win a Grammy Award for the Beatles. And the Bulls went on to win the NBA Championship for the next three seasons.

From rock stars to basketball stars, from entrepreneurs to

enterprises—and everyone in between, "With a Little Help from My Friends" is more than a song—it's a mindset we all should embrace.

And from my experience, it's a vital part of the independent mind.

EVERSON'S ACTION POINT: FOR EVERYONE

For everyone: Start with the Golden Rule because independents are, after all, people. Showing basic manners and gratitude will never go out of style and, I believe, can cut across generational and cultural divides.

For enterprises: Invite (but don't require) independents into social events and opportunities for networking within your company. If a team of employees is heading to a convention or conference, offer to reimburse the costs for independents—especially if they're working with your company on large or long-term projects. Are they needed at these events? Probably not, but don't look at it this way. Consider their participation to be part of building up the three Cs we talked about in this chapter.

For independents: (1) Schedule regular check-in calls and emails to update on project progress and ensure alignment. (2) Especially for meetings with three or fewer people, use video calls instead of just audio calls or email. (3) Seek and give feedback. (4) Remember the details of your client's communication preference and use it. (5) Stay organized because "falling through the cracks" creates relational tension. (6) Be transparent and honest always, but even more so when there are changes to the scope or timeline of the project.

MARGARITAVILLE
(IT'S FIVE O'CLOCK SOMEWHERE)

A Flexible When and Where of Work

> To all the companies calling people back to the office full-time:
> Don't mistake presence for performance. Showing up is not a
> sign of commitment or contribution. It's an act of compliance.
> What matters is the value people create, not the place they
> inhabit.
>
> —Adam Grant[1]

A hot day, a margarita, and a beautiful woman: Could *you* earn a billion dollars from those three items?

Jimmy Buffett wrote most of "Margaritaville" in one sitting, inspired by its namesake cocktail from a bar and grill once located just up the road from where I live. "It was written in five minutes about a hot day in Austin, Texas," he explained years later, "with a margarita and a beautiful woman."

Buffett, who died during the writing of this book, had neither fame nor fortune as a musician when he wrote the song, but it changed the course of his life. Released in February 1977, the song reached #8 on Billboard's US Hot 100 and #1 on its Adult Contemporary list.

He then capitalized on the popularity of the music's laid-back lifestyle ethic by licensing restaurants, resorts, jewelry, beverages, and even retirement communities under his "Margaritaville Holdings" brand. In a recent year, the business earned $1.5 billion, earning Buffett a top-20 ranking on the *Forbes* list of wealthiest celebrities. "Other musicians rank higher (Sean Combs, Jay-Z, and Dr. Dre)," the *Austin Chronicle* wrote, "but none with success stories built upon a single song."[2]

Twenty-five years later, country music star Alan Jackson released "It's Five O'Clock Somewhere"—a duet *with* Buffett for a song that paid homage to Jimmy. The lighthearted lyrics speak of wishing it was already 5 PM—the end to the traditional 9 to 5 work schedule—so the narrator can start drinking. But then it dawns on him that it's already "five o'clock" in other time zones, so there's no need to get hung up on artificially imposed schedules. Bring on the booze.

◆ ◆ ◆

If you Google for images of "remote work," you'll probably see a picture of a person wearing shorts and a T-shirt while sitting next to a scenic body of water with a laptop perched on their legs. Likewise, read any article on "digital nomads" and you'll see a stock photo cliché: a laptopper lounging in a seaside hammock or doing beach yoga while Zooming with a client.

That's what I call the "Margaritaville myth" of remote work—that everyone wants to get out of the office so they can sit oceanside with nothing but Caribbean music and their computer. And yet, if working within sight of the waves, mountains, or even (call me crazy) the comfort of your own home is your jam, then the location flexibility of being an independent worker is for you. And the twin benefit of having a flexible *location* for work is that you also have greater flexibility of *schedule* (the "It's Five O'Clock Somewhere" perk of being independent).

So go ahead, put on your flip-flops and cue up some Jimmy Buffett because the *where* and *when* of work has changed forever. In fact, "one in three remote employees admit they've worked from their car or bed," a recent poll found.[3] What's stopping you? A boss? A job that demands (for good reason or no reason at all) that your body be located in a certain space and time?

Independents know that much of the knowledge work of the digital revolution era can be done remotely and should not be forced into a specific time and location. They want to work *where* it's most efficient and *when* they do their best work. As Adam Grant wrote: "The world is unfair to night owls. School: they're bright as larks, yet get poorer grades—except in afternoon and evening classes. Work: if they start later but deliver identical hours & results, they're still penalized. We should let people engage when they're most alert."[4]

The tech that makes remote work possible has long been in place, but the pandemic accelerated the social acceptance of remote work. Independents prefer to work in flexible locations and schedules, knowing they can maintain a focus on the success of their clients' projects no matter where their body is located.

The US and global workforce simply will *not* be forced into a company office as often as people were before the pandemic, because very talented people choose to work remotely and employers' companies want access to the best talent. Even burgeoning trends like digital nomads—of which the United States has 15.5 million—has become a lifestyle choice for many people. While you can be a remote worker as a full-time employee *or* as an independent, there is a correlation between the acceptance of remote work and those who have the best talent.[5]

* * *

At this point, I should explain why I'll be talking about remote work so much, even though working remotely isn't synonymous with being an independent. Not all remote workers are independents, even though pretty much all independents work remotely in some fashion or other. But here's

the connection: If an enterprise can't get behind and support remote working options for employees, they'll often resist it for independents. Unless
they want chaotic inconsistency, an enterprise can't cut out remote work for
employees without also cutting it out for independents.

Having flexibility in the "where and when" of work has become one of
the highest motivations that people report when asked why they became
independent. That being the case, if an *employee* gets attached to working
remotely, it's a natural progression for them to eventually become independent. Therefore, your remotely working employee may eventually realize they only have one shoe. They've got the flexibility of location but not
of schedule. Innovative enterprises create policies to institutionalize and
support this fact. They will, in fact, make it work well for people to work
remotely.

AUSTIN CITY LIMITS

Austin is a fantastic city to live in, with lots of culture, art, beauty, heat,
and humidity (okay, so those last two aren't so great). I chose to move to
the Lone Star State in 2013 for many reasons, including its lack of an income tax. And over the past decade, tens of thousands have relocated to
Austin too—many from California.[6] *USA Today* reported that in 2021, the
California-to-Texas pipeline was "the most popular interstate move in the
country, with 111,000 people—or 300 people a day—making the change."[7]

In 2021, Elon Musk relocated Tesla's headquarters from Palo Alto,
California, to Austin and began building a vast factory, which has now
become our city's largest employer. In moving the company, Musk mentioned the cheaper cost of living, fewer taxes and regulations, and shorter
commute times for the workforce.[8] And from everything I hear, people like
working at "Gigafactory Texas" and feel fortunate to have the high-paying
jobs.

I bring up Musk—one of the world's wealthiest individuals and certainly
one of the most fascinating entrepreneur-inventors in my lifetime—because

in 2023, he gave one of the most heated opinions ever stated about remote work:

> It's like, really, you're going to work from home and you're going to make everyone else who made your car come work in the factory? You're going to make the people who make your food that gets delivered—that they can't work from home? You know, the people that fix your home—they can't work from home, but you can? Does that seem morally right? That's messed up.[9]

Musk also said that "the laptop class is living in la-la land" referring to Silicon Valley engineers—but also applying to all knowledge workers. His solution? Remote workers need to "get off the goddamn moral high horse with the work-from-home bullshit because they're asking everyone else to not work from home while they do."[10]

Musk's views on remote work are deeply personal and reflect his values and vision for his own relationship with work. He's driven by the conviction that his company's products will advance and maybe even preserve humanity. Therefore, he believes that personal sacrifices must be made to achieve such accomplishments.

"How detached from reality does the work-from-home crowd have to be? While they take advantage of those who cannot work from home," Musk said. "Why did I sleep in the factory so many times? Because it mattered."

Call him an obsessive workaholic if you want, but we live in a free country, and because he's the founder and CEO of these various companies, his preferences win out—for *his* companies and within the rule of law. And as hard driving as he is with his workforce and even with the labor shortages in the United States, Musk doesn't seem to lack for people who line up to work for his companies.

This may surprise you, but I actually agree with Musk's "no remote work" policy for Tesla and SpaceX, and here's why: Tesla builds cars and SpaceX builds rockets. In the "move bytes not atoms" thinking, building cars and rockets means designing and moving a lot of atoms—and that level of physicality mandates in-person work.

Tim Cook, the CEO of Apple, said something similar in November 2022 when defending the company's mandate for employees returning to the office: "We make product, and you have to hold product. You collaborate with one another because we believe that one plus one equals three." Physical product: atoms, engineering, design, materials. This makes sense for many of the employees. But what about the accountants, lawyers, copywriters, and other knowledge workers at Apple? Why do they need to come into an office? Why do they need to live in or live near some of the most expensive zip codes in America? They don't—and many of them won't—if the RTO mandates stick.

The point is that when it comes to remote work, both sides (labor and business) get to choose what works best for them. You can be an engineer *and* work remotely *and* independently—you just can't do it for Elon Musk. Likewise, if you're the CEO who shuts down remote work or ignores independents, you'd better make sure you know what your business plan is for innovation, diversity of thought, cost reduction, agility, and a whole host of factors that can sink your ship.

Besides all that, Musk actually is a remote worker himself—albeit a serially remote worker. Musk may sleep at the factory of one company during a sprint of effort to hit deadlines, but he's still running (i.e., working for) the other companies . . . wait for it . . . at the same *time . . . remotely.*

That's called having flexibility in your work schedule and location—the *when* and *where* of work.

All that said, I don't want to overstate the case to make it seem that independents only work remotely. In other words, the physical location does not dictate the form of relationship between the worker and the enterprise. Though the growing acceptance of remote work has accelerated the adoption of independent work, there are still plenty of independents who work on-site every day. So the larger point is that too many people see it as binary: you either work remotely or you don't. In reality, Musk himself proves that it's the balance of remote and on-site that is often the right answer.

THE PANDEMIC

The pandemic accelerated change in a way that most organizations hadn't planned for. Typically, the impediment to any change is the status quo, but that's been changed for everybody in America. And so, it's an opportune time to reset the table.[11] As economist and Stanford professor Nicholas Bloom put it, "The pandemic is the largest change to hit the labor market since World War II. It turns out we've opened Pandora's box, and what's in Pandora's box is pretty good. It's a new way of working and living."[12]

Coming out of the pandemic, Apple and Musk's companies weren't alone in pressuring workers to return to the office. Alphabet (Google), Meta (Facebook), IBM, Yahoo, Best Buy, Lyft, and Salesforce—to name just a few—all talked big at first about the freedom its workforce would have to work remotely. In 2020, Mark Zuckerberg said, "I'd much rather have us teleport by using virtual reality or video chat than sit in traffic."[13]

But by mid-2022 and 2023, these tech companies began to reverse course, mandating employees back to the office—at least in a hybrid manner of two to three days per week.[14] Even Zoom is pulling employees back into the office—ironic given that the video conferencing company became a verb ("let's Zoom") during the pandemic's rush to remote.[15] I mention that they're all in the technology sector because, ostensibly, it's easiest to work remotely in tech, finance, and other knowledge work. Even so, many are trying to pull their people back into a specific time and place.

By contrast, others have codified a "work from anywhere" hiring policy that was underway even before the pandemic. Quinn Emanuel, one of the largest law firms in the United States, announced it will recruit and hire "new associates who live in places where the firm does not have an office." Founder John Quinn said, "Our lawyers should work from wherever they do their best work. We want to invite the best litigators to join our firm, wherever their desks are. Over the past 18 months, our lawyers have mastered the art of collaborating remotely and at the highest levels—without sacrificing camaraderie or the free sharing of ideas."[16]

Whether corporate America supports remote work or not, the pandemic accelerated and permanently surged forward the total number of employees in the United States who work remotely in some fashion (fully remote or hybrid). A study by Stanford's Bloom says the acceleration of work from home is the "equivalent to almost forty years of pre-pandemic growth." His study shows that the work-from-home share increased from 0.4% to 4.7% in 55 years (1965–2020), then spiked to 61.5% during the lockdown. By 2023, the number settled down to about 30%, or roughly five times higher than pre-pandemic.[17]

I believe there is, and will continue to be, a direct correlation between the accelerated number of remote employees and the increasing number of people who will become independent. Here's why.

Once an employee has enjoyed the perks of remote work and learned how to deal with the challenges, most do not want to give it away and return to the office along the old lines. Many will simply find a new job or become independent if mandated to return full-time to the office. In March 2023, *Harper's* reported that 45% of US workers were "willing to take a pay cut in exchange for the option to work from home."[18] Bloom's study found that "having the option of working from home two days a week is as valuable as an 8 percent pay increase."

In 2022, Gallup published survey stats showing that hybrid or fully remote is the only path forward because only 6% of employees "want to work entirely on-site going forward." Gallup drives the point home: "Doesn't it seem that traditional management and workplace practices are broken if more than 90% of 70 million employees say they don't want to come back to the office full time?" I would answer: Yes! And the solution is twofold: support remote work for *employees* and increase the utilization of independents.

The "work from anywhere" trend is here to stay, and employers must take note that the power is in the hands of the worker, not the employer or client. When it comes to protecting their right to work remotely, US employees embody a phrase we Texans have been using since we first won our independence: "Come and take it."

LET'S GET REAL ABOUT REAL ESTATE

The explosive trend of remote work for employees has disastrously affected corporate real estate. Companies have broken their leases on existing office space. Others continue to occupy their holdings but with only half the people using the facilities. "The value of New York's office buildings could fall nearly $50 billion in the coming years," reported the *New York Times*.[19]

Data from mid-2023 revealed a total of "one billion square feet of empty office space" in America.[20] Salesforce CEO Marc Benioff said that San Francisco's downtown is "never going back to the way it was."[21] The *Washington Post* reported that the "commercial real estate apocalypse threatens the economy and midsize cities," noting that "midsize cities have some of the highest office delinquency rates."[22]

In January 2024, an episode of *60 Minutes* highlighted the crisis of empty urban office space.[23] Journalist Jon Wertheim interviewed Marc Holliday, the CEO of SL Green—"New York's biggest landlord." Wertheim asked: "Do you accept that work from home is this fundamental shift in how we work—and that it's here to stay?"

"It's one of the biggest societal problems we're facing right now, is work from home," Holliday answered. "I think that it's bad for—business. It's bad for cities. It's bad for people."

Give him credit for not beating around the bush or being coy. But oh boy—work from home is "bad for people." Give me a break.

Wertheim then narrated to the viewers that work from home had "also been bad for his [Holliday's] stock price, down 50% since the pandemic."

Touché. In my way of thinking, when someone in Holliday's position offers his opinion on independent or remote work, they should always provide a disclaimer showing their personal financial stake in having people get their butts back into the office buildings they manage. I'm glad *60 Minutes* showed integrity by making that connection, especially since Holliday's firm is their landlord!

And it's not just the office space that suddenly had more supply than demand. The residential real estate market took a hit, too—or got hot, depending on where you live—as remote-work-capable employees left behind the city's density. "In the first two years of the pandemic, one in four workers who moved long-distance was working remotely in a new home—a previously unheard-of scale of remote migration," the *New York Times* reported. "In the two years leading up to the pandemic, for example, about 20,000 remote workers moved away from the San Francisco metro area. Then, during 2020 and 2021, 110,000 did . . . [In the two years before the pandemic], about 40,000 remote workers moved away from metro New York. Then, 200,000 left in two years."[24]

And where did they all move to? Many headed to the suburbs, opting for larger homes that could better accommodate their newly needed home offices. They also gained the destressing benefit of having some grass to cut or a few trees to sit under while doing yoga.

Other workers migrated to the fly-over portions in the middle of the United States, zip codes far from the offices they formerly inhabited forty to sixty hours a week. This could, of course, lead to a natural spreading out of the population and the revitalization of counties that had been in demographic decline. "Some attractive smaller cities will see populations rise," Cal Newport suggests, "some larger cities will see housing costs decrease."[25] Because independents work remotely from their clients, they can live where they want to—which means they can choose to live where affordable housing exists.

For some people, remote work allowed them to move back to the small towns of their youth or be closer to aging parents. Though the limited job offerings of such locations could not hold them to that area when they first entered the workforce decades earlier, remote work and the digital economy has altered that paradigm forever. They get to keep their "NYC job" while living in towns where the livestock population dramatically outnumbers the human population. As Joseph Hearne, an independent entrepreneur living in the rural heartland, wrote on LinkedIn: "Graphic design was promoted as the career where you live in the big city and wear an expensive wide-brimmed fedora. Meanwhile, I'm over here in between projects, wearing Duluth Trading Company overalls, getting an auger and lumber for my chicken coop build, and thinking through whether or not I want dairy goats. I'm an off-brand branding guy."[26]

Some futurists even predict the creation of "remotevilles," brand-new cities built on the edge of major cities, "offering new housing at a lower price while still having access to the amenities of traditional urban hubs."[27]

Indeed, the rules of what Cal Newport calls "car-based work culture" are changing.[28] Even the definition of the words "suburb" and "commute" may expand to include living several hours out from a city. Why? Because if you only go into an office one day a week or one day a month—either as an employee or an independent—then it matters little how long your "commute" takes. *Business Insider* reported that "super commuting is on the rise, thanks to the flexibility of hybrid work," noting a tech executive who lives in Des Moines, Iowa, but works for a "fast-growing private technology company" in San Francisco, California—commuting cross-country one or two times a month.[29]

If something as extreme as "super commuting" can be a reality for employees and executives of companies, how much more is it already true for independents? Or enterprises should go one better: dump the office altogether if you can.

BIG BLUE

In 2017, IBM announced it was reversing its policy on remote work by commanding several thousand of its employees to get back into the office. This move came after being a worldwide pioneer in "telework" (as it was originally called) for forty years! Big Blue's announcement bombshelled the affected workers—for good reason! As one analyst said about IBM's remote work mandate: "If what they're looking to do is reduce productivity, lose talent, and increase cost, maybe they're on to something."[30]

True! Or, stated positively: allowing remote work by employees and using more independents will enhance an enterprise's productivity, help retain talent, and improve the bottom line.

And on that note, it's time to talk about money.

EVERSON'S ACTION POINT: FOR ENTERPRISES

If your enterprise needs *one* more reason to embrace remote work, then let me give you *three*:

1. Do it for the **disabled**. The Hustle reports that the "mainstream adoption of remote work has led record numbers of people with disabilities to join the workforce."[31] Remote work eliminates the inefficiencies of commuting, the reality of offices not being fully optimized for disabled employees, and the hiring biases against the disabled.[32] In the war for talent, tweaking your perspective on remote work could open your business more fully to the 42 million Americans with disabilities—some who desire full-time employment and others who work independently.

2. Do it for the **environment**. "Fully remote workers could produce less than half the climate-warming emissions of people who spend their days in offices," reports the *Washington Post*.[33] And even if offices are half empty, does the energy usage decrease by half because offices don't have to use as much energy on lighting, IT, and climate control systems throughout their building?[34] Could be yes or no, depending on how smart the energy is managed. But there's a strong chance that using more remote workers and independents will save energy and energy expenses for your buildings.

3. Do it for the **children**. Literally. The *Atlantic*'s Derek Thompson reported in 2023 on a study by an economist and a demographer who conceived a theory about remote work and baby making: "Working from home could be making it easier for couples to become parents—and for parents to have more children."[35] Bring on the babies!

HAS LIFE BEEN GOOD TO ME?

Independents, Enterprises, Society, and Money

Show me the money.

—Rod Tidwell and Jerry Maguire

When guitar legend Joe Walsh released the song "Life's Been Good" on May 16, 1978—a satire about the hedonistic excesses of being a rich and famous rock star—he was only 30 and still had another two decades of decadence to go before he changed course. *Rolling Stone* called the song "(maybe) the most important statement on rock stardom anyone has made in the late Seventies."[1]

Though the lyrics sound fictional, Walsh explained that some of the song's claims were, in fact, autobiographical. For example, when his agent bought him a chain saw for his birthday, Walsh took it on tour and used it one night at a Holiday Inn to rip into a wall and create his own connecting room with a friend. But Walsh wasn't even sure he liked the lyrics while drafting the song: "I was thinking, 'Well, they're kind of dumb, and the song will either be looked at as a satirical, funny song or it's gonna not be funny at all and it'll go down the toilet as one of the worst things ever written.'"

Adding satire to satire, Walsh even ran for US president in 1980, campaigning on a pledge to change the national anthem to "Life's Been Good."[2] Five decades after its release, classic rock stations play the song every day. Indeed, life has been good for Joe Walsh.

But as you listen to the lyrics, you soon realize that everyone is in on the song's joke—the musician and the fans alike. Rock stars quickly get world-weary and jaded by the dissatisfying nature of crazed materialism, longing to be "normal" once again. Everyone is a fan, but a true friend is nowhere to be found. Meanwhile, it's the Average Joes who fund the famous Joe's lifestyle with every album and concert ticket purchase, all the while wishing they could live *his* "good life" instead of their own.

But be careful what you wish for. The "Life's Been Good" lifestyle was unstainable even for the Joe Walshes of the world. "I started believing I was who everybody thought I was, which was a crazy rock star. It took me away from my craft," Walsh said years later. "Me and a lot of the guys I ran with, we were party monsters. It was a real challenge just to stay alive."[3]

◆ ◆ ◆

This is the chapter where we talk about money—the "show me the money" material that backs up the bottom-line economic impact independents have on enterprises and how independents are happy with their earnings.

First, from data compiled by MBO, we'll see that independents earn more than they did as full-time employees. It's true that the intangible quality-of-life factors seem to be the primary magnet pulling people into the independent life, but that's not to say the increased pay didn't sway them also. Independents don't sit around wishing they were living the life of a full-time employee.

Second, we'll examine the financial boost for enterprises that utilize independents. It's great that independents earn more pay, but if their contributions don't benefit their clients, then companies would be right to stick mostly with full-time employees. Since it's all about the basis points, there's no trouble there, because independents *do* impact the financials of a company—as we will see.

Finally, I'll answer "the Joe Walsh" question: Is the Free Birds revolution sustainable, and does society benefit from the surging growth of the independent workforce? Do independents create value, or are they like the rock star who can tear up hotel rooms thoughtlessly because everyone else buys his albums? Do first-generation entrepreneurs-turned-billionaires lose touch with reality and lose their relationships for the sake of giving the planet "1,000 songs in your pocket"?[4] Taken as a whole, is the independent workforce a net positive—a giver to society rather than a taker?

INDEPENDENTS EARN MORE

Independent work has its challenges—don't let anyone tell you otherwise. From the MBO research, the challenge cited most frequently is not enough predictable income. In 2023, nearly half of independents (49%) noted such a challenge, up notably from 43% in 2022. In a related finding, the next most cited challenge is worrying about their next job or project pipeline (33%). And in 2023, 29% said that lack of job security was a challenge, up from 25% in 2022. In a sign that inflation, especially in health care, is front and center, 28% of independents cited concern about benefits as a challenge, up from 24% in 2022. So working independently does not remove all economic stress from a person's life.

That said, independents still declare they are better off financially than they were as full-time employees. In 2023, 53% of full-time independents reported that they earned more working on their own than they could at traditional jobs. One of the signal findings of MBO's State of Independence has been a marked increase in independents' professional confidence and security over the years. In 2011, only 32% of independents said they felt more secure working independently. But in 2023, fully 66% answered in the affirmative. And to clarify, "more secure" is in comparison to when they worked as full-time employees.

That's why I often say that if you give your best in whatever you do, you will likely become independent because you will eventually want to trade yourself at your own competitive price. Going independent solves the problem of employees who believe they are insufficiently compensated for their work.

As noted earlier, by the end of 2023, 72 million Americans have chosen the independent route—full-time, part-time, or occasional independents—even as the nation registered a record-breaking 156 million payroll jobs. And one of the fastest-growing segments of independents over the life of MBO's research has been independents who report earning $100,000 or more in the prior year. After declining in 2020 due to the pandemic, the number of $100K+ independents increased by 53% from 2021 to 2023. What factors drive the growth and financial prosperity of the independent workforce in general—and the $100K earners in particular?

First, it's a gold rush. Independent workers are the hot ticket in today's labor market. Labor shortages mean companies are innovating faster than ever. Hiring platforms and advanced collaboration technologies make it less complicated for businesses to identify, employ, and coordinate with independent workers.

This tech-driven approach provides a timely answer to the pressing challenge of filling specialized roles, especially in high-demand sectors such as technology. In fact, according to MBO's August 2022 Contingent Labor Imperative study, which surveyed HR leaders from 600 organizations, the average company reveals that contingent labor now comprises 28% of their workforce. This percentage is forecasted to jump to 38% by 2027.

Second, the supply of independent workers is growing as more people are drawn to the flexibility and autonomy of being independent. The allure of "being your own boss" is compelling, and this sentiment is even stronger among independents when compared to traditional employees. In 2023, 80% of independent workers expressed a lifelong desire for this autonomy, compared to 61% of traditional workers. And 71% of independents dislike reporting to a superior, a sentiment only 49% of their traditional counterparts shared.

Third, tech has got their back. Repeat this axiom as your mantra: "Technology unlocks capacity"—because the tech ecosystem is both a catalyst and support system for independents. Remote working capabilities and talent platforms have democratized access to work and made it lucrative. In 2023, 24% of independents said online talent marketplaces were a top three method of finding work. Forty percent of independents who provide services to businesses said they had used an online talent platform to find work in the past 12 months, and 47% said they planned to do so in the next 12 months.

Increasingly, these platforms are becoming another sales channel for many independent workers who sell services. The average person uses 3.2 platforms, and 34% of those people say it is their primary source of work. These numbers and insights indicate that the independent workforce's growth isn't just a statistical uptick. It represents a profound transformation in the workforce psyche and the broader work landscape in the twenty-first century.

SIDE-GIG ENTREPREHUSTLING

Having noted the surge of independents earning over $100K, it's important to also talk about the role of the gig economy or the side hustle because clearly, the Uber driver who took you to the airport this morning isn't earning six figures, right? The odd jobs (both digital and physical) you outsource to a stranger you hired off platforms like Fiverr, Taskrabbit, or Upwork probably don't amount to $100,000 of annual earnings for these workers. So how should we think about the side-hustling independents?

First, the overall supply of independent workers is growing partly because of the rising importance and mainstreaming of side gigs. As noted in chapter 6, the last several years have seen a huge increase in the number of what we call "occasional independents"—from about 16 million in 2020 to almost 37 million in 2023, an increase of 130% in three years. These are people who carve out a few hours a month to freelance, to take assignments from a digital work platform, or to dabble in gig work or a passion business.

In this environment, side gigs have much to offer. Amid skyrocketing housing costs and inflation, people feel a need to supplement their income.

Also, side gigs are often "passion" businesses for entrepreneurs, speaking to the person's need for fulfillment. In other instances, side gigs can be precursors as people use them to test the waters before making the leap into full-time independent work. And side gigs can function as life rafts, a safe place people can jump to in case their current job or arrangement doesn't work out.

One interesting subsegment of occasional independents would be those who have side gigs providing freelancing or consulting services *in addition* to holding down a traditional job. One in seven traditional jobholders (15%) reported having this type of side gig in 2023. This group uses the skills they've developed in their primary job to tap into the growing demand for freelancers and consulting services.

But to answer the question directly: What function do the work opportunities of the gig economy play in the overall independent workforce? I believe gig work and side hustles provide a starting ground for entrepreneurship, a "minor league" for independents to develop their business skills even as they're earning primary or secondary income. Do they want to drive people around town for the next fifty years? Maybe—and there's nothing shameful about the honest labor of providing safe transport. Or maybe not. But while they're doing this work, they're also learning time management, networking, legal filings, regulatory compliance, taxes, continuing education, marketing and communications, and customer satisfaction—to name just a few skills.

So the business-builder ethos of the gig economy should be encouraged as the seedling of entrepreneurship that it is. And what company doesn't want more entrepreneurially minded workers? That's why "Employers shouldn't discourage side hustles—or hesitate to hire people who have them," Adam Grant wrote, quoting recent academic studies. "[A]fter engaging evenings on their side gigs, people perform better the next day in their full-time jobs. Side hustles aren't a distraction. They're a source of energy and empowerment."[5]

I'm reminded of a *Zits* comic strip I saw in 2023 where the 17-year-old main character, Jeremy, talks with his friends Hector and Pierce about the crazy randomization of the gig economy. They're handed slips of paper with that day's assigned gig: Pierce got to "babysit kittens" while Jeremy "scraped bird poop out of gutters." In real life, of course, gigs show up digitally, not on scraps of paper. And I've never heard of the "luck of the draw" concept.

But here's my takeaway from the comic: the gig economy might just be the work you do when you're low skilled or young but on your way up. Just make sure that you are, in fact, on your way up by means of upskilling and continual growth. You may be scraping bird poop out of gutters today, but this time next year, you could be *installing* gutters for a local company that saw you up on that ladder doing your bird doody duty. And a year after that, you could start your own gutters-and-siding business. Five years later, you might employ your own crew and gross $1M in earnings. And to think, you got your start by downloading a gig economy app and doing low-skill manual labor. The point is: if you're side-gig entreprehustling, congratulations . . . and don't stop now!

ENTERPRISES: "IT'S ALL ABOUT THAT BASIS POINT"

Before coming to MBO, I wondered if a company's market capitalization correlated to the relative share of its independent workforce. I had an external research firm answer this question for me: yes. They discovered that within each sector, the public companies with the highest share of independents in their workforce were commanding an evaluation over 1,000 basis points higher than the rest of their sector. When you're talking about the valuations of an enterprise, 1,000 basis points is a sizeable amount of difference.

Again, I want to stress that this research showed correlation, not causation. But based on three decades of business leadership, I'll hypothesize that the higher evaluation and return on assets (ROA) of the companies using independents comes because of their increased agility, lowered costs (especially human capital expenses), improved processes and client satisfaction, and lessened groupthink.

Companies that utilize independents are more agile. They can move faster, plugging in and out in the areas that matter. The fractional workforce can significantly impact ROA, helping the business succeed as it navigates uncertain waters—like times of recession. Further, studies on cost savings have shown a 15–35% reduction in employment expenses when businesses leverage the external workforce. These numbers don't even tell the whole picture, as successfully implementing independents leads to greater client satisfaction and improved processes.

Companies constantly say they want to hire a diverse workforce, including a diversity of thought. Companies that truly embrace diversity will secure talent from all possible sources—including independents. The bottom line is that using independents is good for the bottom line.

So when a company's invaluable employees go independent, I recommend they congratulate these new entrepreneurs and seek to become one of their first clients. Choose to see them as Jeff Bezos–like entrepreneurs, not Benedict Arnold betrayers of your cause.

* * *

Now, let's break these "agility factors" down a bit further. First, independents focus on doing what they are good at, and they develop deep skills in that area. And yes, they probably honed those skills for several years as an employee of a company (maybe even *your* company, and that's how you know each other). But as they become independent, they instinctively follow one of Peter Drucker's principles for managing oneself: "Just as people achieve results by doing what they are good at, they also achieve results by working in ways that they best perform."[6]

Here's a question that cuts to the heart of the matter: How many annual hours does an *employee* invest in doing "what they are good at" compared to doing things they're not as good at? Or performing low-value tasks that could be done by lesser-paid employees? Would they be spending even 1,000 hours (50% of their annual total) on work they are really good at? Probably not. And even if they were, why would a CEO take joy that half his or her employees' hours *aren't* spent doing what they excel at? That would be like paying LeBron James a full salary but asking him to suit up as a team cheerleader or PA announcer for half the season's games.

This ties into the second factor: Independents know they prove their value through project-based outcomes, not the clocking of hours. Therefore, companies will increasingly utilize project-based outcome arrangements over full-time hourly rates. They'll focus on tapping into specialized, deep skills instead of broad generic skill sets. Your value as a company will be driven by projects and outcomes, not full-time employees and activities.[7]

Related to this, independents don't need "pay transparency" laws to determine what they should earn. Eight states currently have such laws, and in March 2023, the Salary Transparency Act and Pay Equity for All Act were introduced in the US Congress. If both laws were passed, employers would have to disclose the pay ranges for all their job offerings—and they would be forbidden from asking job candidates about their salary history.[8]

Look, I understand why *employees* may desire these laws—and I'm all for greater transparency that improves workers' lives—but independents don't need the government to force clients to disclose employee pay rates. Instead, independents set their own prices for the projects and problems they tackle for clients. The law of supply and demand kicks in after that: If an independent's expertise leads to a price tag that the market will pay, then they win clients and get work. If they're landing too much work, they'll raise the price or hire additional help to fulfill the greater volume. But if they struggle to land work, they'll instinctively know to drop the price or add more value.

And independents know to go where the market leads. "You *aren't* rewarded for hard work," solopreneur Justin Welsh wrote. "You're rewarded for creating something of value. So don't work extra hard on something you're not sure anyone even wants."[9] But what independents *don't* do is show up with an attitude of "I'm a cool independent, and you're lucky to have me." Nor do they allow their labor to be turned into a commodity. "Belief in yourself is overrated. Generate evidence," Ryan Holiday wrote.[10] Independents know they prove their value through project-based outcomes—projects the client definitely wants because these are client-driven projects. When independents finish the projects or solve the client's problems, that's the evidence Holiday wrote about—the evidence of the value that the independent brought to the enterprise.

Third, enterprises seek to accomplish work in quicker sprints. Most companies today would not say, "This is my five-year strategy." They have much shorter cycle times in mind. The sprint to drive change allows you to more demonstrably determine if you're getting the desired outcomes. As a result, you see a rise in project-based work instead of role-based work. Leaders are saying, "Let's get teams together, get things done . . . and then define another project and make another sprint to get even more things done."

◆ ◆ ◆

Combining these three elements, independents will hire themselves to your enterprise based on what they're really good at, using their deep skills to solve problems and complete projects for you. Once your problem is solved, they don't wait around for busywork tasks to fall into their laps to justify an employee paycheck from you. They move on to the next client with problems and projects that are in the independent's wheelhouse. They've fractionalized their labor. They've unbundled their "I'm good at X" skills from full-time employment and have offered X to your business. That's great for you because you need someone who can do X.

As Gary Bolles wrote, "Work is becoming unbundled—but what is work? Work is three things: Skills, applied to Tasks, to solve Problems. (We are paid for work because we're problem-solvers. But we are often rated by how we perform Tasks—rather than how we solve problems.)"[11]

In the past, companies have addressed this specialized, short-term need for specific skills by "bolting on" contractors or consultants to their workforce. This often required hiring a consulting company—with more than one person billing to the work—or working through a staffing agency with limited visibility into candidates and hefty fees to pay.

In these scenarios, the acquired skills can be more liabilities than assets—the cost of the skills interferes with any positive economic benefit. This is no longer necessary. Skills can now be moved entirely to the asset column by creating a fractional workforce—like the 60/30/10 approach I advocated for in chapter 3.

UNIQUE THINKERS SHRINK GROUPTHINK

A fourth way independents add value is by shrinking the groupthink within an enterprise. Companies constantly say they want to hire a diverse workforce, but too often, all they have in mind is gender and race. But what about diversity in thought? Companies make new hires from a variety of experiences and backgrounds, but then their thick company culture standardizes how these fresh employees must do things. The culture envelops them quickly, telling them how they are to think if they are to keep their job. This pressures employees to blend in and become homogenous payroll additions.

I constantly see an intellectual disconnect between the stated desire for diversity and the conformist mindset of corporate culture. Preserve the status quo or promote diversity in thought—which will it be? That's why enterprises need perpetual startup thinking from their workforce.

"Positively defined, a startup is the largest group of people you can convince of a plan to build a different future," venture capitalist and startup guru Peter Thiel wrote. "A new company's most important strength is *new thinking*: even more important than nimbleness, small size affords space *to think* . . . Because that is what a startup must do: *question received ideas and rethink business from scratch*."[12] Or, as Sam Walton—arguably one of the greatest entrepreneurs of the twentieth century—once said, "Ignore the conventional wisdom. If everybody else is doing it one way, there's a good chance you can find your niche by going in exactly the opposite direction."

I recently read an opinion piece in *Forbes* titled "Why Being a Nonconformist Is Exactly What Your Company Needs from You."[13] The article focuses on employees—and I agree with the principle. But even better than *hoping employees* avoid groupthink is this: having nonconformity baked right into your enterprise by your utilization of independents. Independents don't have to be encouraged to be this way—they already are. Unique thinking is a core value for entrepreneurs.

In the previous chapter, we saw how the remote work revolution for employees impacted corporate real estate prices as office spaces emptied. In 2020, Pinterest announced they terminated a lease for a half million square feet of office space in San Francisco, citing remote work as a reason. But in the press release, they touched on what we're talking about here: "A more distributed workforce will allow us to hire people from a wider range of backgrounds and experiences."[14] Sure, Pinterest was simply talking about a distributed workforce of *employees*. But when you add independents into the mix, the "opportunity to hire people from a wider range of backgrounds and experiences" increases exponentially. So hiring independents helps win both the war for talent and the war against groupthink.

Companies that truly embrace diversity will secure talent from all possible sources—including independents. When a company only accesses people who have chosen to be full-time employees, then that workforce becomes homogenous because it is a fixed, captive group. Independents, however, create heterogeneous thinking immediately because they're *not* captive. Yes, companies need both mindsets in their workforce, but without direct action to hire independents, the default setting will be to only have employees. Homogenous thinking will be the norm unless a leader takes proactive measures.

In sum, if business leaders want a workforce that thinks and acts like entrepreneurs, then they need to fish where the independents swim. Those fish are easy to find—especially when you create a pool of independents.

MAY THE DIRECT SOURCE BE WITH YOU

For achieving the maximum financial benefit of finding and using independents, I recommend businesses source directly: identifying candidates for an open project or role using your own internal resources instead of a third party. Many financial benefits flow when businesses use this strategy.[15]

Direct sourcing helps a business develop an agile talent strategy. Savvy enterprises are realizing not only the financial benefits but also the return on investment of having quick access to in-demand skills, staffing flexibility, and the ability to create a talent-centered brand to thrive in the future of work.

Sourcing directly cuts out the middleman and focuses on the connection. With direct sourcing, business leaders and HR managers build their talent pool while saving 30% to 70% of their resources by going directly to these talents instead of relying on a third-party gatekeeper or intermediary.

Direct sourcing creates a frictionless approach to talent management: businesses can access talent on demand, eliminate compliance risks, reduce recruiting and onboarding costs and times, and build and nurture known talents for future projects.

As more workers are joining the independent workforce, companies are realizing they have greater access to top talents than ever before. That is why many of them are looking for new ways to find and manage these talents!

But how do you find quality independent talent with direct sourcing? Curation. A curator in a museum or art gallery helps oversee the tangible assets of an organization and sort those assets into something meaningful for an audience. When applied to the independent workforce, curation is the act of finding and selecting individuals based on a certain set of criteria. The goal of curating independent talent is to offer a tailored and enhanced experience that's beneficial to the end user.

Why is this important in the world of work? Many clients only accept or welcome talents who meet a specific set of criteria. From that first step, they can identify those who are fit for a certain task or project and those who are not. The result? A pool of quality candidates who would make for a far better client user experience!

That's why business leaders and HR managers must never forget that technology, platforms, and terminologies will continue to evolve. As individuals and organizations look to benefit from the future of work, it's essential to be specific *and* correct in using each aspect of direct sourcing.

Successful direct sourcing dramatically impacts a company's revenue and future direction. Because of this, many businesses are moving away from traditional hiring models and adapting to a new generation of workers. If done correctly, this staffing strategy can lead to significant savings in costs and time. It also helps companies directly access the booming contingent workforce.

Making the most of this labor pool is a great weapon in various firms' competition to attract top talents. Companies that find and engage with contingent workers outside of a traditional staffing agency are, by definition, direct sourcing.

There are several options available when pursuing a direct-sourcing strategy. You can access top talents via:

1. *Online marketplaces.* These are open-to-the-public, skills-based platforms that allow access to people who have been prequalified to promote their services online. These can be business-to-consumer or peer-to-peer marketplaces.

   The best marketplace for finding first-rate talents is one based on technology that delivers high-quality matching. Additionally, a marketplace that offers compliance, onboarding, invoicing, and payment processing not only helps mitigate risks but also enables selected talents to get to work fast.

2. *Freelance management systems.* Some companies that use contingent workers may rely on technology that puts top talents into an online marketplace and provides an end-to-end solution to store talents, post and fill projects, and manage invoicing and onboarding. For example, MBO Partners has an online marketplace and an end-to-end contractor management service.

3. *Talent networks, talent clouds, talent communities, and talent benches.* These are the places where organizations store talent. A talent network, cloud, community, or bench is a feature of the free market system. Here, the platform will allow the user to easily share projects and tap into this group of talents whenever a project opportunity comes.

By tapping into the power of direct sourcing to access top talents, you and your business can build a reputation as a "client of choice" of independents with in-demand skills and continue to thrive in the future of work.

SOCIETY BENEFITS

Finally, I want to answer the question posed at the beginning of this chapter: Is the Free Birds revolution sustainable, and does society benefit from the surging growth of the independent workforce? To answer the question, replace the word "independent" with "entrepreneur"—because it's the same query: Is the *entrepreneurship* movement sustainable? Are entrepreneurs an economic benefit to society? Yes!

First, independents build businesses that create jobs and wealth for others, even when their business remains without employees as a solopreneur. As tracked by new business applications from the US Census Bureau, America seems to be undergoing a burst of entrepreneurialism that began with the pandemic and hasn't died down since.

In 2022 and 2023, the bureau defined solopreneur business applications as "other than high propensity," meaning they are not likely to hire employees. According to a report by the Economic Innovation Group, "Americans filed 5.5 million applications to start new businesses in 2023, nearly 1.8 million of which are highly likely to hire employees"—and both figures set new records.[16] But even when independents don't hire anyone else as an employee of their business, the independent has business expenses—products and services they spend money on in support of their business. Those expenditures create jobs and wealth for other people.

Second, entrepreneurs are agents of innovation. *Entrepreneur* and *startup* are nearly synonymous with innovation and invention. Entrepreneurs recognize a market need and embrace the risk involved in starting a business to build a product or service that meets that need and earns the financial reward. Innovation introduces new things into the world, and entrepreneurs turn great ideas into business opportunities. This is a benefit to society, and it's at the heart of what independents do.

Third, as discussed above, it's not just businesses that get stuck in a rut of conventionality—society as a whole falls into the quagmire of closed-loop thinking. But then independents come along and "think outside the box" (a cliché that by its use shows the opposite of "thinking outside the box"). Seriously though, independents succeed because they choose the correct French loanword to shape their business: No to clichés (unoriginal, overused, imitation and replication, group thinking) and yes to niche (bespoke products and services, fresh perspective, invention, unique).

Independents dream and do, imagine and invent, brainstorm and build—and they grab on to any way of going about life except groupthink. In one era, the new thing is "horseless carriages," and in the next generation, it's the assembly line. Now, it's driverless cars, which are really just an app with wheels. In the late 1970s and 1980s, it was about getting personal computers in your home; in the past two decades, it's been about getting personal computers in your pocket. Now with AI and the Internet of Things, it's about having computing power embedded into just about everything imaginable—and that's the key word: *imaginable*. This benefits all of society.

Fourth, independent entrepreneurs fight against poverty by leading innovation, building businesses, and creating tax revenue and jobs. "Entrepreneurs are fighting America's only serious war against poverty," George Gilder wrote in his influential book *Wealth and Poverty*. "The potentialities of invention and enterprise are now greater than ever before in human history."[17] Benjamin Waterhouse, professor of history at University of North Carolina at Chapel Hill—a hotbed of entrepreneurialism and startup culture—says he sees this firsthand:

> If you step onto a college campus like UNC-Chapel Hill, where I teach, you'll see its influence in all the buzz around business start-ups. To be sure, many of the students who take college entrepreneurship courses want to learn how to get rich. But what is striking is the convictions of the socially conscious ones, the altruistic folks who want to do good for the world. They, too, have been swayed by those whispers. For them, fixing social problems doesn't involve political activism, legal reform, or movement building. Rather, the cure is always a new business venture.

In sum, entrepreneur-independents provide a sustainable benefit to society. When MBO commissioned a study to ask full-time independents about their life goals, they were most likely to cite factors like being happy (67%), helping others (66%), spending enough time with family (64%), and ensuring life has purpose (62%). And they were relatively less concerned about the factors in which traditional work offers greater security, like being on track for retirement (39%) and creating wealth (41%).[18]

That's not to say the goals of building financial security and independent work are incompatible. Far from it. Instead, these findings reflect a different set of priorities. By offering greater control and flexibility, independent work provides more space to pursue life goals.

We live in a world in which workers are trying—often without success—to align their life goals and purpose with their work. To a degree that is not always appreciated, independent work can offer a far greater potential to harmonize people's aspirations with their trades, crafts, and professions.

While a high earning potential is a significant factor for becoming independent, it's particularly noteworthy that the reasons independents cite as motivation for their choice of work often have less to do with pay and more to do with powerful values, impulses, and human needs.

MORE THAN "SHOW ME THE MONEY": LIFE GOALS AND THE LISA STORY

By 1991, Joe Walsh was almost ready for sobriety—the key word being "almost"—when he wrote "Ordinary Average Guy" as a sequel and counter to the fantasyland view of the entertainer's life.

"What we do as rock & roll stars, everybody thinks that's a whole lifestyle that we live, and that it's glorious and extravagant and wonderful," Walsh told *Rolling Stone*. "And they think that 24 hours a day we're famous and wearing expensive clothes and riding around in limos. But that's not really true. We're really cool for about an hour and a half onstage. And the rest of the day, we're taking out garbage and picking up dog crap and washing cars and sucking eggs like everybody else on the planet."[19]

Having hit rock bottom with substance abuse, Walsh sought help in 1994 and began attending rehab meetings with former addicts and alcoholics. "I met some old timers," Walsh told *Rolling Stone*. "Gradually they showed me that I'm not a unique individual, one-of-a-kind person. I'm just an alcoholic, and for the first time in my life, I felt like I was somewhere where I belonged."[20]

For the first decades of his career, Joe Walsh's life was as unsustainable as his earnings were high. But since 1994, Walsh has sought something beyond money and momentary pleasure: freedom from his addictions. As Ryan Holiday wrote, "If it's a problem that can be solved by money, you don't have a problem."[21] Walsh joined Alcoholics Anonymous and has been sober ever since—and even helps others down the path of addiction-free living. In the end, it took much more than money for Walsh to experience a lasting "Life's been good" time.

As I began this chapter, I framed it as being "where we talk about money"—and I believe I've done that and could end this chapter right now—mission accomplished. But I want to probe the final sentence of my framing further—to say one final word about "how independents are happy with their earnings."

Here's why: Once you achieve a certain level of earnings to meet your basic physiological needs (the exact amount is relative to your local economy and the cost of goods and services), more money does not buy you more happiness.[22] I'm not going to do armchair sociology or psychology here, but I think most of you have lived long enough to know that wealth doesn't solve all your problems or cure all your ills.

Walsh released the album containing "Life's Been Good" on May 16, 1978. On that exact same day up in the state of Oregon, an unwed, pregnant, 23-year-old named Chrisann Brennan knew the baby she was carrying would soon arrive. The next day, her daughter was born: Lisa.

I've talked a lot about Steve Jobs in this book, using his career as an illustration—a living metaphor—of the independent mind of an entrepreneur. But as we're talking about "Life Is Good" and the relationship entrepreneurs have with money and people, I'm going to tell the story about what's probably the most famous moral failure of Steve Jobs: his years-long denial of paternity for his daughter Lisa. I hope you don't find this distasteful. I bring up this story not to gawk at someone's misstep but for reflection.

And I use the word *famous* because this story is well-known in all the biographical book and film treatments of Jobs. I'm not writing investigative journalism here.

Chrisann Brennan had been Jobs's girlfriend on and off since high school, and at the time of Lisa's conception, Chrisann shared a house with Jobs and a mutual friend. When she told Jobs about the pregnancy, he "turned ugly" and did not want to discuss the situation. He himself had been put up for adoption and told Chrisann, "If you give up this baby for adoption, you will be sorry," and "I am never going to help you."

Brennan went on welfare and cleaned houses for money, having left work at the newly formed Apple due to her shame at the pregnancy that Jobs was indignant about. And Brennan recalls how Jobs began creating a false narrative to shield himself from paternity. Jobs "started to seed people with the notion that I slept around and he was infertile, which meant that this could not be his child."[23]

And so, even as Jobs's company began selling millions of dollars of Apple II products in 1978, Chrisann gave birth to Lisa at the All One Farm in Oregon. Jobs arrived a few days later, in time to help name the infant, choosing the name he would later give to a new computer model he had begun to develop that year.

Everybody *knew* Steve was the father, but nobody could convince Steve to *admit* he was the father. Nobody, that is, except the courts. Jobs continued to deny paternity, and Brennan continued to live in poverty. Years later, Lisa wrote a bestselling memoir and described what happened next:

> Then, in 1980, the district attorney of San Mateo County, California, sued my father for child-support payments. My father responded by denying paternity, swearing in a deposition that he was sterile and naming another man he said was my father.
>
> I was required to take a DNA test. The tests were new then, and when the results came back, they gave the odds that we were related as the highest the instruments could measure at the time: 94.4 percent. The court required my father to cover welfare back payments, child-support payments of $385 per month, which he increased to $500, and medical

insurance until I was 18. The case was finalized on December 8, 1980, with my father's lawyers insistent to close.[24]

Rock historians will rightly note the significance of that date: John Lennon was murdered that very night in New York City. But in her memoirs, Lisa noted the *personal* significance of the timing of the settlement: "Four days later Apple went public and overnight my father was worth more than $200 million."[25]

Even after Jobs began to be a father to Lisa during her childhood and they built a relationship—she even took his last name, legally changing hers to Lisa Brennan-Jobs—even after all that, he still denied the computer connection to her name. She asked him, "Hey, you know that computer, the Lisa? Was it named after me?" She was hoping "he would just give me this one thing"—the idea that he had actually connected with her somehow as a baby. Lisa recalls his answer: "'Nope.' His voice was clipped, dismissive. Like I was fishing for a compliment. 'Sorry, kid.'"[26]

But when Lisa was 27, Steve took her on a yacht trip with her stepmother and step-siblings. Jobs docked somewhere off the coast of France "to meet a friend for lunch"—and the "friend" wound up being Bono, the close friend of Jobs and the lead singer of U2. In yet another example of historical synchronicity, Bono and the other three high schoolers who formed the group that became U2 held their initial practice in September 1976, the same month that Jobs and Wozniak first displayed their Apple I computers to the world at a trade show in Atlantic City (see chapter 1).

Lisa recollected the lunch conversation they shared with Bono that day.

Bono asked my father about the beginning of Apple. Did the team feel alive? Did they sense it was something big and they were going to change the world? My father said it did feel that way as they were making the Macintosh, and Bono said it was that way for him and the band, too, and wasn't it incredible that people in such disparate fields could have the same experience?

Then Bono asked, "So, was the Lisa computer named after her?"

There was a pause. I braced myself—prepared for his answer.

My father hesitated, looked down at his plate for a long moment, and then back at Bono. "Yeah, it was," he said.

I sat up in my chair.

"I thought so," Bono said.

"Yup," my father said.

I studied my father's face. What had changed? Why had he admitted it now, after all these years? Of course it was named after me, I thought then. His lie seemed preposterous now. I felt a new power that pulled my chest up.

"That's the first time he's said yes," I told Bono. "Thank you for asking." As if famous people needed other famous people around to release their secrets.[27]

When Walter Isaacson interviewed Jobs for the biography that was released right after Jobs died in 2011, he told the author: "I wish I had handled it differently. I could not see myself as a father then, so I didn't face up to it . . . But if I could do it over, I would do a better job."[28]

Because Jobs can be used as an uberexample of an entrepreneur—a model of independent spirit and brains whose life is worthy of study and analysis—then it's also good to reflect on where he got it wrong. Especially when thinking about a wrong that Jobs himself said, "if I could do it over, I would do a better job."

Again, I retell this familiar story not to shame Jobs, but to remind myself that what's truly important in life isn't the material stuff. Not the money in bank accounts. Not the accumulation of possessions or stock options. Not the success of our entrepreneurial empires, or even the creation of world-changing consumer products.

So, what *is* most significant? If you can say, "Life's been good" as a reflection of your life, then *why*? Why has "life been good"? That question is a deeply personal one, and I won't try to answer it for you. But, like Joe Walsh and Steve Jobs learned along the way, the answer truly is more than a "show me the money" ethos.

If you're skilled, a lifelong learner, know how to work hard, and become independent, then you *will* earn money—and most independents will earn more of it than they did as a full-time employee.

But even as you are making bank, remember to make a life too.

EVERSON'S ACTION POINT: FOR ENTERPRISES

It's one thing to believe what I'm saying is true—that utilizing independents is good for the bottom line of your business—but what are some baby steps you can take quickly to get started down this path? Here are four action points:

1. Encourage employees to have side gigs and side hustles. They're baby steps of entrepreneurship.
2. In building your workforce, have a bias for competencies versus roles.
3. Get the middleman out and focus on the connection. With direct sourcing, business leaders and HR managers build their talent pool while saving 30% to 70% of their resources by going directly to these talents instead of relying on a third-party gatekeeper or intermediary.
4. When a valuable employee becomes an independent, congratulate them and ask for a meeting: your enterprise should be their first client!

17

NEW KID IN TOWN

Innovation and the Younger Generations

> The personal computer revolution, when it erupted in the mid-1975s, was led by scruffy entrepreneurs in strip malls and garages who started companies with names like Altair and Apple.
>
> —Walter Isaacson[1]

In December 1975, the Eagles announced that Bernie Leadon, an original member of the band, was leaving the group. Glenn Frey and Don Henley wanted to broaden the fan base as wide as possible, Henley later told Marc Eliot, a historian of the band. "[Leadon] thought we were selling out from the very beginning," Henley said. "To me, the point was to reach as many people as possible . . . Glenn and I always wanted to make it all the way, and also to make some money, because we didn't think it was going to last that long. To me, it wasn't just an art or entertainment. It was a job. I looked at it like being in football. After a while your knees go and you have to start selling insurance."[2]

Both sides wanted to be authentic to their vision—but their visions clashed. So, Leadon poured a beer on Frey's head, literally, and headed out the door.

But on the same day the band announced Leadon's departure, the Eagles also heralded the arrival of his replacement, a 28-year-old who was already a star in his own right as a solo act: Joe Walsh.

It might seem hard to imagine how Walsh could immediately influence a band already considered one of the most popular musical acts in the world, but that's exactly what he did. Before Walsh arrived, the Eagles' sound was laid-back country rock. Walsh brought a harder rock-guitar grittiness to the band and more stage theatrics than the Eagles were known for. Walsh made an impact.

The Eagles' first album with Walsh was *Hotel California*—one of the bestselling albums of all time, moving 500,000 units per week during its rollout and over 40 million since. The album's first single, "New Kid in Town," was released December 7, 1976, raced up the charts in January, and hit #1 in February 1977.

It's completely unrelated to the Eagles except for the theme of "new kid in town," but January 1977 was also the month when Jobs and Wozniak incorporated Apple with Mike Markkula's capital.[3]

In February 1977, the title track, "Hotel California," was released, hitting #1 on the charts the first week in May—a few weeks *after* the two Steves launched the Apple II at the West Coast Computer Faire in San Francisco, California, and a few weeks before the debut of *Star Wars*. New guitarist, new album, new personal computer industry, new tech, new company, new special effects, new era of blockbuster films: indeed, there were many new kids in town.

There's no correlation or causation—just fun. But hey, when you're telling the story about your independent startup at its 50-year mark, what fun historical synchronicities will *you* look back and recognize?

The "New Kid in Town" lyrics were about "the fleeting, fickle nature of love and romance," Henley said, and "also about the fleeting nature of fame, especially in the music business. We were basically saying, 'Look, we know we're red-hot right now but we also know that somebody's going to come along and replace us—both in music and in love.'"[4]

Eagles biographer Marc Eliot wrote that the lyrics contained "a suggestion of the fickle nature of both the muse and the masses. After all, there was a new kid in town, Springsteen, and he did seem to steal the band's 'girl.'"[5]

With that fickleness in mind and knowing the limited shelf life of any band—especially a band unwilling to reinvent itself—the Eagles grabbed onto Joe Walsh for his energy, guitar, and wild-man ways. Walsh was the *new* thing the Eagles needed to keep relevant, to fend off challengers like Springsteen, and to stay on top. With Walsh, they could rock and roll in the dollars for decades more—at least, that was the plan.

But like Mike Tyson said, "Everyone has a plan until they get punched in the face."[6] So the Eagles broke up in 1980, and Springsteen became one of the biggest acts of the decade, with his 1984 *Born in the U.S.A.* album having now sold 30 million copies.

SMELLS LIKE TEEN SPIRIT

Woz, Jobs, and all the members of the Eagles: Every one of these guys were in their 20s in 1977. Think about that the next time you're reading some snarky article about Gen Z's faults.

In the February 1982 issue that first put Steve Jobs on the cover of *Time*, here are the opening lines from the article aptly titled "Striking It Rich: A new breed of risk takers is betting on the high-technology future":

> It is among the most durable of American dreams. The young man with a bright idea for a new product or service decides to form his own company. He invests his family's savings in the new venture. He is soon working 18-hour days but does not mind because the company is his own. Sales start sluggishly, and he makes enough mistakes to fill a textbook. Eventually it all pays off. Profits boom; he makes it big. He becomes wealthy beyond his wildest hopes. That is not just some Walter Mitty fantasy. New businesses are being created in the U.S. today as never before. Last year some 587,000 companies were incorporated, 80% more than in 1975 and 53,000 more than in 1980.[7]

Time would put Jobs on the cover and he, who would grace the cover of *Time* seven more times, had these words written about him:

Steven Jobs, 26, the co-founder of five-year-old Apple Computer, practically singlehanded created the personal computer industry. This college dropout is now worth $149 million.[8]

The 1980s became an entrepreneurial decade, and articles like this helped publicize just how young many of the entrepreneurs were and promote the idea that their youthfulness was no coincidence to their success:

> One Wall Street adage has it that if a person has not made his first million dollars by the time he is 30, he is never going to make it. In 1776 Adam Smith wrote that it was young people who had "the contempt of risk and the presumptuous hope of success," precisely the skills needed to found new businesses. Indeed, a large number of entrepreneurs have achieved success at a very early age.

I can't close out this book without mentioning the outsized role that 20-something-year-olds have played as change-agent entrepreneurs in the digital era. When I say "20-something," I actually mean "under 35" because that's double the lifespan of a typical high school graduate. Here is just a small sampling of easily recognizable names from the past 50 years who started now-household-name digital-revolution companies before they turned 35:

Age at Founding	Founder	Company	Year Founded
33	Travis Kalanick	Uber	2009
33	Peter Thiel	PayPal	1998
30	Jeff Bezos	Amazon	1994
29	Jack Dorsey	Twitter	2006
27	Steve Wozniak	Apple	1976
22	Steve Jobs	Apple	1976
22	Andy Fang	DoorDash	2013
21	Evan Spiegel	Snapchat	2011
19	Mark Zuckerberg	Facebook	2004
19	Bill Gates	Microsoft	1975

And if you expand the list to include unknown names of successful 20-something entrepreneurs from outside the digital world, this list could grow one hundred times over.

Perhaps that's why venture capitalist Peter Thiel launched the Thiel Fellowship to fund young entrepreneurs, giving "$100,000 to young people who want to build new things instead of sitting in a classroom." The tagline says it all: "Two years. $100,000. Some ideas can't wait."[9]

* * *

I grew up in a tiny North Dakota town five hours from Minneapolis and three hours south of Canada. Have you seen the movie *Fargo*? I grew up 100 miles west of there. Needless to say, the opportunities for a young entrepreneur were not the same in Jamestown, North Dakota, as they were in a major city. Jamestown wasn't Manhattan or Silicon Valley. Venture capitalists did not land their private jets at the local airport to discuss funding our projects.

But entrepreneurs start wherever they are—no excuses! I started working in my dad's upholstery shop when I was about six, sweeping floors and learning skills to help him. He also owned a car wash, which needed a hard worker to do the glamorous job of cleaning the mud and gunk out of the pits. When I was 11, I started selling Watkins Home Products door-to-door to housewives, carrying a suitcase of items like vanilla, spices, and ointments. At age 14, I became the youngest-ever direct distributor for that company. I had a team of full-time people working for me while I was in high school.

I went to college, earned a degree in accounting, and planned for a career in consulting, acquisitions, and mergers. I had already accepted a job right out of college for a position with Coopers & Lybrand, a few years before they merged to become PricewaterhouseCoopers. But do you know what I did the day after I graduated college? A friend and I opened a women's costume jewelry store—a "side hustle" before that phrase became something everyone uses. Of course, I still took the corporate job, and after the

ED EVERSON and his son, Miles, of Jamestown, talk business with Dave King, vice president of Watkins Products, Inc., Winona, Minn., at a regional dealer meeting in Fargo. Miles, 12, who works with his father, may be the youngest Watkins dealer in the country. King is the great-grandson of J.R. Watkins, who founded the company 109 years ago, selling liniment and vanilla extract door-to-door by horse and wagon. Miles makes his deliveries with a wagon attached to his bicycle.

merger, I became one of the first partners with the new firm, one of the youngest.

Here's the point. To be an entrepreneur, you don't have to grow up somewhere special or have parents who know senators, celebrities, and CEOs on a first-name basis. But you do have to have an independent mind, to work hard and take calculated risks, and to invest your time and capital resources into something with a product or service people are willing to purchase. You cannot be stuck in the mold of what came before. You don't have to be the first to market, but you can't be afraid to be original or unorthodox.

HOW YA DOOIN'? GET MOVING!

With a #1 album and millions of sales in 1977, nobody could have predicted that the Eagles would split up just three years later. Or that they would stay disbanded for fourteen years. The corporate bosses may have known the peak was over, but a total breakup? No way.

"The high-flying Eagles may have believed the world now and forever belonged to them, but the suits knew better," Marc Eliot wrote. "They understood that the biggest rock stars rarely stayed on the charts for more than seven years, the rough equivalent of the peak teenage-to-early-twenties record-buying days."[10]

That's what made their breakup even more surprising: They didn't go bust on account of declining fan support (though the sales of their follow-up to *Hotel California* paled in comparison). But in 1980, the Eagles still had musical mojo in spades—certainly enough to satisfy their fans, many of whom were now in their thirties. The center simply did not hold, and a combination of factors led to the group's parting of ways.

Joe Walsh had brought "new kid in town" energy to the Eagles, leading to the *Hotel California* success that piled on more fame and fortune to the group. But he also added more wildness to the band—the stereotypical "out of control rock star" element—to say nothing of the escalated drug and alcohol use. This volatility came at a time when the Eagles were already fraying.

And it's not as if Walsh had been accepted entirely on his own terms by the likes of Henley and Frey. Walsh was "a real crowd pleaser with a high-caliber star quality all his own," Eliot wrote. "Perhaps to maintain his idea of the status quo, early on Henley told Walsh in no uncertain terms that the Eagles did not 'perform' onstage . . . it was the music, after all, that audiences came to hear."

Even so, "Walsh became the most popular live Eagle. His slightest gyration, grimace, or stylistic wrist-bending flourish never failed to bring roars from the sold-out stadium crowds, and he milked it for all it was worth." In other words, there was a spirited competition between the original members of the band and the "new kid in town."

But the Eagles didn't break up because of Walsh. As Frey explained it years later during his speech in 1998 when the Rock and Roll Hall of Fame inducted the band: "Anybody who's been in a band knows what it's like to go through the changes. The Eagles were a very laid-back band in a high-stress situation . . . We got along fine! We just disagreed a lot! Tell me one worthwhile relationship that has not had peaks and valleys . . . You cannot play music with people for very long if you don't genuinely like them."[11]

That night, all band members stood on stage at the induction ceremony. After being introduced by Jimmy Buffett, they each took turns saying a few words of reflection or thanks. And all of them uniformly wore black tuxedos or suits. Everyone except Walsh, who sported a suit made of fabric designed to look like a red brick wall. Walsh got rowdy applause from the audience, then leaned in to the mic and, smiling, said: "Hey, how ya dooin'?"[12]

Just a reminder to us all that even when you're not the "new kid in town," you can always keep your freedom, authenticity, and your independent mind.

* * *

As I close this chapter and as this chapter closes out the book, here's one final flurry of aphoristic advice: Since you can't predict the future with perfect accuracy, go ahead and get started *now* with what you know you want to be doing *later*. Years before you hit the game-winning homer in the World Series, you'd have to learn your swing in Little League or T-ball. So get going.

Considering the "exponential changes" that "continue to occur," wrote Gary Bolles, "the most important question we can ask ourselves is: In 20 years, what will we wish we had done—today?"[13]

Accept the fact that technology will continue to change under your feet. Don't get locked into past tech or previous ways of doing things. Don't say you're too busy to learn new skills, knowledge, or the "new kid in town" tech.

"Everything doesn't always move toward better," Seth Godin wrote, "but everything moves."

You should too: get moving.

No professional athlete today would compete while wearing equipment and clothing from fifty years ago. Likewise, with the escalated rate of change, your skills and use of tech might be obsolete if you're still doing things as you did ten years ago. Or even five.

So don't wait. If you're going to go independent, then do it. Start now, even if your starting point is "part-time" within the gig economy. Side hustling today beats doing nothing today. "Time is our most irreplaceable asset," wrote Ryan Holiday, "we cannot buy more of it. We can only strive to waste as little as possible."

Finally, as an enterprise leader, if you're thinking of ramping up your use of independents, ignore status quo thinkers. Instead, think independently for your enterprise . . . and think of using independents *for* your enterprise.

EVERSON'S ACTION POINT: FOR EVERYONE

To enterprises, I'd say: Pull in independents when they're young. Hire interns like crazy and find the diamonds in the rough. Pitch them on being independent even as their first job. They'll either love it or hate it—don't try to change minds; just find those who want to be independent. You'll have to build out mentorship programs that work remotely and deliver on them. Do a Peter Thiel sponsorship program—pull bright minds right from college, or even out of college. This may sound radical, but it's the future.

To independents: Jump into the independent workforce at least once in your 20s. The barriers to entry have never been lower, so get started now, even as a side hustle. Learn. Grow. Experience. Will you earn lots of money in these ventures? Maybe, maybe not. But you'll earn entrepreneurship firsthand. That's priceless.

Acknowledgments

There are many people who I'd like to thank and who deserve recognition upon the making of this book. So many that it would create a book unto itself. Which is why I've decided to keep it as brief as I possibly can. But to all those who are not mentioned by name, you know who you are, and believe me, the thanks I have to give you transcends time and space. For you are the individuals who helped me learn to fly free.

To start my thanks, though, I am deeply grateful to my parents, whose unwavering love, support, and encouragement have been the foundation upon which I've built my aspirations and pursuits. Their guidance, wisdom, and belief in my abilities have been a constant source of strength and inspiration throughout this journey. My father recently passed during the same month my book was accepted into publication. To me this was significant because he was the first to ever make me believe in my own ability to create, build, and scale a life of work truly on my own. Thank you for always being there for me, for nurturing my curiosity, and for instilling in me the values of hard work, perseverance, and integrity. And yes, thank you for those forty dollars to launch my first business.

Next, my thanks extend to my children, Luke and Krista. Their boundless energy, curiosity, and laughter have brought light and joy into my life every day. Their enthusiasm for learning, creativity, and adventure reminds me of the importance of embracing life's wonders and possibilities. I want to specifically thank Krista during this process, who helped with the writing, editing, and creative decisions of this work and who lives by the principles of an independent herself, running her own executive branding company, ALLU. Thank you for your patience and understanding during the countless hours I spent immersed in writing, editing, and revision. Your love and support mean the world to me.

I extend my heartfelt appreciation to the editors and publishing professionals who have contributed their expertise, guidance, and support to this project. Your insights, feedback, and dedication have been invaluable in shaping and refining the manuscript, ensuring that it reaches its fullest potential. I am grateful for the collaborative spirit and shared commitment to excellence that have characterized our working relationship. Specifically, I'd like to thank Scott Lamb who researched and helped create my vision for this book to come true.

Next, I would like to express my gratitude to the independent workforce whose contributions have been instrumental in bringing this book to fruition. From cover designers and illustrators to marketing consultants and distribution partners, your talent, professionalism, and dedication have enhanced every aspect of the publishing process. I would be remiss if I did not express my great gratitude to Gene Zaino and MBO Partners. Thank you for providing a space to allow people to pursue their independent business and self-growth.

Finally, I also extend a sincere thank you to Kristin Casey, author and coach, who has not only helped guide this book but who has personally helped me arrive at my own understanding of how I can live authentically and show up as my true self in all aspects of life.

And yet, as I said in the beginning, it would take days to recount all those I'd like to thank. So, to bring this to a close, I finally want to thank anyone who has ever had a dream to live the life they want and live with an independent mind, and anyone who gave their all to fly free. It is those individuals who truly are the backbone of my work *Free Birds*.

Enjoy.

Notes

Introduction

1. Martin Kielty, "Why REO Speedwagon's 'Time for Me to Fly' Took 10 Years to Write," Ultimate Classic Rock, April 20, 2020, https://ultimate classicrock.com/reo-speedwagon-time-for-me-to-fly/.
2. Kielty, "Why REO Speedwagon's 'Time for Me to Fly' Took 10 Years to Write."
3. Mary Campbell, "REO Speedwagon Back on Top," Associated Press, published in the *Post-Star* (Glens Falls, NY), March 2, 1985, 24.
4. Helen Tupper and Sarah Ellis, *The Squiggly Career: Ditch the Ladder, Discover Opportunity, Design Your Career* (London: Portfolio Penguin, 2020).
5. Kielty, "Why REO Speedwagon's 'Time for Me to Fly' Took 10 Years to Write."
6. Campbell, "REO Speedwagon Back on Top."
7. Kielty, "Why REO Speedwagon's 'Time for Me to Fly' Took 10 Years to Write."
8. Campbell, "REO Speedwagon Back on Top."
9. Kevin Cronin, "The 10 Best REO Speedwagon Songs, by Kevin Cronin," loudersound (Louder, May 11, 2016), https://www.loudersound.com/features/reospeedwagon-bestofeverything.
10. Brian Cantor, "REO Speedwagon's 'Time for Me to Fly' Debuts at #34 on Billboard Digital Song Sales Chart Following *Ozark* Season 3 Feature," Headline Planet, April 7, 2020, https://headlineplanet.com/home/2020/04/07/reo-speedwagons-time-for-me-to-fly-debuts-at-34-on-billboard-digital-song-sales-chart-following-ozark-season-3-feature/.
11. Campbell, "REO Speedwagon Back on Top."
12. Reid Hoffman and Ben Casnocha, *The Startup of You: Adapt, Take Risks, Grow Your Network, and Transform Your Career* (New York: Currency, 2022).
13. Dave Everley, "The Story of Free Bird by Lynyrd Skynyrd," loudersound, January 14, 2021, https://www.loudersound.com/features/the-story-of-free-bird-by-lynyrd-skynyrd.
14. Tejas Morey, "How iTunes Changed the Music Industry Forever," mensxp.com, January 9, 2015, https://www.mensxp.com/technology/internet/8798-how-itunes-changed-the-music-industry-forever.html. Also see Pimm Fox, "The Day the Music Stores Died," *Computerworld*, May 24, 2004, https://www.computerworld.com/article/2565199/the-day-the-music-stores-died.html.
15. Do you even know the name of that album? It's called *You Can Tune a Piano,*

But You Can't Tuna Fish—with awful album art to match the dad joke. The Skynyrd album that houses "Free Bird" actually has three or four other tracks that still get airtime on classic rock stations: "Tuesday's Gone," "Give Me Three Steps," and "Simple Man."

16. Nicholas Negroponte, *Being Digital* (New York: Vintage Books, 1995).

17. Robert Tercek, *Vaporized: Solid Strategies for Success in a Dematerialized World* (Vancouver: Lifetree Media, 2015), x. (Italics added.)

18. Tercek, *Vaporized*, 177. Tercek writes about "The Rise of the Peer-to-Peer Economy": "The vaporized concept is just a metaphor, and every metaphor breaks at some point. It's always instructive to find out where. I recognize that certain things will never be replaced by software—for example, we all need buildings and food, bridges, and vehicles—which is why the motto is not 'Everything will be vaporized,' but rather 'Whatever can be vaporized will be.'"

19. "Median Tenure with Current Employer Was 4.1 Years in January 2020," U.S. Bureau of Labor Statistics, September 29, 2020, https://www.bls.gov /opub/ted/2020/median-tenure-with-current-employer-was-4-point-1-years -in-january-2020.htm.

20. "Employee Tenure Summary—2022 A01 Results," U.S. Bureau of Labor Statistics, September 22, 2022, https://www.bls.gov/news.release/tenure.nr0.htm.

21. Karen Bennett, "2023 Job Seekers: A Regional Overview," Bankrate, May 24, 2023, https://www.bankrate.com/banking/job-seekers-regional-overview/.

22. Ken Schnee, "2022 Tech Trends Impact the Great Resignation, Talent War, and More," Sterling, January 24, 2022, https://www.sterlingcheck.com/blog /2022/01/2022-tech-trends-impact-the-great-resignation/; Rebecca Chen, "The True Cost of Employee Turnover in Tech," Bucketlist, December 1, 2023, https://bucketlistrewards.com/blog/the-true-cost-of-employee-turnover-in-tech/.

23. Tammy Kim, "The Gig Economy Is Coming for Your Job," *New York Times*, January 10, 2020, https://www.nytimes.com/2020/01/10/opinion/sunday /gig-economy-unemployment-automation.html.

24. Jia Tolentino, "The Gig Economy Celebrates Working Yourself to Death," *New Yorker*, March 22, 2017, https://www.newyorker.com/culture/jia -tolentino/the-gig-economy-celebrates-working-yourself-to-death.

25. Sarah June Kessler, "The Gig Economy: Lower Wages, More Injuries, Horrible Benefits," Literary Hub, April 3, 2019, https://lithub.com/the-gig -economy-lower-wages-more-injuries-horrible-benefits/.

26. Steven Greenhouse, "False Freedom: Sharing the Scraps from the Perilous Gig Economy," Literary Hub, August 4, 2019, https://lithub.com/false-freedom -sharing-the-scraps-from-the-perilous-gig-economy/.

27. Mike Bebernes. "The Gig Economy: Opportunity or Exploitation?" Yahoo! News, August 25, 2021, https://news.yahoo.com/the-gig-economy-opportunity-or-exploitation-194706864.html.

28. GiveGet, "Yes, the Gig Economy Sucks; No, It's Not Fulfilling Its Promise of Freedom," Medium, May 20, 2019, https://giveget.medium.com/yes-the-gig-economy-sucks-no-its-not-fulfilling-its-promise-of-freedom-af9738939f16.

29. Malcolm Gladwell, "That Jerk at the Café? C'est Moi | Malcolm Gladwell on Writing in Coffee Shops," *Wall Street Journal*, September 25, 2010, https://www.wsj.com/articles/SB10001424052748704147804575455923448456324.

30. Robert Johnson, "The Fax Machine: Technology That Refuses to Die," *New York Times*, March 27, 2005, https://www.nytimes.com/2005/03/27/business/yourmoney/the-fax-machine-technology-that-refuses-to-die.html.

31. "Steve Jobs Introducing the iPhone at Macworld 2007," YouTube, December 3, 2010, https://www.youtube.com/watch?v=x7qPAY9JqE4&t=4s&ab_channel=superapple4ever.

32. Li Jin, "Unbundling Work from Employment," *Li's Newsletter*, July 29, 2020, https://li.substack.com/p/unbundling-work-from-employment.

33. Peter Carlson, "Self-Employment: Nice If You Can Get It," *Washington Post*, December 9, 1997, https://www.washingtonpost.com/archive/lifestyle/1997/12/09/self-employment-nice-if-you-can-get-it/932fe22f-9fbf-47d7-be78-3bf962b22ed7/.

34. 2,000 hours of work per year x a 45-year work span (age 22–67) = 90,000 hours.

Chapter 1

1. Nassim Nicholas Taleb, *The Black Swan: The Impact of the Highly Improbable* (New York: Random House, 2016), 10.

2. R. S. Jones, "Comparing Apples and Oranges," *Interface*, July 1976.

3. Jim Collins, The Flywheel Effect, accessed February 8, 2024, https://www.jimcollins.com/concepts/the-flywheel.html.

4. For "nearly half-million" see Steven Levy, *Hackers: Heroes of the Computer Revolution: 25th Anniversary Edition* (Sebastopol, CA: O'Reilly, 2010), 186. See Jack Nicas, "Apple Becomes First Company to Hit $3 Trillion Market Value," *New York Times*, January 3, 2022, https://www.nytimes.com/2022/01/03/technology/apple-3-trillion-market-value.html.

5. Levy, *Hackers*, 190–191.

6. Levy, *Hackers*, 229.

7. "March 5, 1975: A Whiff of Homebrew Excites the Valley," *Wired*,

March 5, 2009, https://www.wired.com/2009/03/march-5-1975-a-whiff-of
-homebrew-excites-the-valley-2/.

8. Steve Wozniak and Gina Smith, *iWoz: Computer Geek to Cult Icon: How I Invented the Personal Computer, Co-Founded Apple, and Had Fun Doing It* (New
York: W. W. Norton, 2007), 153–154.

9. Wozniak and Smith, *iWoz*, 155, 156.

10. Wozniak and Smith, *iWoz*, 157.

11. Walter Isaacson, *Steve Jobs* (New York: Simon & Schuster, 2011), 102.

12. Steve Wozniak, "The Apple II," *Byte* magazine (Volume 2, Number 5),
May 1, 1977, https://archive.org/details/byte-magazine-1977-05/page/n35
/mode/2up?view=theater, 34.

13. "The Model T," Ford Corporate, n.d., https://corporate.ford.com/articles
/history/the-model-t.html.

14. Miles Everson, modified from "Money ≠ Happiness: What are the secrets
to unlocking a genuinely happy and meaningful life? [Fridays: Mindfulness
by Miles]," LinkedIn, October 21, 2022, https://www.linkedin.com/pulse
/money-happiness-what-secrets-unlocking-genuinely-happy-miles-everson,
modified from here, by Miles.

15. The ad was placed in the July 1977 edition of *Byte* magazine. For a discussion of those early ad campaigns for the Apple II, see Jesse Adams Stein,
"Domesticity, Gender and the 1977 Apple II Personal Computer," *Design
and Culture*, July 2011, https://www.researchgate.net/publication/272146002
_Domesticity_Gender_and_the_1977_Apple_II_Personal_Computer.

16. This information comes from the documentation for Apple Computer's December 12, 1980, IPO.

17. Margaret Canning, "Call That Launched the Mobile Era," *Belfast Telegraph*,
April 3, 2013, https://www.belfasttelegraph.co.uk/business/technology/call
-that-launched-the-mobile-era/29170824.html and Zachary M. Seward,
"The First Mobile Phone Call Was Made 40 Years Ago Today," *The Atlantic*, April 3, 2013, https://www.theatlantic.com/technology/archive/2013/04
/the-first-mobile-phone-call-was-made-40-years-ago-today/274611/.

18. D. Weisman, "Where Have All the Payphones Gone?," *Escondido Grapevine*,
April 4, 2023, https://www.escondidograpevine.com/2023/04/02/where
-have-all-the-payphones-gone/.

19. Vannevar Bush, "As We May Think," *The Atlantic*, July 8, 2022, https://www
.theatlantic.com/magazine/archive/1945/07/as-we-may-think/303881/. Also,
see the discussion of Bush's article "As We May Think": Walter Isaacson, *The
Innovators: How a Group of Hackers, Geniuses, and Geeks Created the Digital
Revolution* (New York: Simon & Schuster, 2014), 263–264.

20. David Sheff, "Playboy Interview: Steven Jobs," AllAboutSteveJobs.com, February 1, 1985 (the original Playboy interview), https://allaboutstevejobs.com/verbatim/interviews/playboy_1985.

21. John Hagel, John Seely Brown, and Lang Davison, *The Power of Pull: How Small Moves, Smartly Made, Can Set Big Things in Motion* (New York: Basic Books, 2010), 57–58.

22. Miles Everson, "Four Forces Driving the New World of Work," MBO Partners, https://www.mbopartners.com/wp-content/uploads/2020/04/FourForces-Designed.pdf.

23. The term *telecommute* was coined in the early 1970s by Jack Nilles, a futurist and pioneer in the field of telecommuting. Nilles used the term in his 1973 book *The Telecommunications-Transportation Tradeoff: Options for Tomorrow*, which explored the potential benefits of telecommuting and other remote work arrangements. The term *telecommuting* originally referred specifically to working from home or another remote location using telecommunications technology, such as a telephone or a computer. Over time, the term has broadened to encompass a wider range of remote work arrangements, including those that involve working from coffee shops, coworking spaces, or other locations outside of a traditional office environment.

24. Frank W Schiff, "Working at Home Can Save Gasoline," *Washington Post*, September 1, 1979, https://www.washingtonpost.com/archive/opinions/1979/09/02/working-at-home-can-save-gasoline/ffa475c7-d1a8-476e-8411-8cb53f1f3470/.

25. Bill Murphy, "Apple Sent This 8-Sentence Memo to Its Top People 39 Years Ago," *Inc.*, October 16, 2019, https://www.inc.com/bill-murphy-jr/apple-sent-this-8-sentence-memo-to-its-top-people-39-years-ago-results-were-game-changing-and-yes-you-should-copy-it.html.

26. "Typewriters of Electronic Era," *New York Times*, November 23, 1984, https://www.nytimes.com/1984/11/23/business/typewriters-of-electronic-era.html.

27. That's why Apple's stringent return-to-work policies after the COVID-19 pandemic are rather ironic: Mark Gurman, "Apple (AAPL) Sets Return-to-Office Deadline of Sept. 5 After Covid Delays," Bloomberg, August 15, 2022, https://www.bloomberg.com/news/articles/2022-08-15/apple-sets-return-to-office-deadline-of-sept-5-after-delays.

28. "Machine of the Year 1982: The Computer Moves In," *Time*, January 3, 1983.

29. Steve Jobs, "Steve Jobs Interview - 2/18/1981," YouTube, https://www.youtube.com/watch?v=DbfejwP1d3c&ab_channel=SirMix-A-LotRareMusic.

30. Sean Burch, "The US Festival, 40 Years Later: An Oral History," *Spin*, May 27, 2023, https://www.spin.com/2023/05/us-festival-40th-anniversary

-oral-history/. See also: "Largest Rock Festival Attendance," Guinness World Records, accessed February 8, 2024, https://www.guinnessworldrecords.com /world-records/69627-largest-rock-festival-attendance.

31. Wozniak and Smith, *iWoz*, 256.

Chapter 2

1. "The Police Setlist at US Festival 1982," setlist.fm, https://www.setlist.fm /setlist/the-police/1982/glen-helen-regional-park-san-bernardino-ca-3ded953 .html. Also, Woz's accurate lunar recollection: "Moon Phase for Friday September 3rd, 1982," Nine Planets, https://nineplanets.org/moon/phase/9-3-1982/.

2. John Pidgeon, "On Tour with the Police," *Guardian*, August 24, 2007, https:// www.theguardian.com/music/2007/aug/24/popandrock1.

3. For "favorite song": "Jools Holland Interviews Sting (The Police)," YouTube, May 20, 2007, https://youtu.be/ci-yIVsDIdk?feature=shared. For remainder of Sting quote: "Sting: Discography: Message in a Bottle, 7," Sting.com, accessed February 8, 2024, https://www.sting.com/discography/album/144 /Singles+(The+Police).

4. Ying Lin, "How Many Emails Are Sent per Day in 2023? [Jan 2023 Update]," Oberlo, https://www.oberlo.com/statistics/how-many-emails-are-sent-per-day.

5. Jenny Gross, "Can You Have More than 150 Friends?," *New York Times*, May 11, 2021, https://www.nytimes.com/2021/05/11/science/dunbars -number-debunked.html.

6. Yes, that's an insider joke for fans of the Police and their bestselling, final album, *Synchronicity*.

7. USPS—March 9, "A Decade of Facts and Figures," Postal Facts—U.S. Postal Service, March 9, 2022, https://facts.usps.com/table-facts/.

8. Miles Everson, "Four Forces Driving the New World of Work," MBO Partners, https://www.mbopartners.com/wp-content/uploads/2020/04/FourForces -Designed.pdf.

9. Bret Swanson, "The $101,000,000 iPhone," American Enterprise Institute, accessed March 1, 2023, https://www.aei.org/technology-and-innovation /the-101000000-iphone/.

10. Ash Turner et al., "2.94 Billion More Phones than People in the World!," *BankMyCell*, February 7, 2023, https://www.bankmycell.com/blog/how -many-phones-are-in-the-world.

11. Alexander Taylor, "Striking It Rich: A New Breed of Risk Takers Is Betting on the High-Technology Future," *Time*, February 15, 1982, https://content .time.com/time/subscriber/article/0,33009,925279,00.html.

12. "Compaq Portable 386," Wikipedia, January 25, 2023, https://en.wikipedia.org/wiki/Compaq_Portable_386.

13. Steve Cichon, "Everything from 1991 Radio Shack Ad I Now Do with My Phone," Trending Buffalo, January 14, 2014, https://www.trendingbuffalo.com/life/uncle-steves-buffalo/everything-from-1991-radio-shack-ad-now/.

14. Cichon, "Everything from 1991 Radio Shack Ad I Now Do with My Phone."

15. Otto Friedrich, "The Computer Moves In," *Time*, January 3, 1983, https://time.com/archive/6699317/the-computer-moves-in/.

16. Harry McCracken, "The Rise—Yes, Rise—of RadioShack," *Fast Company*, February 5, 2015, https://www.fastcompany.com/3042101/the-rise-of-radioshack.

17. Steve Wozniak and Gina Smith, *iWoz: Computer Geek to Cult Icon: How I Invented the Personal Computer, Co-Founded Apple, and Had Fun Doing It* (New York: W.W. Norton, 2007), 190–191.

18. Wozniak and Smith, *iWoz*, 190–191

19. Tim Stevens, "Atari Pong Review (1976)," Engadget, April 1, 2012, https://www.engadget.com/2012-04-01-atari-pong-review.html.

20. Jack Nicas, "Apple Becomes First Company to Hit $3 Trillion Market Value," *New York Times*, January 3, 2022, https://www.nytimes.com/2022/01/03/technology/apple-3-trillion-market-value.html.

21. John McCallum, "Memory Prices 1957+," Historical Memory Prices 1957+, n.d., https://jcmit.net/memoryprice.htm.

22. "Dire Straits—Money for Nothing (Official Music Video)," YouTube, February 23, 2010, https://www.youtube.com/watch?v=wTP2RUD_cL0.

23. Gordon Moore, "Cramming More Components onto Integrated Circuits," *Electronics* magazine, April 19, 1965.

24. Chris Miller, *Chip War: The Fight for the World's Most Critical Technology* (London: Simon & Schuster UK Ltd., 2022), xxiii.

25. George Gilder coined and used the phrase "Metcalfe's law" multiple times throughout his book *Telecosm: How Infinite Bandwidth Will Revolutionize Our World*. The term is mentioned in several sections of the book, including the introduction, chapter 1, and chapter 8, among others. The concept is discussed in depth in chapter 8, which is titled "The Law of the Telecosm." In any case, it's important to note that the concept of Metcalfe's Law predates Gilder's book, as Robert Metcalfe himself had described the idea in the 1980s. However, Gilder popularized the term and helped bring it to wider attention.

26. "Mobile Network Evolution from 1G to 5G," ViserMark, August 16, 2023, https://www.visermark.com/post/mobile-network-evolution-from-1g-to-5g.

27. Jeff Bezos, "Amazon's Original 1997 Letter to Shareholders," US About Am-

azon, March 21, 1997, https://www.aboutamazon.com/news/company-news
/amazons-original-1997-letter-to-shareholders.

28. John Hagel, John Seely Brown, and Lang Davison, *The Power of Pull: How
Small Moves, Smartly Made, Can Set Big Things in Motion* (New York: Basic
Books, 2010), 44.

29. Everson, "Four Forces Driving the New World of Work."

30. "San Francisco Exodus as Tech Giants Lean In to Remote Work," *Arab
News*, September 14, 2020, https://www.arabnews.com/node/1734086/ajax
/jserrors/aggregate.

31. Emily Dreibelbis, "Startup Success: Laid-off Tech Workers Are Becoming
Their Own Bosses," *PCMag*, February 9, 2023, https://www.pcmag.com/news
/startup-success-laid-off-tech-workers-are-becoming-their-own-bosses.

32. Joe Lazer, "Many Workers Say They're Fed Up with Full-Time Work," *Fast
Company*, January 1, 2023, https://www.fastcompany.com/90841746/after
-brutal-layoffs-many-workers-say-theyre-fed-up-with-full-time-work-is-this
-the-great-betrayal.

Chapter 3

1. Matt Rickard, "Economics of Bundling and Unbundling," *MattRickard.com*,
January 2021, https://matt-rickard.com/bundling-unbundling-economics.

2. Alexandre Tanzi, "The Share of Americans Who Are Mortgage-Free Is
at an All-Time High," Bloomberg.com, November 17, 2023, https://www
.bloomberg.com/news/articles/2023-11-17/amid-high-mortgage-rates-higher
-share-of-americans-outright-own-homes.

3. Charles Dickens, *A Tale of Two Cities*, Project Gutenberg EBook of *A Tale of
Two Cities*, by Charles Dickens, accessed November 20, 2023, https://www
.gutenberg.org/files/98/98-h/98-h.htm#link2H_4_0001.

4. Thankful to Jin's article for producing the list of the work-related infrastructure. Li Jin, "Unbundling Work from Employment," *Li's Newsletter*, July 29,
2020, https://li.substack.com/p/unbundling-work-from-employment.

5. Jin, "Unbundling Work from Employment."

6. And some people spend money on both. See Abby McCain, "23 Incredible Cord Cutting Statistics [2023]: Why Americans Are Moving Away
from Cable," Zippia, March 1, 2023, https://www.zippia.com/advice/cord
-cutting-statistics/.

7. Leif O'Leary, "Are Employer-Sponsored Health Plans on Their Way
Out?," *Harvard Business Review*, May 19, 2021, https://hbr.org/2021/05
/are-employer-sponsored-health-plans-on-their-way-out.

8. Miles Everson, "How a Fractional Workforce Can Help You Improve Your Return on Assets," *Fast Company*, November 8, 2022, https://www .fastcompany.com/90807087/how-a-fractional-workforce-can-help -you-improve-your-return-on-assets.

Chapter 4

1. Linus Torvalds and David Diamond, *Just for Fun: The Story of an Accidental Revolutionary* (New York: HarperBusiness, 2002), 212.

2. These numbers fluctuate annually, but current figures can be found at the "Linux" entry at Wikipedia. Also, see here: "Linux Statistics 2024," TrueList, January 9, 2023, https://truelist.co/blog/linux-statistics/. And here: "90% of the Public Cloud Runs on Linux," Developer.com, March 25, 2021, https:// www.developer.com/news/90-of-the-public-cloud-runs-on-linux/.

3. Steven Levy, *Hackers: Heroes of the Computer Revolution: 25th Anniversary Edition* (Sebastopol, CA: O'Reilly, 2010), 227.

4. Levy, *Hackers*, 227, 230.

5. Levy, *Hackers*, 232.

6. Levy, *Hackers*, 233–234.

7. Levy, *Hackers*, 232–233. Also see Walter Isaacson, *Steve Jobs* (New York: Simon & Schuster, 2011), 61–62.

8. Levy, *Hackers*, 234.

9. There are no sources for Torvalds's wealth, but for Gates, see: "Real Time Billionaires," *Forbes*, accessed February 8, 2024, https://www.forbes.com /real-time-billionaires/#534f4e083d78.

10. Miles Everson, "Four Forces Driving the New World of Work," MBO Partners, https://www.mbopartners.com/wp-content/uploads/2020/04/FourForces -Designed.pdf.

11. Dan Levine and James Kelleher, "Chinese Espionage Cases Touch DuPont, Motorola," Reuters, February 9, 2012, https://www.reuters.com/article/us -dupont-espionage-idUKTRE81805L20120209/. Also see: "Kolon Industries Inc. Pleads Guilty for Conspiring to Steal DuPont Trade Secrets Involving Kevlar Technology," Office of Public Affairs, U.S. Department of Justice, April 30, 2015, https://www.justice.gov/opa/pr/kolon-industries-inc-pleads -guilty-conspiring-steal-dupont-trade-secrets-involving-kevlar.

12. Kirsten Korosec and Mark Harris, "Anthony Levandowski Sentenced to 18 Months in Prison as New $4B Lawsuit against Uber Is Filed," TechCrunch, August 5, 2020, https://techcrunch.com/2020/08/04/anthony-levandowski -sentenced-to-18-months-in-prison-as-new-4b-lawsuit-against-uber-is-filed/.

13. T. George Harris and Peter Drucker, "The Post-Capitalist Executive: An Interview with Peter F. Drucker," *Harvard Business Review*, May–June 1993, https://hbr.org/1993/05/the-post-capitalist-executive-an-interview-with-peter-f-drucker.

14. Everson, "Four Forces Driving the New World of Work."

15. Bo Burlingham and George Gendron, "The Entrepreneur of the Decade," *Inc.*, April 1, 1989, https://www.inc.com/magazine/19890401/5602.html.

16. Burlingham and Gendron, "The Entrepreneur of the Decade."

17. Miles Everson, John Sviokla, and Kelly Barnes, "Leading a Bionic Transformation," Strategy+business, October 29, 2018, https:// https://www.strategy-business.com/article/Leading-a-Bionic-Transformation.

18. See Carla de-Juan-Ripoll et al., "Virtual Reality as a New Approach for Risk Taking Assessment," *Frontiers*, November 27, 2018, https://www.frontiersin.org/journals/psychology/articles/10.3389/fpsyg.2018.02532/full. And see Ken Wunderlich, "Mitigating Risk in Virtual World," blog.imec.org, accessed June 4, 2024. Also, Mary K. Pratt, "Today's Virtual Reality Use Cases and Industry Applications," *CIO*, March 5, 2024, https://www.techtarget.com/searchcio/tip/Todays-virtual-reality-use-cases-and-industry-applications.

19. Jeff Howe, "The Rise of Crowdsourcing," *Wired*, June 2006, https://www.wired.com/2006/06/crowds/.

20. Stacy Schiff, "Know It All," *New Yorker*, July 24, 2006, https://www.newyorker.com/magazine/2006/07/31/know-it-all.

21. Torvalds and Diamond, *Just for Fun*, ix.

22. See John Hagel and Marc Singer, "Unbundling the Corporation," *Harvard Business Review*, August 1, 2014, https://hbr.org/1999/03/unbundling-the-corporation.

23. Torvalds and Diamond, *Just for Fun*, 230.

24. Torvalds and Diamond, *Just for Fun*, 230.

25. Torvalds and Diamond, *Just for Fun*, 229.

26. Torvalds and Diamond, *Just for Fun*, 232. (Italics added.)

Chapter 5

1. Kaitlin Balasaygun, "The Talent War Is Over. Talent Won, Says PwC U.S. Chairman Tim Ryan," CNBC, October 27, 2022, https://www.cnbc.com/2022/10/26/the-war-for-talent-is-over-talent-won-says-pwc-us-chairman.html.

2. John Lydon, "Sex Pistols Vinyl Reissues 2007." JohnLydon.com, accessed July 7, 2023, https://www.johnlydon.com/press/pistols.html.

3. Chris Campion, *Walking on the Moon: The Untold Story of the Police and the Rise of New Wave Rock* (Hoboken: John Wiley & Sons, 2010), Chapter 2.

4. Campion, *Walking on the Moon*, Chapter 2.

5. Technically, Stewart Copeland was born in the United States and grew up in Beirut. Fun fact: His father helped begin the CIA. So taken together, this father and son are responsible for the origins of the CIA and the Police.

6. Christopher Connelly, "The Police: Alone at the Top," *Rolling Stone*, June 1, 1984, https://www.rollingstone.com/music/music-news/the-police-alone -at-the-top-2-68372/.

7. "Queen Setlist at Bingley Hall, Stafford," setlist.fm, accessed November 20, 2023, https://www.setlist.fm/setlist/queen/1977/bingley-hall-stafford -england-6bdcb692.html.

8. Mick Wall, "Queen vs. Sex Pistols: How Freddie Took On Punk and Won with News of the World," Louder, October 31, 2022, https://www .loudersound.com/features/queen-the-story-of-news-of-the-world-album.

9. Terry Gross, "Fresh Air's Summer Music Interviews: Queen Guitarist Brian May," NPR, August 29, 2022, https://www.npr.org/2022/08/29/1119640665 /fresh-airs-summer-music-interviews-queen-guitarist-brian-may.

10. Gross, "Fresh Air's Summer Music Interviews: Queen Guitarist Brian May."

11. *Bohemian Rhapsody*, directed by Bryan Singer (2018; Beverly Hills, CA: 20th Century Fox).

12. "'We Will Rock You' Now Part of History," Long Beach Press, December 2, 2008, https://www.presstelegram.com/2008/12/02/we-will-rock-you-now -part-of-history/.

13. Tom Goodwyn, "Queen's 'We Are the Champions' Is the Catchiest Song Ever, Say Scientists," *NME*, September 30, 2011, https://www.nme.com /news/music/queen-101-1274133.

14. Editors of *Life*. (2018). *Life Queen*. Retrieved as ebook from https://www .amazon.com/LIFE-Queen-Editors-ebook/dp/B07JW58WX1.

15. "Gartner Survey Reveals Talent Is Top Challenge Facing CFOs Through 2023," Gartner, September 16, 2022, https://www.gartner.com/en/newsroom /press-releases/2022-09-16-gartner-survey-reveals-talent-is-top-challenge -facing-cfos-through-2023.

16. "Gartner Survey Reveals Talent Is Top Challenge Facing CFOs through 2023."

17. "Concepts and Definitions (CPS)," US Bureau of Labor Statistics, accessed June 6, 2024, https://www.bls.gov/cps/definitions.htm#laborforce.

18. Q.ai—Powering a Personal Wealth Movement, "Unemployment Is Low, but So Is the Labor Force Participation Rate—What's Going on in the U.S. Labor Market?," *Forbes*, January 27, 2023, https://www.forbes.com/sites /qai/2023/01/25/unemployment-is-low-but-so-is-the-labor-force-participation -rate---whats-going-on-in-the-us-labor-market/.

19. EMSI report, as read here: Brad Phillips, "From Pandemic to 'Sansdemic': Major Impacts on Higher Ed and the Future Workforce," *Newsweek*, June 29, 2022, https://www.newsweek.com/pandemic-sansdemic-major-impacts -higher-ed-future-workforce-1719995. And here: "Demographic Drought," *Lightcast*, accessed November 20, 2023, https://lightcast.io/resources /research/demographic-drought.

20. "Demographic Drought," *Lightcast*.

21. "Charts Related to the Latest 'The Employment Situation' News Release." U.S. Bureau of Labor Statistics, https://www.bls.gov/charts /employment-situation/civilian-labor-force-participation-rate.htm. Also see: "Civilian Labor Force Participation Rate U.S. 2022," Statista, November 3, 2023, https://www.statista.com/statistics/191734/us-civilian-labor -force-participation-rate-since-1990/.

22. Austen Hufford and Gwynn Guilford, "Americans Have Quit Quitting Their Jobs," *Wall Street Journal*, July 7, 2023, https://www.wsj.com /articles/americans-have-quit-quitting-their-jobs-4feda9bb; Courtnay Brown, "The Great Resignation Is Over," Axios, May 31, 2023, https://www.axios .com/2023/05/31/great-resignation-quitting-boom. Looking to the underlying data here (https://fred.stlouisfed.org/graph/?g=16ObU) shows that the number peaked at 3% in November 2021 and then again in April 2022.

23. "How Historic Has the Great Resignation Been?," SHRM, March 9, 2022, https://www.shrm.org/topics-tools/news/talent-acquisition/interactive-chart -how-historic-great-resignation.

24. See the 2022 report here: "MBO Partners State of Independence in America Report 2022." MBO Partners. https://www.mbopartners.com/state-of -independence/soi-22/. And the 2023 report here: https://www.mbopartners .com/state-of-independence/.

25. Linus Torvalds and David Diamond, *Just for Fun: The Story of an Accidental Revolutionary* (New York: HarperBusiness, 2002), 220.

26. Jordan Teicher, "Facing Layoffs, HR Leaders Embrace Freelancers over Ftes." a.Team, October 20, 2022, https://www.a.team/mission/2023-hr -hiring-outlook-report.

27. Stephen Davies, "The Great Horse-Manure Crisis of 1894," Foundation for Economic Education, September 1, 2004, https://fee.org/articles /the-great-horse-manure-crisis-of-1894/.

28. Will Knight, "The Last AI Boom Didn't Kill Jobs. Feel Better?," *Wired*, June 22, 2023, https://www.wired.com/story/fast-forward-the-last-ai-boom-didnt-kill-jobs/.

29. "American Manufacturing Makes a Comeback," *Wall Street Journal*, May

21, 2012, https://www.wsj.com/video/american-manufacturing-makes-a-comeback/A0612D1D-4D2E-4BDD-8603-723F428C28BA.html.

30. Adele Peters, "You Might Want to Ditch Your Desk Job to Become an Electrician," *Fast Company*, June 6, 2023, https://www.fastcompany.com/90910359/ditch-your-desk-job-to-become-an-electrician. Also see Nate DiCamillo, "There's Never Been a Better Time in the US to Be an Electrician," *Quartz*, June 7, 2023, https://qz.com/there-s-never-been-a-better-time-in-the-us-to-be-an-ele-1850508041.

31. Laura Vozzella, "Virginia Gov. Youngkin Scraps Degree Requirement for Most State Jobs," *Washington Post*, May 30, 2023, https://www.washingtonpost.com/dc-md-va/2023/05/30/youngkin-college-degree-state-workforce/.

32. Vozzella, "Virginia Gov. Youngkin Scraps Degree Requirement for Most State Jobs."

33. Sarah Wood, "How Much Student Loan Debt Does the Average College Graduate Have?," *U.S. News & World Report*, September 22, 2023, https://www.usnews.com/education/best-colleges/paying-for-college/articles/see-how-student-loan-borrowing-has-changed.

34. Emily Dreibelbis, "Startup Success: Laid-Off Tech Workers Are Becoming Their Own Bosses," *PCMag*, February 9, 2023, https://www.pcmag.com/news/startup-success-laid-off-tech-workers-are-becoming-their-own-bosses.

35. MBO Partners, "C-Suite Leaders Hold the Key to Unlocking a Future of Work Paradigm Shift," LinkedIn, August 8, 2023, https://www.linkedin.com/pulse/c-suite-leaders-hold-key-unlocking-future-work-paradigm-shift/.

36. See Vozzella, "Virginia Gov. Youngkin Scraps Degree Requirement for Most State Jobs."

Chapter 6

1. "'Satisfaction' Comes to Keith Richards in His Sleep," History.com, accessed February 9, 2024, https://www.history.com/this-day-in-history/satisfaction-comes-to-keith-richards.

2. Tyler Golsen, "The 25 Songs the Rolling Stones Have Played Live the Most," *Far Out Magazine*, January 12, 2022, https://faroutmagazine.co.uk/the-25-songs-the-rolling-stones-played-live-the-most/.

3. "Educational Attainment in the U.S. 1960–2022," Statista, October 6, 2023, https://www.statista.com/statistics/184260/educational-attainment-in-the-us/.

4. Kim Parker, "Chapter 5: Americans' Time at Paid Work, Housework, Child Care, 1965 to 2011," Pew Research Center's Social & Demographic Trends

Project, March 14, 2013, http://pewrsr.ch/OLAaxT. See also: "Women in the Labor Force: A Databook: BLS Reports," US Bureau of Labor Statistics, April 1, 2021, https://www.bls.gov/opub/reports/womens-databook/2020/home.htm.

5. "Federal Reserve Economic Data: Your Trusted Data Source since 1991," Employees on Nonfarm Payrolls by Industry Sector and Selected Industry Detail, Seasonally Adjusted, accessed November 21, 2023, https://fred.stlouisfed.org/release/tables?rid=50&eid=4881&od=1965-05-01#.

6. The statistics that appear in the remainder of this chapter come from the "MBO Partners State of Independence in America Report 2023."

Chapter 7

1. "Looking Back Looking Forward: A Conversation with James D. Watson and Edward O. Wilson," YouTube, October 14, 2014, https://www.youtube.com/watch?v=N8_W2cBAO7s&list=PLcuB9ocQRZCm4-n_TuQKie_L2jlC9Pq2h&ab_channel=HarvardMuseumofNaturalHistory.

2. Adapted from Miles Everson, "3 Ways to Incorporate Independent Workers into Your Talent Strategy," BenefitsPRO, July 8, 2022, https://www.benefitspro.com/2022/07/08/3-ways-to-incorporate-independent-workers-into-your-talent-strategy/.

3. Carmel McCoubrey, "Don't Quote Them on It," *New York Times*, February 14, 2017, https://www.nytimes.com/2017/02/14/opinion/dont-quote-them-on-it.html.

4. "Life Expectancy in the USA, 1900–98," Berkeley Demography, accessed November 21, 2023, https://u.demog.berkeley.edu/~andrew/1918/figure2.html.

5. Imperial College London. "Average life expectancy set to increase by 2030." ScienceDaily, accessed November 21, 2023, www.sciencedaily.com/releases/2017/02/170221222528.htm.

6. "Employee Tenure Summary—2022 A01 Results," US Bureau of Labor Statistics, September 22, 2022, https://www.bls.gov/news.release/tenure.nr0.htm.

7. "Gen Z Is Leading a New Era of Salary Transparency," Handshake, February 22, 2023, https://joinhandshake.com/network-trends/gen-z-salary-transparency/. Also, see: Emma Goldberg, "It's All That Young Job Seekers Are Asking For: Stability," *New York Times*, December 2, 2022, https://www.nytimes.com/2022/12/02/business/dream-job-pandemic-layoffs.html.

8. "Charts Related to the Latest 'The Employment Situation' News Release." US Bureau of Labor Statistics, https://www.bls.gov/charts/employment-situation/civilian-labor-force-participation-rate.htm; Austen Hufford and Gwynn Guilford, "Americans Have Quit Quitting Their Jobs," *Wall Street Journal*, July 7, 2023, https://www.wsj.com/articles/americans-have-quit

-quitting-their-jobs-4feda9bb. Also see: Courtnay Brown, "The Great Resignation Is Over," Axios, May 31, 2023, https://www.axios.com/2023/05/31/great-resignation-quitting-boom. And, looking to the underlying data here (https://fred.stlouisfed.org/graph/?g=16ObU) shows that the number peaked at 3% in November 2021 and then again in April 2022.

9. Miles Everson, "The Great Realization Is Here. Now What?," *Fast Company*, July 11, 2022, https://www.fastcompany.com/90765434/the-great-realization-is-here-now-what.

10. Matt Pearce, "Gen Z Didn't Coin 'Quiet Quitting'—Gen X Did," *Los Angeles Times*, August 27, 2022, https://www.latimes.com/entertainment-arts/story/2022-08-27/la-ent-quiet-quitting-origins.

11. Arianna Huffington, "Why Quiet Quitting Is Not the Solution to Our Burnout Crisis," Thrive Global, September 2, 2022, https://community.thriveglobal.com/arianna-huffington-quiet-quitting-workplace-burnout-crisis/.

12. As this book was going to print, the California Supreme Court upheld Proposition 22, which carved out an exemption for some independent workers, like app-based gig workers. See here: Miles Everson, "A California Victory for 'Free Birds' Everywhere," LinkedIn, August 6, 2024, https://www.linkedin.com/pulse/return-driven-strategy-california-victory-free-birds-miles-everson-epnqc/.

13. Modified and adapted from MBO Partners, "Certified Self-Employed," MBO Partners, August 15, 2019, https://www.mbopartners.com/wp-content/uploads/2019/08/MBO-CSE-2019.pdf.

14. Seth Godin, "Dawani's Law," *Seth's Blog*, October 20, 2022, https://seths.blog/2022/10/dawanis-law/.

15. Adam Grant (@AdamMGrant), "'Quiet quitting' isn't laziness. Doing the bare minimum is a common response to bullshit jobs, abusive bosses, and low pay," Twitter (now X), August 26, 2022, 10:01 pm, https://twitter.com/AdamMGrant/status/1563164741987893248.

Chapter 8

1. Dave Byrne, "Steve Jobs' Lesson About Storytelling," LinkedIn, February 8, 2021, https://www.linkedin.com/pulse/steve-jobs-lesson-storytelling-dave-byrne/. Also see: Dirk Strauss, "Steve Jobs: Anecdotes of a Genius, A Life Well Lived," *Programming and Tech Blog*, January 7, 2019, https://dirkstrauss.com/steve-jobs-anecdotes-of-a-genius/.

2. "Taylor Swift on 'Lover' and Haters," CBS News, August 25, 2019, https://www.cbsnews.com/news/taylor-swift-on-lover-and-haters/. Also see: Joe Coscarelli, "Taylor Swift Escalates Battle with Scooter Braun and Big Machine,"

New York Times, November 15, 2019, https://www.nytimes.com/2019/11/15/arts/music/taylor-swift-scooter-braun.html.

3. Kevin Perry, "Taylor Swift Sets Staggering Vinyl Sale Record," *Independent*, January 16, 2024, https://www.independent.co.uk/arts-entertainment/music/news/taylor-swift-vinyl-sales-b2479792.html.

4. "Taylor Swift Masters Dispute," Wikipedia, accessed February 9, 2024, https://en.wikipedia.org/w/index.php?title=Taylor_Swift_masters_dispute&oldid=1205012983. And: "Battle of Gettysburg," Wikipedia, accessed February 9, 2024, https://en.wikipedia.org/w/index.php?title=Battle_of_Gettysburg&oldid=1201659025.

5. "Superforecasting: The Art and Science of Prediction by Philip E. Tetlock," Wharton School Press, https://wsp.wharton.upenn.edu/book/superforecasting/. Also see: "Superforecasting: The Art and Science of Prediction Book Summary," You Exec, https://youexec.com/book-summaries/superforecasting-the-art-and-science-of-prediction. And of course, the book itself: Philip E. Tetlock and Dan Gardner, *Superforecasting: The Art and Science of Prediction* (New York: Broadway Books, 2016).

6. Seth Godin, *All Marketers Are Liars: The Power of Telling Authentic Stories in a Low-Trust World* (New York: Portfolio, 2005), 2.

7. Rebecca Schiller, "Taylor Swift Accepts Woman of the Decade Award at Billboard's Women in Music: Read Her Full Speech," *Billboard*, December 13, 2019, https://www.billboard.com/music/awards/taylor-swift-woman-of-the-decade-speech-billboard-women-in-music-8546156/.

Chapter 9

1. Marc Andreessen (@pmarca), "I can't convince you to want freedom. But if you do want freedom, it can't come to you in the form of a centralized system…," Twitter (now X), March 9, 2023, 2:55 am, https://twitter.com/pmarca/status/1633738311922782209.

2. Ray Dalio, *Principles: Life and Work* (New York: Simon & Schuster, 2017), 406.

3. Peter H. Diamandis, MD (@PeterDiamandis), "What made Steve Jobs, Jeff Bezos, or Elon Musk succeed? Was it their technology or their mindset? Personally, I think mindset is…," Twitter (now X), November 29, 2020, 5:09 pm, https://twitter.com/PeterDiamandis/status/1333171373460611072.

4. Peter Thiel and Blake Masters, *Zero to One* (New York: The Crown Publishing Group, 2014), 195.

5. Caryn Ganz, "100 Best Singles of 1984: Pop's Greatest Year," *Rolling Stone*, August 30, 2019, https://www.rollingstone.com/music/music-lists/100-best

-singles-of-1984-pops-greatest-year-163322/bruce-springsteen-dancing-in
-the-dark-170866/ (emphasis added).

6. "Braveheart," IMDb, accessed February 9, 2024, https://www.imdb.com
   /title/tt0112573/characters/nm0570954.

7. "Braveheart," IMDb.

8. "The Surprising History of 'Freelance,'" *Merriam-Webster*, accessed November
   21, 2023, https://www.merriam-webster.com/wordplay/freelance-origin-meaning.

9. Witold Nowiński et al., "Perceived Public Support and Entrepreneurship
   Attitudes: A Little Reciprocity Can Go a Long Way!," *Journal of Vocational
   Behavior* 121 (2020): 103474, https://doi.org/10.1016/j.jvb.2020.103474.

10. "Steve Jobs Interview—2/18/1981," YouTube, February 1, 2021, https://
    www.youtube.com/watch?v=DbfejwP1d3c.

11. Dr. Seuss, *Oh, The Places You'll Go!* (New York: Random House, 2020).

12. Linus Torvalds and David Diamond, *Just for Fun: The Story of an Accidental
    Revolutionary* (New York: HarperBusiness, 2002), 215.

13. Sean McGever, "Early Americans Read the Bible in a Way That Nearly
    Destroyed America," ChristianityToday.com, July 18, 2023, https://www
    .christianitytoday.com/ct/2023/july-web-only/mark-noll-america-book-bible
    -independence-civil-war.html.

14. Genevieve Roch-Decter, CFA (@GRDecter), "Elon Musk should hire
    Tucker Carlson and start a video service to compete with YouTube," Twit-
    ter (now X), April 24, 2023, 4:04 pm, https://twitter.com/GRDecter/status
    /1650591453343543297.

15. Ryan Morgan, "Elon Musk Suggests Twitter as New Platform for Tucker
    Carlson After Fox News Departure," *The Epoch Times*, April 27, 2023,
    https://www.theepochtimes.com/article/elon-musk-suggests-twitter-as-new
    -platform-for-tucker-carlson-after-fox-news-departure-5220284.

16. Miles Everson, "Embracing the Age of Personal Agency," *Fast Company*, June
    27, 2023, https://www.fastcompany.com/90911898/embracing-the-age-of
    -personal-agency-unlocking-the-power-of-the-great-realization.

Chapter 10

1. Victoria Miller, "Lindsey Buckingham & Stevie Nicks: Inside Their Rocky
   Relationship," Heavy.com, May 22, 2021, https://heavy.com/entertainment
   /lindsey-buckingham-relationship-with-stevie-nicks/.

2. Brian Hiatt, "Stevie Nicks: A Rock Goddess Looks Back," *Rolling
   Stone*, May 21, 2020, https://www.rollingstone.com/music/music-news
   /stevie-nicks-a-rock-goddess-looks-back-179984/7/.

3. Marc Myers, "How 'Go Your Own Way' Helped Lindsey Buckingham Get Over Stevie Nicks," *Wall Street Journal*, September 14, 2021, https://www .wsj.com/articles/how-go-your-own-way-helped-lindsey-buckingham-get -over-stevie-nicks-11631620801.

4. "Go Your Own Way by Fleetwood Mac," Songfacts, accessed November 21, 2023, https://www.songfacts.com/facts/fleetwood-mac/go-your-own-way.

5. Ken Caillat and Steven Stiefel, *Making Rumours: The Inside Story of the Classic Fleetwood Mac Album* (Hoboken, NJ: John Wiley & Sons, 2012), xv.

6. "Make Your Day," TikTok, accessed December 13, 2023, https://www .tiktok.com/@music_is_powerful/video/7172715582616472878. Note: This TikTok reproduces a previously produced video of this interview, though I was unable to ascertain the original source.

7. Bill Murphy, "In 2005, Steve Jobs Gave an Incredible Speech. Here's What to Steal . . . ," *Inc.*, May 24, 2020, https://www.inc.com/bill-murphy-jr/in-2005 -steve-jobs-gave-an-incredible-speech-heres-what-to-steal-from-it.html.

8. Stanford University, "'You've Got to Find What You Love,' Jobs Says," *Stanford News*, June 12, 2005, https://news.stanford.edu/2005/06/12/youve -got-find-love-jobs-says/.

9. Arthur C. Brooks, "The Only Career Advice You'll Ever Need," *The Atlantic*, October 20, 2023, https://www.theatlantic.com/ideas/archive/2023/05 /career-advice-happiness-know-thyself/674087/.

10. Steve Wozniak and Gina Smith, *iWoz: Computer Geek to Cult Icon: How I Invented the Personal Computer, Co-Founded Apple, and Had Fun Doing It* (New York: W. W. Norton, 2007), 198–199.

11. Brent Schlender and Rick Tetzeli, *Becoming Steve Jobs: The Evolution of a Reckless Upstart into a Visionary Leader* (New York: Crown Business, 2016), 50–51.

12. "Apple—Here's to the Crazy Ones (1997)," YouTube, May 24, 2010, https:// www.youtube.com/watch?v=tjgtLSHhTPg&ab_channel=vintagemacmuseum (emphasis added).

13. "PwC's Global Workforce Hopes and Fears Survey 2022," PwC, May 24, 2022, https://www.pwc.com/gx/en/issues/workforce/hopes-and-fears-2022.html.

14. As quoted in Jack Kelly, "It's Time to Normalize Frequent Job Changes," *Forbes*, May 3, 2022, https://www.forbes.com/sites/jackkelly/2022/05/01 /its-time-to-normalize-frequent-job-changes/.

15. Peter Economy, "Glassdoor Just Announced the Surprising Results of Its 2019 Mission and Culture Survey (How Does Your Company Stack Up?)," *Inc.*, July 11, 2019, https://www.inc.com/peter-economy/glassdoor-just

-announced-surprising-results-of-its-2019-mission-culture-survey-how
-does-your-company-stack-up.html.

16. Originally published in Miles's newsletter; see here: Miles Everson, "Are You in the Right Job? Here Are Ways to Know Whether or Not You're on the Right Career Path! [Tuesdays: Return Driven Strategy]," Valens Research, November 22, 2022, https://www.valens-research.com/dynamic-marketing -communique/are-you-in-the-right-job-here-are-ways-to-know-whether -or-not-youre-on-the-right-career-path-tuesdays-return-driven-strategy/.

17. Mick Fleetwood and Anthony Bozza, *Play On: Now, Then, and Fleetwood Mac* (New York: Little, Brown and Company, 2014), 15–16.

18. "Miles Everson & Daniel Pink," YouTube, April 9, 2023, https://www .youtube.com/watch?v=Wo_mnVWjsjs&ab_channel=ToneFilms.

19. Daniel Pink, "Land of the Free," *Fast Company*, April 1, 2001, https://www .fastcompany.com/42901/land-free.

20. Ryan Holiday, *The Obstacle Is the Way: The Timeless Art of Turning Trials into Triumph* (New York: Portfolio/Penguin, 2014), xiv.

Chapter 11

1. *40 Years of Rocky: The Birth of a Classic*, directed by Derek Wayne Johnson (2020; Newtown, PA: Virgil Films).

2. *Rocky*, directed by Sylvester Stallone (1976; New York: Chartoff-Winkler Productions).

3. Mike Young and Victor Dulewicz, "General Intelligence, Personality Traits, and Motivation as Predictors of Performance, Potential, and Rate of Advancement of Royal Navy Senior Officers," *Military Psychology*, 2023, 1–14, https://doi.org/10.1080/08995605.2023.2244818. As discussed by Tyler Cowen here: Tyler Cowen, "What Makes for a Good Royal Navy Senior Officer?," Marginal Revolution, August 14, 2023, https://marginalrevolution .com/marginalrevolution/2023/08/what-makes-for-a-good-royal-navy-senior -officer.html.

4. Ryan Holiday, *The Obstacle Is the Way: The Little Book for Flipping Adversity into Opportunity* (New York: Portfolio/Penguin, 2014).

5. *The Lord of the Rings: The Fellowship of the Ring*, directed by Peter Jackson (2001; New York: New Line Cinema; Wellington, New Zealand: WingNut Films).

6. Alex Hormozi (@AlexHormozi), "The fact that you don't know if it's gonna work," X, August 1, 2023, 3:45 pm, https://x.com/AlexHormozi/status /1693710883535585519.

7. Jamy Bechler (@CoachBechler), "Get the Right Guys on the Bus," Twitter

(now X), February 25, 2021, 10:00 am, https://twitter.com/CoachBechler/status/1364953383266885650.

8. Tony Robbins, "Barriers to Entry," tonyrobbins.com, December 9, 2019, https://www.tonyrobbins.com/business/barriers-to-entry/.

Chapter 12

1. "Some Age Others Mature," YouTube, June 14, 2007, https://www.youtube.com/watch?v=wIzSki7ZcTM&ab_channel=viletouch.

2. Aaron O'Neill, "United States: Life Expectancy 1860–2020," Statista, June 21, 2022, https://www.statista.com/statistics/1040079/life-expectancy-united-states-all-time/.

3. Peter H. Diamandis, "Fountain of Youth?," Peter Diamandis—Innovation & Entrepreneurship Community, July 13, 2021, https://www.diamandis.com/blog/fountain-of-youth.

4. Peter H. Diamandis, MD (@PeterDiamandis), "Entrepreneurship is beautiful because," Twitter (now X), July 23, 2022, 4:59 pm, https://twitter.com/PeterDiamandis/status/1550948648929853446?s=20.

5. Dana G. Smith, "What Is the Ideal Retirement Age for Your Health?," *New York Times*, April 3, 2023, https://www.nytimes.com/2023/04/03/well/live/retirement-age-health.html.

6. James Root et al., "Better with Age: The Rising Importance of Older Workers," Bain, July 26, 2023, https://www.bain.com/insights/better-with-age-the-rising-importance-of-older-workers/.

7. Richard N. Bolles, *The Three Boxes of Life: And How to Get Out of Them: An Introduction to Life/Work Planning* (Berkeley: Ten Speed Press, 1981).

8. David Brooks, "The New Old Age," *The Atlantic*, August 30, 2023, https://www.theatlantic.com/culture/archive/2023/08/career-retirement-transition-academic-programs/675085/.

9. Brooks, "The New Old Age."

10. Brooks, "The New Old Age."

11. "No One on His Deathbed Ever Said, 'I Wish I Had Spent More Time on My Business,'" Quote Investigator, April 1, 2021, https://quoteinvestigator.com/2021/03/31/deathbed-wish/.

12. David A. Graham, "Track of the Day: 'Forever Young' for Bob Dylan's Birthday," *The Atlantic*, March 22, 2022, https://www.theatlantic.com/culture/archive/2016/05/track-of-the-day-forever-young/623937/.

13. *The Holy Bible: Containing the Old and New Testaments* (Nashville: Thomas Nelson, 2020), Numbers 6:24–26.

14. "Star Trek Spock's Vulcan Salute Is Really Hebrew High Priest Blessing!

Halleluyah!!!," YouTube, October 28, 2011, https://www.youtube.com/watch?v=BBiTRaHnXt4&ab_channel=YeshuaisLordforever.

15. Hugh Rawson and Margaret Miner, *The Oxford Dictionary of American Quotations* (Oxford: Oxford University Press, 2008), p. 382. The dictionary says London said this "to friends, 1916, reported in San Francisco Bulletin, Dec. 2, 1916."

Chapter 13

1. Justin Birnbaum, "Michael Jordan Is Now Worth $3 Billion and Joins the Forbes 400," *Forbes*, October 18, 2023, https://www.forbes.com/sites/justinbirnbaum/2023/10/02/michael-jordan-joins-forbes-400-worth-3-billion/.

2. Tom Huddleston, "How Michael Jordan Became Great: 'Nobody Will Ever Work as Hard as I Work,'" CNBC, April 21, 2020, https://www.cnbc.com/2020/04/21/how-michael-jordan-became-great-nobody-will-ever-work-as-hard.html. Also, see the documentary itself.

3. Tom Huddleston, "How Michael Jordan Became Great." Also, see the documentary itself.

4. Ryan Holiday, "These 14 Small Mindset Shifts Will Change Your Life," RyanHoliday.net, September 20, 2023, https://ryanholiday.net/these-14-small-mindset-shifts-will-change-your-life/.

5. Marcel Schwantes, "In 4 Sentences, Elon Musk Gives Leaders His 'Single Best Piece of Advice,'" *Inc.*, August 11, 2021, https://www.inc.com/marcel-schwantes/in-4-sentences-elon-musk-gives-leaders-his-single-best-piece-of-advice.html.

6. Ryan Holiday, *Ego Is the Enemy* (New York: Portfolio, Penguin, 2016), 40.

7. From an interview with Miles found here: Phil La Duke, "Miles Everson of MBO Partners on the Top Five Trends to Watch," *Authority Magazine*, October 13, 2021, https://medium.com/authority-magazine/preparing-for-the-future-of-work-miles-everson-of-mbo-partners-on-the-top-five-trends-to-watch-in-7b2d529953b3.

8. "Machine of the Year 1982: The Computer Moves In," *Time*, January 3, 1983.

9. "Machine of the Year 1982: The Computer Moves In," *Time*.

10. Tim Hanrahan and Jason Fry, "Google's Algorithmic Oath," *Wall Street Journal*, December 29, 2003, https://www.wsj.com/articles/SB107211693855181300.

11. MBO Partners, "New Study Shows Wave of AI-Upskilling Among Independent Workers," MBO Partners, March 11, 2024, https://www.mbopartners.com/blog/press/new-study-shows-wave-of-ai-upskilling-among-independent-workers/.

12. Carol S. Dweck, *Mindset: Changing the Way You Think to Fulfill Your Potential* (London: Robinson, 2017).

13. Dweck, *Mindset*, 15–16.

14. Bill Gates, "Bill Gates On . . . ," *Time*, June 14, 1993, https://content.time .com/time/subscriber/article/0,33009,978678,00.html.

15. Keaton Swett, LinkedIn, 2022, https://www.linkedin.com/posts/keatonswett _crowdsourcing-openinnovation-activity-6988940781684146176-ITbT.

16. James Clear, "3-2-1: Outsmarting Yourself, Staying Adaptable, and Choosing More Empowering Self-Talk," JamesClear.com, October 20, 2022, https:// jamesclear.com/3-2-1/october-20-2022.

17. Holiday, *Ego Is the Enemy*, 40.

18. "'Right a Lot' Amazon Leadership Principle Explained by Jeff Bezos—Best Explanation Ever," YouTube, April 28, 2023, https://www.youtube.com /watch?v=C3Y3z5ZJmss&ab_channel=AndrewDetiffe%28founderatMocki .co%29.

19. Dweck, *Mindset*, 15–16.

20. John Hagel III and John Seely Brown, "Great Businesses Scale Their Learning, Not Just Their Operations," *Harvard Business Review*, July 7, 2017, https://hbr .org/2017/06/great-businesses-scale-their-learning-not-just-their-operations.

21. "A Duck with One Leg Swims in Circles," Reddit, accessed November 22, 2023, https://www.reddit.com/r/Showerthoughts/comments/1516ln4/a_duck _with_one_leg_swims_in_circles/.

22. Charles Clay Doyle, Wolfgang Mieder, and Fred R. Shapiro, *The Dictionary of Modern Proverbs* (New Haven, CT: Yale University Press, 2012), 153.

23. "Is College Necessary for Success? Todd Rose and Mike Rowe Discuss," *Forbes*, December 18, 2023, https://www.forbes.com/sites/stand-together/2023/09/05 /is-college-necessary-for-success-todd-rose-and-mike-rowe-discuss.

24. Seth Godin, "Anti-Smart," *Seth's Blog*, August 1, 2023, https://seths.blog /2023/08/anti-smart/.

25. Philipp Frank, *Einstein: His Life and Times* (New York: Alfred A. Knopf, Inc., 1947), 185.

26. "'These Horrible People Do Everything'—Jordan Peterson on Price's Law," YouTube, September 16, 2017, https://www.youtube.com/watch?v= UmUdcWk6Vfw&ab_channel=TheArchangel911. As gleaned from Darius Foroux, "Price's Law: What It Is and Why You Should Care," *Darius Foroux*, December 20, 2020, https://dariusforoux.com/prices-law/.

27. Ashish Mathur, "Michael Jordan Credited Phil Jackson for Helping Him Calm His Body and Emotions during Pressure-Filled Games," Sportscasting, August 6, 2021, https://www.sportscasting.com/michael-jordan-credited -phil-jackson-helping-calm-body-emotions-during-pressure-filled-games

-bulls/. Also see: Nikhil Naik, "The Student and the Master. How Phil Jackson Moulded Michael Jordan the Leader," EssentiallySports, August 11, 2021, https://www.essentiallysports.com/nba-basketball-news-the-student-and-the-master-how-phil-jackson-moulded-michael-jordan-the-leader/.

28. "'The Last Dance': What to Watch for in Episodes 7 and 8, Including the Most Human of Michael Jordan Moments," CBSSports.com, May 10, 2020, https://www.cbssports.com/nba/news/the-last-dance-what-to-watch-for-in-episodes-7-and-8-including-the-most-human-of-michael-jordan-moments/.

29. "How Upskilling Impacts Talent Retention and Recruiting," PwC ProEdge RSS, accessed February 9, 2024, https://proedge.pwc.com/upskilling-and-talent-strategies. And see here: "The American Upskilling Study," Gallup .com, July 20, 2023, https://www.gallup.com/analytics/354374/the-american-upskilling-study.aspx.

30. John Hagel, John Seely Brown, and Lang Davison, *The Power of Pull: How Small Moves, Smartly Made, Can Set Big Things in Motion* (New York: Basic Books, 2010), 24, 25.

Chapter 14

1. Daniel Pink (@DanielPink), "Three-word summary of this smart new book: Friends are medicine," Twitter (now X), January 18, 2023, 11:03 am, https://twitter.com/DanielPink/status/1615741772830842882. Pink's tweet was a blurb to promote the 2023 book *The Good Life* by Marc Schulz and Robert Waldinger.

2. Ali Thanawalla, "Steve Kerr, Michael Jordan Discuss Infamous 1995 Fight in 'Last Dance,'" NBC Sports Bay Area; California, May 4, 2020, https://www.nbcsportsbayarea.com/nba/golden-state-warriors/steve-kerr-michael-jordan-discuss-infamous-1995-fight-in-last-dance/1365015/. The article quotes the 2020 Jordan documentary from ESPN, "The Last Dance": "'The Last Dance': The Untold Story of Michael Jordan's Chicago Bulls," ESPN, accessed November 22, 2023, https://www.espn.com/nba/story/_/id/28973557/the-last-dance-untold-story-michael-jordan-chicago-bulls.

3. Aikansh Chaudhary, "Steve Kerr surprisingly explained that Michael Jordan punching him in the face . . ." Fadeaway World, Yardbarker, October 11, 2022, https://fadeawayworld.net/steve-kerr-surprisingly-explained-that-michael-jordan-punching-him-in-the-face-improved-their-relationship-michael-was-definitely-testing-me-and-i-responded-i-feel-like-i-kind-of-passed-the-test.

4. Paulina Dedaj, "Warriors' Steve Kerr Credits Successful NBA Career to

Michael Jordan: 'I Owe Him Everything,'" Fox News, May 29, 2020, https://www.foxnews.com/sports/warriors-steve-kerr-credits-successful-nba-career-to-michael-jordan-i-owe-him-everything.

5. Allistair McCaw (@AllistairMcCaw), "Steve Kerr on describing a strong #culture," X, August 3, 2023, 10:03 am, https://x.com/AllistairMcCaw/status/1687101980173631489.

6. The material in this section is revised or comes directly from the 2022 "State of Independence in America," the annual report published by MBO Partners, found here: MBOpartners, "Happier, Healthier & Wealthier: State of Independence in America 2022," November 30, 2022, https://www.mbopartners.com/state-of-independence/soi-22/.

7. George Vlahakis, "Entrepreneurs Benefit More from Emotional Intelligence than Other Competencies, Such as IQ," *Kelley School of Business*, January 28, 2021, https://blog.kelley.iu.edu/2021/01/28/entrepreneurs-benefit-more-from-emotional-intelligence-than-other-competencies-such-as-iq/. Also: Nate Nead, "4 Ways Emotional Intelligence Makes You a Better Entrepreneur," *Entrepreneur*, April 24, 2022, https://www.entrepreneur.com/leadership/4-ways-emotional-intelligence-makes-you-a-better/423485.

8. Vlahakis, "Entrepreneurs Benefit More from Emotional Intelligence"; Nead, "4 Ways Emotional Intelligence."

9. Brené Brown, *Rising Strong: How the Ability to Reset Transforms the Way We Live, Love, Parent, and Lead* (New York: Random House, 2017), chapter 1.

10. "The Most Misquoted Song Lyrics," uDiscover Music, January 6, 2022, https://www.udiscovermusic.com/stories/the-most-misquoted-song-lyrics/. And see the Babylon Bee's satirical piece, https://babylonbee.com/news/lifelong-pearl-jam-fan-close-to-figuring-out-three-of-the-lyrics.

11. Gene Zaino, "Independent Professionals: Who They Are, What They Need and Why It Matters," *Forbes*, September 7, 2018, https://www.forbes.com/sites/forbeshumanresourcescouncil/2018/09/07/independent-professionals-who-they-are-what-they-need-and-why-it-matters/.

12. Modified from Miles's article, found here: "Embracing the Age of Personal Agency: Unlocking the Power of the Great Realization," *Fast Company*, June 27, 2023, https://www.fastcompany.com/90911898/embracing-the-age-of-personal-agency-unlocking-the-power-of-the-great-realization.

13. Note that the Beatles have released yet another song even while I was writing this book, but this time with the help of AI. See: Jenni Reid, "A New Beatles Song Is Set for Release After 45 Years—with Help from AI," CNBC, November 2, 2023, https://www.cnbc.com/2023/11/02/a-new-beatles-song-is-set-for-release-after-45-years-with-help-from-ai.html.

Chapter 15

1. Adam Grant (@AdamMGrant), "What matters is the value people create, not the place they inhabit," Twitter (now X), June 13, 2023, 1:59 pm, https://twitter.com/AdamMGrant/status/1668679477742673944.

2. Doug Freeman, "How Jimmy Buffett's 'Margaritaville' Became the Most Valuable Song of All Time," *The Austin Chronicle*, July 21, 2017, https://www.austinchronicle.com/music/2017-07-21/how-jimmy-buffetts-margaritaville-became-the-most-valuable-song-of-all-time/.

3. "1 in 3 Remote Employees Admit They've Worked from Their Car or Bed: Poll," *New York Post*, May 2, 2023, https://nypost.com/2023/05/02/1-in-3-remote-employees-admit-theyve-worked-from-their-car-or-bed-poll/.

4. Adam Grant (@AdamMGrant), "The world is unfair to night owls . . . ," X, September 3, 2023, 11:15 am, https://x.com/AdamMGrant/status/1698354009352933492.

5. "Preparing for the Future of Work: Miles Everson of MBO Partners on the Top Five Trends to Watch In. . .," Authority, October 13, 2021, https://medium.com/authority-magazine/preparing-for-the-future-of-work-miles-everson-of-mbo-partners-on-the-top-five-trends-to-watch-in-7b2d529953b3.

6. Swapna Venugopal Ramaswamy, "'We Kept Getting Outbid': Californians Moving to Texas Explain Why They're Changing States," *USA Today*, August 3, 2023, https://www.usatoday.com/story/money/2023/08/02/californians-moving-to-texas/70488867007/.

7. Venugopal Ramaswamy, "'We Kept Getting Outbid.'"

8. Niraj Chokshi, "Tesla Will Move Its Headquarters to Austin, Texas, in Blow to California," *New York Times*, October 7, 2021, https://www.nytimes.com/2021/10/07/business/tesla-texas-headquarters.html.

9. Nicholas Gordon, "Musk Says 'Laptop Class' Should Stop 'the Work-from-Home' BS," *Fortune*, May 17, 2023, https://fortune.com/2023/05/17/elon-musk-work-from-home-remote-tesla-twitter-unfair/.

10. Grace Kay, "Elon Musk Says Remote Work Is 'Morally Wrong,'" *Business Insider*, May 16, 2023, https://www.businessinsider.com/elon-musk-remote-work-morally-wrong-get-off-high-horse-2023-5. Also: Rohan Goswami, "Elon Musk: Working from Home Is 'Morally Wrong' When Service Workers Still Have to Show Up," CNBC, May 17, 2023, https://www.cnbc.com/2023/05/16/elon-musk-work-from-home-morally-wrong-when-some-have-to-show-up.html.

11. MBO Partners, Miles Everson, and Bryan Pena, "Building an Agile Workforce in a Post-COVID World," YouTube, June 17, 2020, https://www.youtube.com/watch?v=0FR91SqMltI.

12. Emma Goldberg, "The R.T.O. Whisperers Have a Plan," *New York Times*, April 11, 2023, https://www.nytimes.com/2023/04/11/magazine/return-to -office-consultants.html.

13. Brittany Hosea-Small, "San Francisco Exodus as Tech Giants Lean In to Remote Work in Covid-19 Era," *Barron's*, September 13, 2020, https://www .barrons.com/news/san-francisco-exodus-as-tech-giants-lean-in-to-remote -work-in-covid-19-era-01599961208.

14. Carolyn Fong, "Tech, an Early Booster of Remote Work, Wants People Back in the Office," *Wall Street Journal*, July 19, 2023, https://www.wsj.com /articles/tech-an-early-booster-of-remote-work-wants-people-back-in-the -office-6565b840.

15. Stephanie Vozza, "Why Zoom Implemented a Return-to-Office Policy," *Fast Company*, September 17, 2023, https://www.fastcompany.com/90948921 /what-zoom-learned-from-bringing-employees-back-to-the-office.

16. "Quinn Emanuel Tells Its Lawyers: 'Work from Anywhere,'" Quinn Emanuel Urquhart & Sullivan, LLP, December 20, 2021, https://www.quinnemanuel.com /the-firm/news-events/quinn-emanuel-tells-its-lawyers-work-from-anywhere/.

17. Gwynn Guilford, "Work-from-Home Era Ends for Millions of Americans," *Wall Street Journal*, June 9, 2023, https://www.wsj.com/articles/work -from-home-era-ends-for-millions-of-americans-8bb75367. Also see: Jena McGregor, "Full-Time Remote Work Is Falling—But Still Five Times Pre-Pandemic Levels, Survey Finds," *Forbes*, March 31, 2023, https://www .forbes.com/sites/jenamcgregor/2023/03/30/full-time-remote-work-is-falling -but-still-five-times-pre-pandemic-levels-survey-finds/.

18. "Percentage of U.S. Workers Willing to Take a Pay Cut in Exchange for the Option to Work from Home," *Harper's Magazine*, January 2023, https:// harpers.org/harpers-index/2023/01/percentage-of-u-s-workers-willing-to -take-a-pay-cut-in-exchange-for-the-option-to-work-from-home/.

19. Emma Goldberg and Haruka Sakaguchi, "All That Empty Office Space Belongs to Someone," *New York Times*, September 1, 2023, https://www .nytimes.com/2023/09/01/business/office-vacancies-gural-gfp.html. The authors credit "researchers at Columbia and New York University" for the data.

20. Dorothy Neufeld and Christina Kostandi, "Visualizing 1 Billion Square Feet of Empty Office Space," Visual Capitalist, August 8, 2023, https://www .visualcapitalist.com/visualizing-1-billion-square-feet-of-empty-office-space/.

21. Anne D'Innocenzio and Janie Har, "Marc Benioff Says Downtown San Francisco Is 'Never Going Back to the Way It Was' as Experts Grapple with Turning Around the Ghost Town," *Fortune*, July 16, 2023, https://fortune

.com/2023/07/16/marc-benioff-san-francisco-never-going-back-to-way-it
-was-experts-grapple-with-ghost-town/.

22. Rachel Siegel, "How the 'Urban Doom Loop' Could Pose the Next Economic
Threat," *Washington Post*, August 28, 2023, https://www.washingtonpost.com
/business/2023/08/28/commercial-real-estate-economy-urban-doom-loop/.

23. Jon Wertheim, "Real Estate Owners Saddled with Half-Empty Office
Buildings as Hybrid Work Trend Continues," CBS News, January 14, 2024,
https://www.cbsnews.com/news/real-estate-owners-saddled-with-half-empty
-offices-as-hybrid-work-continues-60-minutes-transcript/.

24. Emily Badger, Robert Gebeloff, and Josh Katz, "The Places Most Affected
by Remote Workers' Moves Around the Country," *New York Times*, June
17, 2023, https://www.nytimes.com/interactive/2023/06/17/upshot/17migration
-patterns-movers.html.

25. Cal Newport, "Why Remote Work Is So Hard—and How It Can Be
Fixed," *New Yorker*, May 26, 2020, https://www.newyorker.com/culture
/annals-of-inquiry/can-remote-work-be-fixed.

26. Joseph Hearne, "Graphic design was promoted as the career where . . . ,"
April 18, 2023, https://www.linkedin.com/posts/joseph-hearne_graphicde-
sign-branding-activity-7054084839553044481-dkqH.

27. Matthew E. Kahn, "Don't Move Just Yet," *Business Insider*, June 15, 2022,
https://www.businessinsider.com/great-resignation-work-from-home-new
-cities-real-estate-housing-2022-6.

28. Newport, "Why Remote Work Is So Hard."

29. Aki Ito, "'Super Commuting' Is on the Rise," *Business Insider*, October 30,
2023, https://www.businessinsider.com/super-commuters-hybrid-work-wfh
-business-travel-office-2023-10.

30. Jerry Useem, "When Working from Home Doesn't Work," *The Atlantic*,
October 3, 2017, https://www.theatlantic.com/magazine/archive/2017/11
/when-working-from-home-doesnt-work/540660/.

31. Rob Litterst, "WFH Is a Game Changer for Disabled Workers," The Hustle,
October 6, 2022, https://thehustle.co/10062022-wfh/.

32. Litterst, "WFH Is a Game Changer for Disabled Workers."

33. Allyson Chiu, "Working from Home Now Has Another Powerful Benefit," *Washington Post*, September 19, 2023, https://www.washingtonpost.com
/climate-solutions/2023/09/18/work-from-home-carbon-footprint/.

34. Nate Berg, "Are Half-Empty Offices Wasting Energy?," *Fast Company*,
August 14, 2023, https://www.fastcompany.com/90933498/empty-offices
-are-surprisingly-better-for-the-climate. Also see Berg's earlier reporting:

Nate Berg, "Empty Office Buildings Are Still Devouring Energy. Why?," *Fast Company*, January 21, 2021, https://www.fastcompany.com/90595577/empty-office-buildings-are-still-devouring-energy-why.

35. Derek Thompson, "The Surprising Effects of Remote Work," *The Atlantic*, March 7, 2023, https://www.theatlantic.com/newsletters/archive/2023/03/us-remote-work-impact-fertility-rate-babies/673301/.

Chapter 16

1. Dave Marsh and John Swenson, *The Rolling Stone Record Guide: Reviews and Ratings of Almost 10,000 Currently Available Rock, Pop, Soul, Country, Blues, Jazz, and Gospel Albums* (New York: Random House, 1979).

2. Richard Bienstock, "Joe Walsh: My Life in 15 Songs," *Rolling Stone*, November 16, 2019, https://www.rollingstone.com/music/music-lists/joe-walsh-my-life-in-15-songs-66390/turn-to-stone-1972-149251/.

3. Luke Edwards, "Life's Been Good: Behind Joe Walsh's Exposé of Rock Star Excess," Dig!, November 21, 2022, https://www.thisisdig.com/feature/lifes-been-good-joe-walsh-song-story/.

4. "Apple Music Event 2001. The First Ever Ipod Introduction," YouTube, April 3, 2006, https://www.youtube.com/watch?v=kN0SVBCJqLs&ab_channel=JoshuaG.

5. Adam Grant (@AdamMGrant), "Employers shouldn't discourage side hustles…," Twitter (now X), October 3, 2022, 10:32 am, https://twitter.com/AdamMGrant/status/1576943208180826112.

6. Peter F. Drucker, "Managing Oneself," *Harvard Business Review*, April 26, 2023, https://hbr.org/2005/01/managing-oneself.

7. MBO Partners, "Driving the Future of Work: How the Great Resignation Is Turning into the Great Realization," MBOPartners.com, January 20, 2023, https://www.mbopartners.com/blog/independent-workforce-trends/driving-the-future-of-work/.

8. Christina Marfice, "Pay Transparency Laws: A State-by-State Guide," *Rippling*, August 14, 2020, https://www.rippling.com/blog/pay-transparency-laws-state-by-state-guide. Also see: Margot Tierney, "The Rise of Pay Transparency Laws and Their Driving Forces," *University of Cincinnati Law Review Blog*, August 3, 2022, https://uclawreview.org/2022/08/03/rise-of-pay-transparency-laws-and-their-driving-forces/.

9. Justin Welsh (@theJustinWelsh), "You aren't rewarded for hard work . . . ," X, September 7, 2023, 2:16 pm, https://x.com/thejustinwelsh/status/1699849191248269534.

10. Ryan Holiday (@RyanHoliday), "Belief in yourself is overrated. Generate evidence," Twitter (now X), November 18, 2021, 9:01 am, https://twitter.com/RyanHoliday/status/1461333644195377156.

11. Gary A. Bolles, "Unbundling Work: Learning to Thrive in Disruptive Times (Lite Version)," Medium, January 18, 2018, https://medium.com/@gbolles/unbundling-work-learning-to-thrive-in-disruptive-times-lite-version-4a215450dc5e.

12. Peter Thiel and Blake Masters, *Zero to One* (The Crown Publishing Group, 2014), 10–11. (Italics added.)

13. William Arruda, "Why Being a Nonconformist Is Exactly What Your Company Needs from You," *Forbes*, September 12, 2023, https://www.forbes.com/sites/williamarruda/2023/09/06/why-being-a-nonconformist-is-exactly-what-your-company-needs-from-you/.

14. "Press Release," Pinterest, August 28, 2020, https://investor.pinterestinc.com/press-releases/press-releases-details/2020/Pinterest-Announces-Termination-of-Future-Lease-Contract/default.aspx. See Bobby Marhamat, "Five Predictions for the Future of In-Office Work," *Forbes*, December 10, 2021, https://www.forbes.com/sites/forbesbusinessdevelopmentcouncil/2021/07/23/five-predictions-for-the-future-of-in-office-work/.

15. Miles Everson, "Mindfulness by Miles: Looking for Ways to Access Top Talents with In-Demand Skills? Check Out This Staffing Strategy!," LinkedIn, September 2, 2022, https://www.linkedin.com/pulse/mindfulness-miles-looking-ways-access-top-talents-skills-everson/?trk=pulse-article_more-articles_related-content-card.

16. Anne Austin, "Business Applications Eked Out a New Record in 2023," Economic Innovation Group, January 12, 2024, https://eig.org/2023-business-formation/.

17. George Gilder, *Wealth and Poverty* (New York: Basic Books, 1981).

18. "2023 Life Goals Report: Why Independent Workers Outperform Other Workers in Achieving Life Goals," MBO Partners, February 2023, https://www.mbopartners.com/state-of-independence/life-goals-report/.

19. Bienstock, "Joe Walsh: My Life in 15 Songs."

20. "Eagles Band Member Joe Walsh Is an Amazing AA Speaker," Intensive Outpatient Program for Addiction in Houston, Texas—First Step Recovery, June 6, 2022, https://fstrecovery.com/2020/07/16/eagles-band-member-joe-walsh-is-amazing-aa-speaker/. Also see the original source from *Rolling Stone* magazine here: Sarah Grant, "Joe Walsh, Ringo Starr and the Mission to End America's Addiction Crisis," *Rolling Stone*, March 17, 2019,

https://www.rollingstone.com/music/music-features/joe-walsh-ringo-starr
-facing-addiction-interview-790689/.

21. Ryan Holiday (@RyanHoliday), "If it's a problem that can be solved by money, you don't have a problem," X, November 4, 2023, 5:00 pm, https://x.com /RyanHoliday/status/1720908847194456389.

22. Adela Suliman, "Can Money Buy Happiness? Scientists Say It Can," *Washington Post*, March 8, 2023, https://www.washingtonpost.com /business/2023/03/08/money-wealth-happiness-study/.

23. Chrisann Brennan, *The Bite in the Apple: A Memoir of My Life with Steve Jobs* (New York: St. Martin's Press, 2013), 190.

24. Lisa Brennan-Jobs, *Small Fry* (New York: Grove Press, 2018), 13.

25. Brennan-Jobs, *Small Fry*, 13.

26. Brennan-Jobs, *Small Fry*, 250.

27. Brennan-Jobs, *Small Fry*, 365–366.

28. Walter Isaacson, *Steve Jobs* (New York: Simon & Schuster, 2011), 91.

Chapter 17

1. Walter Isaacson, *The Innovators* (New York: Simon & Schuster, 2014), 274.

2. Marc Eliot, *To the Limit: The Untold Story of the Eagles* (Cambridge, MA: Da Capo, 2005), 132–134.

3. Walter Isaacson, *Steve Jobs* (New York: Simon & Schuster, 2011), 102.

4. From the liner notes of *The Very Best of the Eagles* (CD; Warner Music Group, 2003).

5. Eliot, *To the Limit*, 149.

6. "Everybody Has Plans Until They Get Hit for the First Time," Quote Investigator, October 28, 2021, https://quoteinvestigator.com/2021/08/25/plans-hit/.

7. Alexander Taylor, "Striking It Rich: A New Breed of Risk Takers Is Betting on the High-Technology Future," *Time*, February 15, 1982, https://content .time.com/time/subscriber/article/0,33009,925279,00.html.

8. Taylor, "Striking It Rich."

9. "Thiel Fellowship," Thiel Fellowship, n.d., https://thielfellowship.org/. And Vinnie Mirchandani, *The New Technology Elite: How Great Companies Optimize Both Technology Consumption and Production* (Hoboken, NJ: Wiley, 2012), 73.

10. Eliot, *To the Limit*, 143.

11. Eliot, *To the Limit*, 259.

12. Eliot, *To the Limit*, 258–259.

13. Bolles, "Unbundling Work."

About the Authors

Miles Everson

Photo by Mark Guerra

Miles Everson joined MBO Partners in 2019 as Chief Executive Officer.

Most recently, Everson served as Global Advisory and Consulting CEO for Pricewaterhouse Coopers, LLP (PwC), leading the company's Asia Pacific Americas Advisory and Consulting businesses.

Before joining MBO, Everson had a rich career with PwC, almost three decades in total. He began in the firm's Assurance practice, moving to leadership roles within Advisory/Consulting in both Canada and the United States, including several Financial Services leadership roles, and eventually became the US Advisory/Consulting Vice Chairman. In 2015, he stepped into the new role of Asia Pacific Americas Advisory and Consulting Leader to help globalize the Advisory/Consulting practice.

Everson has worked with many of the world's largest and most prominent organizations, specializing in executive management. He helps companies balance growth, reduce risk, maximize return, and excel in strategic business priorities.

He is a sought-after public speaker and contributor and has been a case study for success from Harvard Business School.

Everson is a Certified Public Accountant, a member of the American Institute of Certified Public Accountants and Minnesota Society of Certified Public Accountants. He graduated from St. Cloud State University with a BS in accounting.

In 2023, Miles was named as a member of Staffing Industry Analysts (SIA) 2023 Staffing 100 North America. Now in its 12th year, the annual list recognizes influential staffing leaders throughout North America who helped their businesses successfully emerge from one of the most difficult periods in recent world history.

Walter Scott Lamb

Scott Lamb is a chronic biographer of interesting people with stories worth telling. He's the owner of Calliope Media Group and has agented, edited, or authored dozens of books.